THOSE WHO BELONG

Bawaajimo: A Dialect of Dreams in Anishinaabe Language and Literature, Margaret Noodin 978-1-61186-105-1

Centering Anishinaabeg Studies: Understanding the World through Stories, edited by Jill Doerfler, Niigaanwewidam James Sinclair, and Heidi Kiiwetinepinesiik Stark 978-1-61186-067-2

Document of Expectations, Devon Abbott Mihesuah 978-1-61186-011-5

Dragonfly Dance, Denise K. Lajimodiere 978-0-87013-982-6

Facing the Future: The Indian Child Welfare Act at 30, edited by Matthew L. M. Fletcher, Wenona T. Singel, and Kathryn E. Fort 978-0-87013-860-7

Follow the Blackbirds, Gwen Nell Westerman 978-1-61186-092-4

The Indian Who Bombed Berlin and Other Stories, Ralph Salisbury 978-0-87013-847-8

Masculindians: Conversations about Indigenous Manhood, edited by Sam McKegney 978-1-61186-129-7

Mediating Indianness, edited by Cathy Covell Waegner 978-1-61186-151-8

The Murder of Joe White: Ojibwe Leadership and Colonialism in Wisconsin, Erik M. Redix 978-1-61186-145-7

National Monuments, Heid E. Erdrich 978-0-87013-848-5

Ogimawkwe Mitigwaki (Queen of the Woods), Simon Pokagon 978-0-87013-987-1

Ottawa Stories from the Springs: Anishinaabe dibaadjimowinan wodi gaa binjibaamigak wodi mookodjiwong e zhinikaadek, translated and edited by Howard Webkamigad 978-1-61186-137-2

Plain of Jars and Other Stories, Geary Hobson 978-0-87013-998-7

Sacred Wilderness, Susan Power 978-1-61186-111-2

Seeing Red—Hollywood's Pixeled Skins: American Indians and Film, edited by LeAnne Howe, Harvey Markowitz, and Denise K. Cummings 978-1-61186-081-8

Shedding Skins: Four Sioux Poets, edited by Adrian C. Louis 978-0-87013-823-2

Stories through Theories/Theories through Stories: North American Indian Writing, Storytelling, and Critique, edited by Gordon D. Henry Jr., Nieves Pascual Soler, and Silvia Martinez-Falquina 978-0-87013-841-6

That Guy Wolf Dancing, Elizabeth Cook-Lynn 978-1-61186-138-9

Those Who Belong: Identity, Family, Blood, and Citizenship among the White Earth Anishinaabeg, Jill Doerfler 978-1-61186-169-3

Visualities: Perspectives on Contemporary American Indian Film and Art, edited by Denise K. Cummings 978-0-87013-999-4

Writing Home: Indigenous Narratives of Resistance, Michael D. Wilson 978-0-87013-818-8

THOSE WHO BELONG

*Identity, Family, Blood,
and Citizenship among the
White Earth Anishinaabeg*

Jill Doerfler

Michigan State University Press
East Lansing

⊚ The paper used in this publication meets the minimum requirements of ANSI/NISO
Z39.48-1992 (R 1997) (Permanence of Paper).

Michigan State University Press
East Lansing, Michigan 48823-5245
Printed and bound in the United States of America.

21 20 19 18 17 16 15   1 2 3 4 5 6 7 8 9 10

Library of Congress Control Number: 2015930553
ISBN: 978-1-61186-169-3 (pbk.)
ISBN: 978-1-60917-457-6 (ebook: PDF)
ISBN: 978-1-62895-229-2 (ebook: ePub)
ISBN: 978-1-62896-229-1 (ebook: Kindle)

Book design by Scribe Inc. (www.scribenet.com)
Cover design by TG Design.
Cover artwork is *Autumn's Wind*, 38x30 inches, acrylic on canvas ©2010 Frank Big Bear
and is used courtesy of the Bockley Gallery (bockleygallery.com). All rights reserved.

green
press
INITIATIVE   Michigan State University Press is a member of the Green Press Initiative and
is committed to developing and encouraging ecologically responsible publishing
practices. For more information about the Green Press Initiative and the use of recycled
paper in book publishing, please visit www.greenpressinitiative.org.

Visit Michigan State University Press at www.msupress.org

*For all my relations and the families of the
White Earth Nation, may we live mino-bimaadiziwin
today, tomorrow, and always.*

Contents

Preface

We are touched into tribal being with words, made
whole in the world with words and oratorical gestures.

—GERALD VIZENOR, *WORDARROWS*

WE CREATE AND RE-CREATE OURSELVES IN THE PAST, PRESENT, AND future in story. The power of stories cannot be measured. The relationship between past, present, and future cannot be separated; it is unbreakable and calls to mind the ways in which familial relationships intertwine individuals together in enduring ways across time and space. As Choctaw scholar LeAnne Howe has argued, "A Native writer remains in conversation with the past and the present to create the future."[1] In Western academia, history and literature are traditionally divided between nonfiction and fiction. Anishinaabe[2] stories defy this schism, emerging in a border area where these categories overlap.[3] In *The Everlasting Sky*, renowned Anishinaabe scholar Gerald Vizenor asserts, "The *oshki anishinabe* writer tells stories now as in the past—stories about people not facts."[4] These stories form our identities and, as Anishinaabe scholar Kimberly Blaeser has observed, "empower us in the imagination of our destinies."[5]

Anishinaabeg have a long and rich literary tradition. For generations, Anishinaabeg told a vast range of diverse stories as a means to educate and to provide entertainment. Stories were and are in constant motion. They are often changed to fit particular audiences and contexts, continually being told and retold, published and republished. During the eighteenth and nineteenth centuries, the Anishinaabeg began to engage printed literature as a tool to make their political perspectives available to non-Indians and Indians—to tell their stories. Scholar Maureen Konkle has noted that during the first half of the nineteenth century, Anishinaabe writers produced and published the largest body of American Indian narratives.[6] These narratives are encoded with instructions regarding appropriate behavior toward other humans, plants, and animals. They set the moral code and give insight into the tribal governmental structure, political stances, and general worldview.[7] Anishinaabe scholar John Borrows has argued that stories express law and share a close relationship with common law, asserting that Native Nations can "look to their stories as a body of knowledge that fulfills many of the same functions as common law precedent."[8]

There are many creation stories told by Anishinaabeg, each with their own distinct variations. The White Earth Reservation Curriculum Committee agreed upon the version recounted in *White Earth: A History* in 1989:

> Long ago Kitchi Manido had a dream. He dreamed of the "sun, earth, moon, and stars;" and the "trees, flowers, grass, and fruit;" and "all manner of beings walking, flying, crawling, and swimming. . . . After his dream, Kitchi Manido made rock, water, fire, and wind. Into each he breathed life, and to each he gave a different essence and nature. . . . Although his last and weakest of his creations, humans were given the greatest gift of all—the power to dream."[9]

Kitchi Manido had a vision and then took action to make it a reality. This story not only serves to explain creation but to remind Anishinaabeg of our place in the world as the last and weakest of all creatures. Despite this weakness, Anishinaabeg have the power to dream, which is the very way that Kitchi Manido conceived of all creation. Therefore, I argue that the Anishinaabeg carry the power of creation. We create ourselves. We carry the power to create a nation that honors ancestors and also envisions an everlasting future. It was my dream that we use our stories to transform the citizenship requirements of the White Earth Nation (WEN). I wanted to see the nation return to citizenship requirements that do not measure blood but, instead, practice our Anishinaabe values and (re)create a nation with family at its very core. I was elated when White Earth citizens voted to adopt a constitution, which requires lineal descent for citizenship, in 2013. We are now beginning the process of recentering around our families.

As is so often the case, this book is the result of a long journey. I joined the American Studies program at the University of Minnesota in the fall of 2001. Directly after my undergraduate work at the Morris campus of the University of Minnesota, I went to learn and write about the politics of tribal citizenship, especially the one-quarter Minnesota Chippewa Tribe blood-quantum requirement for tribal citizenship used by the Minnesota Chippewa Tribe (MCT)[10] since the middle of the twentieth century. Growing up on the White Earth Reservation, I was all too familiar with the divisions that the use of blood quantum as the sole requirement for tribal citizenship caused, and knew that many Anishinaabeg do not consider it a valid measure of either cultural knowledge or political loyalties. This important issue came up on numerous occasions, but was especially visible during a strong effort for constitutional reform in the late 1990s. At the heart of the issue was whether the WEN and the MCT should continue to use one-quarter MCT blood quantum for tribal citizenship or whether another method, possibly lineal descent, should be implemented. At White Earth there was concern about the vast numbers of Anishinaabeg being excluded under the racial requirement; families were literally divided, with some possessing the blood quantum required for citizenship and others lacking it.

The regulation of tribal citizenship directly impacts my family and me; therefore, I have an interest in, and passion for, this topic that goes beyond scholarly research. While I know who I am as an Anishinaabekwe, I was excluded from citizenship within the White Earth Nation prior to the adoption of the constitution in 2013 because I lacked the required amount of Minnesota Chippewa Tribe blood. I was recognized as a "first degree descendant," which felt like an acknowledgment of my "heritage" but rejection of my identity. My official exclusion from citizenship was a source of disappointment and frustration. My mother is a citizen and raised me with fundamental Anishinaabe values. I had a wonderful childhood and grew up with close bonds to my extended family. I fondly remember walking or riding my bike over to my grandparents' home, where I would play outside for endless hours with my brother and cousins. I do my best to live *mino-bimaadiziwin* (the good life). I also try to be guided by the seven teachings of courage/bravery, truth/sincerity, respect, love, honesty, wisdom, and humility. I have always been proud of who I am as an Anishinaabekwe. My family instilled a sense of responsibility in me, and, with support and encouragement, I came to the conclusion that I could make a contribution to White Earth, the MCT, and other Native nations and peoples through a study of Anishinaabe identity and citizenship.

In my graduate studies, I wanted to address the complex issue of tribal citizenship not only because it impacts me personally but also because it impacts the WEN, the MCT, and other Native nations. As the number of eligible citizens declines, the nation loses power and will eventually "disappear" because no one will qualify for citizenship.[11] Most importantly, the idea that blood alone determines identity runs counter to Anishinaabe values and historic conceptions of identity. The blood-quantum citizenship requirement created a nation based on Western pseudoscientific concepts of race.

Just a few months after my arrival in Minneapolis for graduate school, I was struck by the headline in an issue of *The Circle* (an American Indian newspaper based in Minneapolis), which read, "Blood Quantum v. Lineal Descent." I thought my topic was timely and knew that it was not without controversy, but seeing those words made me realize the broader extent of the issue and the ways in which each side had pitted itself against the other. The issue has put Natives against Natives, and efforts have been focused on fighting each other rather than on positive endeavors to (re)build strong families and nations.[12] Anishinaabe journalist Robert Desjarlait wrote the article, noting that tribes, including Anishinaabeg, have used blood quantum as a requirement for tribal citizenship for about fifty years. Articulating the problems the use of blood quantum has created, Desjarlait asserted: "These federally imposed qualifiers have strongly influenced Indian Country's perceptions of racial acceptability within tribal communities. They result in a eugenic tribal pecking order that has deeply scarred and fragmented the Indian community."[13] Desjarlait discussed the ways in which several nations had recently worked to change their citizenship requirements from blood quantum to lineal descent, in part because, as one person interviewed said, "we want to put our families back together. We don't want them to split because of blood degree."[14] Similarly, I would find that the theme of family would surface again and again in my research.

When I discussed my research with Anishinaabeg, they often shared emotional stories of exclusion and division. Many elders told of grandchildren and great-grandchildren who were ineligible for enrollment because they did not possess the minimum amount of required "blood." Parents were disappointed that their children could not become citizens and expressed concerns about the future of the nation. People told of aggravations and feelings of abandonment because they were not tribal citizens. Others were concerned about their future children—was love or blood more important when selecting the father or mother for one's children? In addition, there are many blended families with only some of their children enrolled.[15] I heard many stories about families divided by fictional fractions of blood, creating a bleeding nation.

In 2007, just as I was finishing my dissertation, Erma Vizenor, chairwoman of the WEN, announced her intention to begin an effort for constitutional reform. I was privileged to be a part of that process, which I detail in chapter 3. Ultimately a new constitution that requires lineal descent for citizenship was created. On November 19, 2013, citizens of the WEN voted to approve the proposed constitution by a margin just short of 80 percent.

My primary purpose is to explore the multifaceted issue of citizenship among the Anishinaabeg of the White Earth Nation and the Minnesota Chippewa Tribe. My concentration in this book on the regulation of tribal citizenship and constitutional reform contributes to the burgeoning field of tribal constitutionalism. I tell the story of identity and citizenship of the White Earth Anishinaabeg to contribute to the complex discussion of tribal citizenship regulations. I delineate the ways in which the United States has infringed upon Anishinaabeg sovereignty and pushed for racial constructions of tribal citizenship, as well as the ways in which Anishinaabeg have resisted these constructions and insisted upon family and relationships as the most appropriate means to determine citizenship. The transparent use of race/blood quantum to define American Indians both within tribal nations as well as by the United States should be challenged. While I place identity and citizenship into dialogue with each other in a specific tribal setting, this work also has implications for the many Native nations currently engaging in or considering constitutional reform. There is no perfect solution to the problem of citizenship regulation for the WEN or any Native nations.

Legal scholar Carol Goldberg has argued, "Citizenship is intimately entangled with fundamental cultural, social, economic, and political dimensions of tribal life."[16] There is a complex relationship between citizenship and identity, beginning in the late nineteenth century and ending with contemporary efforts for change in citizenship requirements via constitutional reform. The Anishinaabeg of White Earth negotiated multifaceted identities both before and after the introduction of blood quantum as a marker of identity and as the sole requirement for tribal citizenship.

Chapter 1, "No, No There Was No Mixed-Bloods: Mapping Anishinaabe Conceptions of Identity," looks at a 1913 federal investigation that assessed the genealogy and racial ancestry of two hundred families at White Earth. This investigation was undertaken to determine the legality of hundreds of land sales because legislation passed by Congress in 1906 tied an individual's ability to sell their land with their biological race. Hundreds of individuals were interviewed regarding their perceptions of identity. These unique and rare interviews provide insightful perspectives on Anishinaabe conceptions of identity and citizenship and help us to understand how political, social, and cultural factors were shaping and reshaping Anishinaabe identity formation during the early twentieth century. The interviews show a wide variety of diverse ideas and conceptions of identity; the only thing they hold in common is the refusal to accept simplistic racial categories set forth by the United States government. It is clear that during the early twentieth century, the Anishinaabeg of White

Earth did not use blood quantum or biological ideas of race to determine a person's identity. Anishinaabeg engaged in survivance by continually refuting those categories while asserting their right to determine identity through fluid understandings of cultural practices and kinship.

The next chapter, "Consider the Relationship: Citizenship Regulations of the Minnesota Chippewa Tribe" begins with the creation of the Minnesota Chippewa Tribe in 1936 and investigates the motivations for changes in citizenship requirements that occurred in the middle of the twentieth century. The MCT is an umbrella government with six member nations (also referred to as bands), including White Earth. There are particular circumstances and influences that led to the implementation of a one-quarter-degree blood-quantum requirement for citizenship in 1961. Previously unexamined administrative documents of the MCT generate an intimate look at how elected tribal leaders thought about citizenship. Documents from the National Archives Records Administration give a more complete picture of the pressures faced by the elected leaders to use blood quantum as the sole determiner for tribal citizenship. The dissatisfaction with the blood-quantum requirement and efforts to change it through the end of the twentieth century are explored here.

The third chapter, "It is Time to Take Our Own Leadership: The Constitution of the White Earth Nation," details the 2007–present effort for constitutional reform with a focus on citizenship requirements. I have been intimately involved in this effort, writing more than forty articles for *Anishinaabeg Today*, which is the official newspaper of the White Earth Nation; giving presentations at constitutional conventions; and serving the team that drafted the constitution. Some of the newspaper articles have been republished in *The White Earth Nation: Ratification of a Native Democratic Constitution*, which I co-wrote with Gerald Vizenor.[17] In this chapter, I draw heavily upon my own notes to describe the discussions about citizenship at each of the four Constitutional Conventions. During the Constitutional Conventions, constitutional delegates frequently noted that citizenship was a very difficult issue, and a wide range of opinions were expressed. While most delegates desired change, there was also a significant degree of apprehension about what change would really mean. This chapter examines the process by which delegates came to decide that family and relationship should once again form the basis of the White Earth Nation.

The book concludes with the Earthdiver story, which tells of the time when Nanaboozhoo, in cooperation with many animals, re-created the earth after the great flood. What can that story mean for us today and how does it apply to citizenship and governance? Creating a citizenship requirement based on values and traditions is a beginning point. We must take action. We must do our best to live and practice our core values in all facets of our lives. It is from this position that we can rebuild our families, communities, and nation.

As a scholar, I have endeavored to create a study that is critical and academically rigorous while also keeping my writing sensitive and respectful to my family and home community, the White Earth Nation, and Anishinaabe peoples. Even though my career has physically removed me away from White Earth, my heart remains there, and I make the 250-mile drive home every chance I get. I humbly offer this text as a gift, an effort at reciprocating for all of the wonderful gifts that I have been given. This is a creation story.

Acknowledgments

THIS BOOK IS ULTIMATELY ABOUT FAMILY, AND WORDS CANNOT express my gratitude to family for their love and support through this entire process. *Miigwech* to my parents, grandparents, uncles and aunties, brother, cousins—all my relations.

Chi-miigwech to my best friend Heidi Kiiwetinepinesiik Stark for helping me work though countless challenges and for her patience, understanding, brilliance, and humor.

Gerald Vizenor's work was a significant source of imagic inspiration. I never could have imagined that we would work on the Constitution of the White Earth Nation together. His friendship and generous advice have been invaluable.

There are so many Anishinaabeg at White Earth that have guided my work. Joe LaGarde's support means the world to me. He has worked on issues related to constitutional reform since before I was born, and his steady resolve that we would get the work done was critical. Erma Vizenor's unwavering determination is a source of inspiration. I have learned so much from her and am grateful she allowed me to be a part of the constitutional reform effort. I must also include the late Andy Favorite, who shared many stories about the history of White Earth and of my own family members, and the late Paul Schultz, who always made me feel welcome and shared good humor on many occasions. Those who have approached me at community events and those who send me e-mails to see how the work is coming and to thank me—mean so much to me.

My wonderful undergraduate liberal arts education at the University of Minnesota–Morris showed me a new world. Wilbert Ahern's kindness and brilliant teaching motivated me to learn. He served as my advisor and mentor for four years and first introduced me to the idea that I might consider graduate school.

This book started as a dissertation in Department of American Studies at the University of Minnesota. I began the research for what is now chapter 2 while participating in the Community of Scholars summer program, which was designed to help students make a successful transition from undergraduate to graduate studies. White Earth Anishinaabe scholar Jeani O'Brien generously agreed to supervise my independent study credits that summer and would later agree to serve as my dissertation advisor. I owe her a great debt; she provided me, and continues to provide me, with guidance and mentorship. I was privileged to learn from brilliant faculty, including Patricia Albers, Brenda Child, LeAnne Howe, Carol Miller, John Nichols, David Treuer, and David Wilkins. The participants in the American Indian Studies Workshop at the University of Minnesota helped me work through many challenges, offering support and useful critiques during both the dissertation and more recent versions of what is now chapter 3. *Miigwech* to David Chang, Christina Gish Hill, Kasey Keeler, Matthew Martinez, Chantal Norrgard, Katie Phillips, Keith Richotte, Jimmy Sweet, Jenny Tonepahhote, and others. My fellow comrades in American Studies, Sonjia Hyon, Anne Martinez, Kim Park Nelson, and Jason Ruiz, provided friendship and motivation.

I finished the dissertation while on the Pre-Doctoral Fellowship at Michigan State University and thank all of the faculty there, but especially the late Susan Applegate-Krouse, who helped me get through that last year. She, her husband Ned, and Nancy DeJoy showed me much hospitality and made my year in East Lansing enjoyable.

The Chancellor's Postdoctoral Fellowship in American Indian Studies at the University of Illinois (2007–2008) allowed me some important time for reflection. I was welcomed as a part of the community there and had such a vibrant experience. *Miigwech* to my fellow fellow Tol Foster and the fabulous faculty and staff: Jodi Byrd, Jan Davis, Brenda Farnel, Matthew Sakiestewa Gilbert (who allowed me to share the "third mesa" with him), Fred Hoxie, John McKinn, Molly Springer, and Robert Dale Parker.

I joined the American Indian Studies Department at the University of Minnesota-Duluth in 2008 and am fortunate to work with excellent colleagues: Joseph Bauerkemper, Linda LeGarde Grover, Tadd Johnson, Ed Minnema, and Erik Redix. I also appreciate the support that our dean, Sue Mahr, has shown for AIS as a whole and for my work. Rochelle Zuck (English) has shared important advice and friendship.

I have presented various versions of this book at several different venues. My community at the Native American Literature Symposium has been especially important. *Miigwech* to Jane Hafen, Gordon Henry, Patrice Hollrah, Margaret Noodin, Niigaanwewidam James Sinclair, and Gwen Westerman, and to Theo Van Alst, Scott Andrews, David Carlson, Royce Freeman, Becca Gerckin, Dustin Gray, Brian Hudson, Denise Low-Weso,

James MacKay, Nancy Pederson, Julie Pelletier, Angela Semple, Steve Sexton, Miriam Brown Spiers, David Stirrup, Chanette Romero, Martha Viehmann, and Laura Adams Weaver. Annual meetings, including those for the American Society for Ethnohistory, American Studies Association, and the Native American and Indigenous Studies Association, have also provided opportunities to share earlier versions of this work. I have been fortunate to have colleagues, including Joanne Barker, Jean Denison, Mishauna Goeman, Kim Tallbear, Malinda Maynor Lowery, Jacki Rand, and Audra Simpson, who have kindly listened to my presentations and offered new insights.

Conversations with colleagues in Anishinaabe studies whose work I admire and who have helped make the field so vibrant have helped me along this journey. *Miigwech* to Kimberly Blaeser, John Borrows, Heid Erdrich, Matthew L. M. Fletcher, Rebecca Kugel, Scott Lyons, Molly McGlennen, Melissa Nelson, Cary Miller, and Bruce White.

I have been fortunate to receive funding support for this project from a variety of sources. I am grateful to the University of Minnesota (Sylvia and Samuel Kaplan Fellowship in Social Justice Studies, Graduate School Block Grant Summer Dissertation Award, the IDEA Multicultural Research Award with the Office of Equity and Diversity, and the Residential Fellowship at the Institute for Advanced Study), Newberry Library (Frances C. Allen Fellowship for Women of American Indian Heritage), University of Minnesota-Duluth (Single-Semester Leave), Michigan State University (Pre-Doctoral Fellowship, American Indian Studies), and University of Illinois (Chancellor's Postdoctoral Fellowship).

Finally, *miigwech* to the wonderful staff at Michigan State University Press, including Bonnie Cobb, Julie Loehr, and Anastasia Wraight for their helpful comments and necessary corrections.

Introduction

CROSS-EXAMINATION OF AY-DOW-AH-CUMIG-O-QUAY BY MR. VAN Meter, 1914:

Q. You know Mis-quah-nah-quod, or Joseph Black?

A. Yes, sir, he was here. He lived here. He was, he had a garden here.

Q. Was he a full blood or a mixed-blood Indian?

A. He was an Indian.

Q. What do you mean by an "Indian,"—a mixed blood may be an Indian.

A. It must be so.

Q. You don't know—you don't know whether he was a mixed blood or a full blood?

A. He is dead long ago. I don't know exactly what he was. You can go dig him out of his grave, and then you can find out.

Q. Who told you to say this to me about digging the grave?

A. I say that just for fun.

Q. Has anybody talked with you about these families, whether they are full bloods or not? Didn't you and the Indians talk about—

A. No, not at all. What I have said came from my own memory.

Q. Then you and the other Indians didn't talk about them in council the last few days?

A. No, sir, I never heard anyone say anything about it.[1]

The exchange between Ay-dow-ah-cumig-o-quay and Mr. Van Meter gives us a glimpse into the competing definitions and complexities of identity in the early years of the twentieth century. Ay-dow-ah-cumig-o-quay and the examiner seem to be using the term "Indian" to mean Anishinaabe. Additionally, Ay-dow-ah-cumig-o-quay was either confused about the categories of mixed-blood and full-blood, or refused to use them in the biological way that the examiner was asking, or both. For many White Earth Anishinaabeg, there were no simple or sensible answers to questions regarding racial identity or blood quantum. Indeed, Ay-dow-ah-cumig-o-quay even took the questions as funny, making a joke, which was not appreciated by the serious examiner. Half a century later, there was no humor to be found when the elected leaders of the Minnesota Chippewa Tribe (MCT) decided that one-quarter Minnesota Chippewa blood would become the sole requirement for tribal citizenship.

The use of blood quantum as the sole requirement for tribal citizenship has had serious and significant consequences. Many Anishinaabeg have been excluded from citizenship because they have less than one-quarter MCT blood. This trend has been projected to continue and to rapidly increase in the coming decades. At the July 2012 quarterly meeting of the Tribal Executive Committee of the MCT, Robert C. Gillespie of Gillespie Processing and Analysis presented the results of a population study he completed for the MCT to determine what the population projections were, based on the one-quarter MCT blood-quantum requirement. Gillespie delivered alarming information: around 2040 it is unlikely that any children being born will have one-quarter or more MCT blood, and thus there will be no new MCT citizens. At that point the number of MCT citizens will decline every year as the population ages and passes away. By 2090 no one will qualify for citizenship within the MCT and the nation will dissolve.[2] See figure 1.

In addition, Gillespie prepared specific data for each of the six MCT nations. He found that the population of White Earth was just over 19,000 and aging rapidly. In fact, about 75 percent of the population were over the age of forty. He estimated that in thirty years the population of White Earth would be about 8,000. In about 2050, the population would continue to decline, and in approximately 2080 there would be no individuals eligible for White Earth citizenship and the White Earth Nation would no longer exist.[3] Despite these stark statistics, some Anishinaabeg accept blood quantum as both a real measure of "Anishinaabeness" and an acceptable means to regulate tribal citizenship. In sharp contrast to the early twentieth century, many now easily answer questions like "how much Indian are you?" with a specific fraction. The existence and validity of blood quantum has become unquestioned by some. Yet, others continue to argue that blood quantum is an alien proposition that is in direct conflict with Anishinaabe values and concepts of identity. Beginning in 2007, the White Earth Nation (WEN) embarked upon an effort for constitutional reform, which included the consideration of citizenship requirements. Constitutional delegates concluded that blood quantum was not the best means of defining citizenship and opted to require lineal descent. The constitution was adopted by referendum vote on November 19, 2013. White Earth citizens decided that citizenship would once again be based on Anishinaabe values, which are rooted in relationships and family.

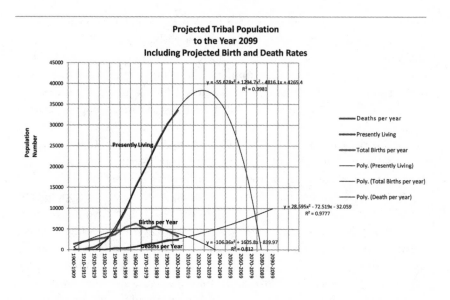

**Projected Tribal Population
to the Year 2099
Including Projected Birth and Death Rates**

DATA SOURCE: MINNESOTA CHIPPEWA TRIBE
GRAPH PRODUCED BY ROBERT C. GILLESPIE, GILLESPIE PROCESSING AND ANALYSIS

NAMES

As they were in the twentieth century, names and terminology continue to be used in diverse ways. Today the Anishinaabeg are known by a variety of names, including Ojibwe and Chippewa.[4] "Chippewa" is considered an altered form of "Ojibwe" and was the name used in treaties with the United States. Chippewa is still the legal name for most government bodies.[5] Ojibwe (also spelled Ojibway and Ojibwa) is thought to be how neighboring tribes referred to Anishinaabeg.[6] Dennis Jones, an Ojibwe language instructor, has found that "when one looks at the history of the word, it has many origins and meanings."[7] The most common definition of Anishinaabe(g) is "original people." While all of the aforementioned names are acceptable, my preference is for Anishinaabe(g), and thus that will be the term used most often in this work.[8] However, I do use other names when quoting others and when naming the official political bodies recognized by the United States. Anishinaabeg acknowledge and value a collective identity but consist of many distinct, separate nations, which are often referred to as bands both in government agreements, such as treaties, and in some scholarship.[9] Despite the care that I, and many other scholars, take with names, the *indian* remains a prominent figure in the American imagination and has, in many ways, pushed the Anishinaabeg and other Native peoples out.

White Earth Anishinaabe scholar Gerald Vizenor has asserted: "The *indian* is a simulation, an invention, and the name could be the last grand prize at a casino."[10] The *indian* is stuck in the 1800s. He (yes, not she) wears a Plains-style headdress, has long black hair in two braids, copper-colored skin, and always has a stern and stoic pose. The *indian* has a static identity that holds tight to the past, prohibiting change and adaptation. He is the pure and authentic "full-blood," simultaneously romantic and tragic. He is posed in museums and photographs but never gets to speak. The *indian* has no tribal affiliation. In his groundbreaking critique of anthropologists, Vine Deloria Jr. noted, "Not even Indians can relate themselves to this type of creature who, to the anthropologists, is the 'real' Indian. Indian people begin to feel that they are merely shadows of a mythical super-Indian."[11] Indeed, for many it is difficult to imagine anything other than the imagery in history textbooks, museums, and Hollywood movies; "the *indian*" has left no room for Natives.[12] I will demonstrate some of the ways that White Earth Anishinaabeg were, and continue to be, measured against the *indian* in impossible and terrible ways.

White Earth Anishinaabeg have in certain ways fervently resisted the imposition of the *indian* and insisted that the power to define identity rests with the people. As a means to escape "the *indian*," Vizenor has suggested "postindian" as a new and useful way in which to characterize identity today. He asserts that as an identity, postindian more effectively encompasses all the complexities of modernity and refutes the static and plastic image of the *indian*. In an interview Vizenor said, "The point is that we are long past the colonial invention of the *indian*. We come after the invention and we are the postindians. . . . The postindian stands for an active, ironic resistance to dominance, and the good energy of native survivance."[13] Vizenor characterizes the *indian* as mere colonial invention, implying that it has no connection with the realities experienced by postindians. Yet, Vizenor also articulates, "the postindian names, in an ironic sense, are the actual names of native creation, such as *anishinabe*, that transpose the *indian* simulations."[14] In the absence of *indian* there is room for diversity, modernity, and victory. Postindians resist dominance by creating and living healthy, principled lives that enact Anishinaabe values.

Vizenor has pushed the *indian* out, declaring, "*Oshki anishinabe* is my postindian name for the new natives of the vast woodland area of the western Great Lakes."[15] He translates *oshki* as "new" or "for the first time." Describing the *oshki anishinabe*, Vizenor has written:

The *oshki anishinabe* are many colors and many different religions, and they have black eyes and blue eyes, blond hair and straight black hair, and they live on and off the reservation, in small towns, remote communities and in the city. . . . Whatever the color of the skin and the politics, the *oshki anishinabe* come together with complex cultural diversity and speak of themselves as being of one tribe.[16]

Religious, political, geographical, and phenotype differences are accepted among the *oshki anishinabe*. In Vizenor's description, phenotype is erased as a determiner of authenticity. Unlike the *indian*, the *oshki anishinabe* are diverse and divergent. The more specific name allows for greater diversity. *Oshki anishinabeg* envision identity and tribal citizen requirements that go beyond colonial constructions of race.

Vizenor's vision of *oshki anishinabe* fits well with the current diversity that exists among White Earth Anishinaabeg. There are White Earth citizens that are Midewiwin, Catholic, Episcopal, Lutheran, Mormon, atheist, and more. There are those who have light skin, dark skin, and skin of a medium shade. There are those who are Green Party, Democrats, Republicans, and those who refuse participation in U.S. politics. There are those who are poor, middle-class, and wealthy. There are those who cherish their children and those who neglect and abuse them; those who follow the traditional seasonal round and those who purchase food at grocery stores and Wal-Mart—and sometimes these are the same people. Similarly, Anishinaabe scholar Scott Lyons has written about the current diversity within the Leech Lake Nation. He notes:

I know devout Christians who speak fluent Ojibwemowin, professors who spend their summers running Midewiwin ceremonies, and softball-playing, English-speaking, nonreligious types who are tremendously talented in the woods, understanding perfectly the language of animal tracks, wind patterns, and habits of game. . . . In fact, now that I think of it, I'm not sure I've ever met anyone whose life perfectly conformed to the standards of Ojibweness as they might be imagined by a purist (language: Ojibwemowin; religion: Midewiwin; mode of production: hunting and gathering; phenotype: brown/black; check, check, check, check).[17]

The *indian* does not exist. In addition, blood quantum has no bearing on the ways in which individuals choose to live their lives. Higher blood quantum does not equal greater fluency in Ojibwemowin. Instead, individuals carry the responsibility to do their best at living Anishinaabe traditions and passing them on to new generations.

BLOOD QUANTUM

Defining American Indian identity on a racial basis has been a primary way the United States has used conceptions of identity to dispossess American Indians of their resources and erase their political obligations. Since the late nineteenth century, the United States has used blood quantum as a way of defining who is and who is not Indian.[18] During the nineteenth century, European and European American scientists believed that blood carried a wide range of hereditary traits. They believed that each race had a unique blood type. It was thought that those blood types determined styles of music and dance, language, and behaviors such as crime. British scholar Francis Galton, often called the "father of eugenics," developed a theory of fractional inheritance. Galton contended that each person received one-half of their hereditary endowment from each parent, one-fourth of which was from each grandparent, one-eighth of which was from each great-grandparent, and so on.[19] Consequently, the mixing of blood that occurred in people who had parents of different races resulted in an amalgamation of behaviors and traits.

During the nineteenth and early twentieth centuries, many Europeans and European Americans considered blood to be an objective measure of American Indian identity. Pseudoscientific theory held that the more "white" blood an American Indian had, the more he or she was socially, culturally, and politically assimilated.[20] In *Native Acts*, Lenape scholar JoAnne Barker discerns that for some, blood was thought to be an impartial and accurate alternative to the "complexities posed by Native customs and epistemologies—which offered alternative perspectives on belonging and kinship that would have included a generosity regarding intermarriage, adoption, and naturalization as well as alternative understandings of belonging and kinship that would have tied members back to their lands and governments as citizens with multiple kinds of responsibilities."[21] In short, Native systems for determining identity were diverse and multifarious; blood quantum was an easy and convenient way for the U.S. government to define identity. Additionally, defining identity via blood ensured that once enough "mixing" took place, American Indians would disappear into the melting pot of American social and political life.

Several states created a variety of laws that utilized blood as the basis for legal definitions of identity. While African Americans were often defined by the one-drop rule, American Indians were often, and continue to be, defined by the one-quarter rule. As scholar Patrick Wolfe has observed, "Race for black people became an indelible trait that would survive any amount of admixture, race for Indians became an inherently descending quantity that was terminally susceptible to dilution."[22] These dramatically different standards for the differing groups highlight the political motivations behind these pseudoscientific determiners of identity: while the United States hoped to define many people as African American because of their prior status as slaves, the federal government desired, and still desires today, to define the least number of people as American Indian in order to limit the number of people they have political and financial obligations to, and to gain control of American Indian resources.[23]

Recently, scholars have begun to expose the political and economic motivations behind blood quantum and its use to define the identity of individuals.[24] In *Hawaiian Blood*, J. Kēhaulani Kauanui asserts, "Blood quantum is a manifestation of settler colonialism that works to deracinate—to pull out by the roots—and displace indigenous peoples."[25] Similarly, scholar Chadwick Allen has concluded, "A standard of racial identification, blood quantum originally served as a device for documenting 'Indian' status for the federal government's purposes of dividing and subsequently alienating collectively held Indian lands."[26] Both Kauanui and Allen address the serious political and economic consequences racialization has had for indigenous peoples.

Blood quantum has served the dual purpose of dispossession and disappearance.[27] In her interdisciplinary study of American Indian identity, *Real Indians*, sociologist Eva Garroutte notes,

> The original, stated intention of blood quantum distinctions was to determine the point at which the various responsibilities of the dominant society to Indian people ended. The ultimate and explicit federal intention was to use the blood quantum standard as a means to liquidate tribal lands and to eliminate government trust responsibility to tribes, along with entitlement programs, treaty rights, and reservations.[28]

The work of these scholars demonstrates that the federal government's use of blood quantum has not been an application of unbiased scientific fact, but rather a calculated political attempt to legally abolish American Indians and gain control of American Indian resources. Additionally, the federal government's attempt to define American Indians on a racial rather than political basis undercuts the sovereign right of American Indian nations to define their own citizenry. This is a serious and conspicuous attack on the sovereignty of Native nations.

Likewise, American Indian nations who utilize blood quantum as a requirement for citizenship participate in a colonial system. They choose to privilege the colonial construct of race above their relatives, who are denied recognition and participation within the nation. Blood quantum places pseudoscientific measures of ancestry above familial relationships and excludes relatives from ever becoming legally recognized citizens. This practice goes against the long history of adoption, incorporation, and intermarriage with both other tribes and non-Indians that many American Indian nations have.[29] In fact, American Indians are considered the most racially diverse of any "group" in the United States. American Indians continue to have the highest rates of intermarriage, which diminishes the American Indian "blood" quantum of their children, putting their ability to enroll as citizens in Native nations at risk.[30] As urbanization and globalization continue, there is little reason to believe that this trend will reverse. Indeed, Cherokee demographer Russell Thornton argued, "A point will be reached—perhaps not too far in the future—when it no longer will make sense to define American Indians in genetic terms, only as tribal members."[31] Consequently, those nations that continue to utilize the pseudoscientific requirement of a specific amount of blood risk having a declining number of citizens, which could result in the nation being in serious jeopardy of vanishing.

In 2007, all eleven of Minnesota's Native nations attended a ceremony at which they signed an agreement with the State of Minnesota designed to ensure that social service agencies recognize the importance of children maintaining contact with their tribes. Kevin Leecy, chairman of the Bois Forte Band of Chippewa and then president of the Minnesota Indian Affairs Council, noted, "Tribal identity is the most critical factor for the health and identity of our children."[32] As Leecy suggests, the essential impact of identity spans all dimensions of life. Citizenship is a fundamental way in which the children that Leecy speaks of can maintain a strong, formal connection with their tribe. In response to studies that have found a connection between high-risk activities, including suicide, and identity acceptance among Native youth in Canada, Mi'kmaq scholar Pamela D. Palmater responds, "It would seem prudent then to find solutions that ensure that Indigenous youth are included in their communities and nations, and that their identities as Indigenous peoples are recognized, legitimized, and encouraged."[33] Allowing children who lack the one-quarter MCT blood quantum to become citizens is a step towards fully welcoming them into a network of extended families, into the nation. In turn, the children will facilitate the continuance of the nation. Relationship becomes the basis for both identity and tribal citizenship.

SOVEREIGNTY AND SURVIVANCE

There has been much legal and scholarly debate about the degree of sovereignty possessed and exercised by American Indian nations. Colonization brought dramatic changes to how sovereignty was understood and practiced. The paradoxical linkages between "race," "culture," and "nation" created a plethora of challenges when it comes to ascertaining the sovereignty of American Indian nations. While there is no single, agreed-upon definition of tribal sovereignty, Wilkins and Stark assert that it is "the spiritual, moral, and dynamic cultural force within a given tribal community empowering the group toward political, economic, and, most important, cultural integrity, and toward maturity in the group's relationships with its own members, with other peoples and their governments, and with the environment."[34] Tribal sovereignty is not static; it is complex and dynamic. It is fundamentally about actions and relationships. Barker astutely argues that "sovereignty must be situated within the historical and cultural relationships in which it is articulated."[35] Understandings of sovereignty are in motion and will continue to change.

U.S. Supreme Court decisions have addressed some questions about the status of American Indian nations.[36] A series of cases in the early 1800s now known as the "Marshall Trilogy" are among the most influential rulings. Chief Justice John Marshall defined the Cherokee as "domestic dependent nations."[37] He argued that "Indian nations had always been considered as distinct, independent political communities, retaining their natural rights, as undisputed possessor of the soil from time immemorial, with the single exception imposed by irresistible power, which excluded them from intercourse with any other European potentate than the first discoverer of the coast of the particular region claimed."[38] Marshall further explained that "weak" states like Indian nations might place themselves under more powerful states without relinquishing the rights of self-government.[39] These rulings remain enforceable legal precedent today. Thus American Indian nations occupy a unique legal and political status, which continues to be explicitly defined in current court cases and legislation.

While it is beyond the scope of this work to detail the dynamic political status of Native nations and their respective degrees of sovereignty, sovereignty is a critical aspect of this work due to my focus on tribal citizenship.[40] The concept and definition of sovereignty as it does or does not apply to American Indians has been defined and redefined by scholars. Mohawk scholar Taiaiake Alfred discusses the notion of sovereignty at length in *Peace, Power, and Righteousness*, asserting, "There is real danger in the assumption that sovereignty is the appropriate model for indigenous governance."[41] Alfred concludes that sovereignty is an "exclusionary concept rooted in an adversarial and coercive Western notion of power."[42] Therefore, he argues, sovereignty is an inappropriate concept for tribal nations because it is incompatible with Indigenous understandings of power. White Earth Anishinaabe scholar Gerald Vizenor explores the idea of sovereignty in *The Heirs of Columbus*, writing: "The notion of tribal sovereignty is not confiscable, or earth bound; sovereignty is neither fence nor feathers. The essence of sovereignty is imaginative, an original tribal trope, communal and spiritual, an idea that is more than metes and bounds in treaties."[43] Vizenor's refusal to define sovereignty in Western terms, as Alfred does, is a way of claiming the term and asserting control to define it.

Vizenor has further argued that Native sovereignty is not the static state of absolute power but a changing state of motion and transformation. In *Fugitive Poses* he writes: "Native sovereignty is the right of motion, and transmotion is personal, reciprocal, the source of survivance, but not territorial."[44] While some have argued that Natives somehow become less authentic or real by changing, Vizenor indicates that, in fact, engaging in motion and transmotion *is* sovereignty.[45] Motion inherently implies action, and thus the motion of sovereignty can be related as a series of actions. Sovereignty is something created through various endeavors, deeds, and acts—through motion. He further asserts, "Sovereignty is in the visions of transformation."[46]

If motion and transformation form significant aspects of sovereignty, then change and adaptation add to the vitality of the people and Native nations. The popular, static representations of *indians* ensure colonial dominance.[47] Imaginative adaptations of the English language are another example of the Native exercise of sovereignty. As Pueblo scholar Simon Ortiz argued in his groundbreaking essay "Towards a National Indian Literature" in 1981,

> The indigenous peoples of the Americas have taken the languages of the colonialists and used them for their own purposes. Some would argue that this means that Indian people have succumbed or . . . have forgotten or been forced to forsake their native selves. This is simply not true. . . . This is the crucial item that has to be understood, that it is entirely possible for a people to retain and maintain their lives through the use of any language.[48]

Ortiz demonstrates the sovereign power of Natives to employ any language to engage in survivance. In this case, change allows for the retention and maintenance of cultural values and political practices. Vizenor's use of the

English language to redefine sovereignty is a direct example of the ways in which Natives use language to redefine and create distinct understandings. Vizenor's assertion that sovereignty is both "imaginative" and an "original tribal trope" forces a reconsideration of the term and ways in which it can be defined. His placement of sovereignty in the realm beyond treaties creates an opening for tribal nations to define sovereignty on their own, independent of Western conceptions of the term.

In *American Indian Literary Nationalism*, Creek scholar Craig Womack articulates the value of sovereignty, writing:

> It is philosophically untenable to assume sovereignty constitutes an inherent demand for purity, isolation, and authenticity. Since sovereignty, by definition, has to do with government-to-government relations, it has everything to do with intersections and exchanges between inside and outside worlds. . . . The beauty of sovereignty is that it liberates tribes from anthropologically based cultural definitions by recognizing them as legally defined political entities, thus providing an alternative to the problem of ahistorical essentialist modes of analysis.[49]

Thus another example of the motion of sovereignty is the "exchanges between inside and outside worlds." Sovereignty is a nexus of relationships. Native sovereignty is not a fixed and static state, but is constantly being (re)defined and (re)created through words, gestures, and actions.

While Womack asserts that a focus on sovereignty can be useful because it frees Native nations from cultural and ahistorical assessments of identity, in fact, culture, time, economics, and more also influence understandings of sovereignty. In *Cash, Color, and Colonialism*, Renee Ann Cramer explores the ways in which the popular misconceptions that American Indians are a racial group(s) and are fixed in the historic past function in the federal acknowledgment process.[50] Despite the rigorous and exhaustive evidence necessary to gain federal acknowledgment, the argument that those applying for (or that have) federal recognition are not "real Indians" is common. Cramer quotes real-estate mogul Donald Trump at Senate hearings regarding proposed changes in the Indian Gaming Regulatory Act in 1992: "When you go up to Connecticut and look—now [the Pequots] don't look like real Indians to me, and they don't look like real Indians to other Indians."[51] Trump cannot "see" the Pequots because they do not look like the racial image in his imagination, and therefore to him they simply do not exist as Indians. Trump goes so far as to assert that "other Indians" do not recognize the Pequots, implying that Natives have a phenotypic and/or racial conception of identity.[52] Even though the United States has recognized the sovereignty of the Pequots, Trump (and others) refuse to acknowledge that political status based in racial and cultural appraisals. He cannot "see" the Pequots because they are not *indians*; they lack the phenotype and poverty expected.

The complexities of American Indian identity and perceptions of American Indian identity are shaped by a wide variety of cultural, political, historical, and racial factors. Cramer acknowledges that

> By socially constructing a mythic Indian and then measuring demands for recognition against it, federal recognition processes seem more often to depend on how many traits the petitioning tribe has in common with the mythic notion of Indian or tribe, than to truly understand the history and reality of the petitioning group.[53]

The racialized image of the American Indians becomes the very standard American Indians are judged against, and this has very real political consequences.[54] Indeed, these racialized definitions have had significant impacts on the White Earth Anishinaabeg.

While the concept of sovereignty remains useful, especially within a political context, it is time to push the boundaries further.[55] Alfred calls for Natives to rethink the concept of sovereignty and replace it with a conception of power that is aligned with both broad and specific tribal ideas of power.[56] In this vein is Vizenor's concept of survivance. Vizenor introduced the term in *Manifest Manners*, published in 1994. While the term has a longer history, Vizenor has put his own twist on the term and it has since come into wide use.[57] In *Manifest Manners* he wrote: "Native survivance stories are renunciations of dominance, tragedy, and victimry. Survivance means the right of succession or reversion of an estate, and in that sense, the estate of native survivancy."[58] Thus, a primary aspect of survivance is continuance, including the genealogical succession of families. The ultimate renunciation of dominance and tragedy is a Native vision of sovereignty, which is survivance.

Survivance is a reimagination of sovereignty that brings control to tribal nations and encompasses political status, resistance, cultural values, and traditions. Indeed, survivance is an original tribal trope. When asked to define survivance, Vizenor responded:

> Survivance in my use of the word, means a native sense of presence, the motion of sovereignty and will to resist dominance. Survivance is not just survival but also resistance, not heroic or tragic, but the tease of tradition, and my sense of survivance outwits dominance and victimry.[59]

Survivance is itself a form of resistance in that it provides an opportunity to challenge and critique sovereignty as it has been defined and utilized by Western nation-states. The motion and actions of sovereignty are an aspect of the comprehensive and inclusive concept of survivance. Survivance is an active word that goes beyond mere survival to include "the tease of tradition" while evading victimization. I use the term survivance in this work as a means to assert Anishinaabe understandings of power.

Survivance is related to the time-honored concept of *mino-bimaadiziwin*, which is defined as "live well, have good health, lead a good life" by John D. Nichols and Earl Nyholm.[60] This broad philosophical concept involves the actions and process necessary to make admirable, moral decisions. Anthropologist Melissa Pflug has defined the good life as "the good, healthy, and moral collective life."[61] Likewise, Vizenor's delicate articulations of the actions and principles of survivance include balance, humor, and continuance. He has also noted, "Survival is a response; survivance is a standpoint, a worldview, and a presence."[62] Like survivance, *mino-bimaadiziwin* is not about mere physical survival. It is a worldview in which individuals and groups actively work to create a rewarding, ethical, and nourishing life. In examining the relationship of both *mino-bimaadiziwin* and survivance in relation to identity and tribal citizenship, I employ Vizenor's theoretical framework to produce scholarship that supports the political, cultural, and intellectual autonomy of American Indian nations and enacts the process of survivance by overturning the "racial hocus-pocus" of blood quantum.[63]

NATIONS AND CITIZENSHIP

The issue of how tribal citizenship should be regulated is directly related to the distinct political status of American Indians. In fact, American Indians are separate from "minority" groups or "people of color" because of their unique political status as nations. American Indians are citizens of Native nations, not minorities.[64] The United States (and several other nations) negotiated treaties with American Indian nations through the nineteenth century and continues to negotiate various agreements today. Anishinaabe scholar Scott Lyons argues that "the moment of treaty was literally the invention of the modern Indian nation."[65] These treaties and political agreements are not based on the racial status of the American Indian, but solely on political status, and they established the foundation for the nation-to-nation relationship that is not experienced by people of color or minorities.

Leading legal scholar Felix S. Cohen has asserted, "In dealing with Indians, the federal government is dealing with members or descendants of political entities, that is, Indian tribes, not with persons of a particular race."[66] While many American scientists and social scientists once accepted race as biological, today many scholars believe that race is a social construction.[67] In the American Anthropological Association's statement on race, they assert, "Physical variations in the human species have no meaning except the social ones that humans put on them."[68] Yet, the United States has attempted to conflate "biological" constructions of race with the political status relating to nations in dealings with American Indians.[69]

Recently there has been a surge in the scholarly debate about the definition of "nation." What defines a nation? How and when do nations form? The answers to these questions are complex.[70] The word "nation" has been used since at least the thirteenth century and comes from the Latin word *natio*, which carries connotations of birth, and often referred to "race," "stock," or "breed." As time went on, the term became more political and cultural.[71]

There are many different ways of conceptualizing nationhood. For example, Alfred explains: "'Mohawk' and 'nationhood' are inseparable. Both are simply about *being*. Being is who you are, and a sense of who you are is arrived at through your relationships with other people—your people. So who we are, is tied with what we are: a nation."[72] Wilkins and Stark define nation as

> a social group that shares a common ideology, common institutions and customs, and a sense of homogeneity; controls a territory viewed as a national homeland; and has a belief in a common ancestry. A prerequisite of nationhood is an awareness or belief that one's own group is unique in a most vital sense; therefore, the essence of a nation is not tangible but psychological, a matter of attitude rather than of fact. A nation may constitute part of a state, be contentious with a state, or extend beyond the borders of a single state.[73]

Our understandings of nationhood have changed over time and will continue to develop as our interpretations and perceptions evolve.

Anishinaabe understandings of nationhood are diverse and have transformed over time as well. In "Marked by Fire," Stark examines Anishinaabe conceptions of nationhood during the nineteenth century. She argues that Anishinaabe conceptions of "nationhood were and remain expressly linked to their inherent constructions of their identity."[74] Stark asserts that Anishinaabe nationhood has been shaped by many factors and has undergone transformation over time. Anishinaabe leaders continued to engage in practices that reaffirmed their notions of nationhood, which were flexible and inclusive, and resisted the imposition of Western constructions of nationhood. Stark reasons: "The Anishinaabe have always engaged in the process of transformation, understanding what nationhood has meant for their people while carefully and strategically shifting what it would become, expressing who they were while envisioning what they would be."[75] Indeed, this process has been ongoing during the 2007–present constitutional reform effort at White Earth; Anishinaabeg have grappled with difficult questions regarding nationhood, sovereignty, and citizenship.

Citizenship is a critical issue for all nations: citizens form the foundation of the nation. Citizenship requirements are one phenomenon to turn to when examining the fundamental characteristics of nations. In *Citizenship and Nationhood in France and Germany*, Roger Brubaker asserts: "The state-centered assimilationist understanding of nationhood in France is embodied and expressed in an expansive definition of citizenship, one that automatically transforms second-generation immigrants into citizens, assimilating them—legally—to other French men and women."[76] Alternatively, the "ethnocultural, differentialist" conception of nationhood in Germany is reflected in citizenship options open to ethnic German immigrants but closed to non-Germans.[77] Conceptions of citizenship are shaped by the distinct political histories, geographic territory, and cultural practices of each nation. In addition, citizenship requirements have changed over time and the process of change has not gone uncontested.[78] Brubaker argues that the expansive French conception of citizenship and the restrictive German definition of citizenship center around cultural understandings of nationhood and are not reflections of economic, demographic, or military concerns.[79]

One of the vital powers all nations have, including Native nations, is the regulation of citizenship. Cohen asserts: "The courts have consistently recognized that one of an Indian tribe's most basic powers is the authority to determine questions of its own membership. A tribe has power to grant, deny, revoke, and qualify membership."[80] This right was initially recognized in the 1905 South Dakota court case *Waldron v. United States*.[81] In 1978 the ruling was further clarified in *Martinez v. Santa Clara Pueblo* when the Supreme Court held that tribal nations have the right to determine tribal citizenship.[82] As expressed by Justice Thurgood Marshall, "A tribe's right to define its own membership for tribal purposes has long been recognized as central to its existence as an independent political community."[83] Legal scholar Matthew Fletcher has observed that *Martinez* "is easily the most heavily-cited Indian law case of the modern era and is one of the strongest judicial statements in favor of tribal self-determination and preservation of tribal culture."[84] While Cohen and other scholars use the term "membership," I use the term "citizenship" with the explicit purpose of evoking the political status of American Indians and American Indian nations. Membership is a term often used with regard to clubs and organizations. Citizenship refers to a specific political status; a citizen is commonly defined as an "enfranchised member of a state or nation."[85] Today American Indians have dual citizenship status. In 1924, Congress naturalized all American Indians via the Indian Citizenship Act.[86] This law conferred U.S. citizenship on all noncitizen American Indians, without their consent.[87] Federal officials hoped that U.S. citizenship would facilitate the assimilation process and eliminate the separate status of Native nations. However, American Indians retained citizenship within their tribal nations, and many continue to participate in their Native nations.[88]

Many American Indian nations establish citizenship requirements and practices within their constitutions. Numerous American Indian nations wrote constitutions in the 1930s after the passage of the Indian Reorganization Act and were highly influenced by U.S. officials.[89] As Vine Deloria Jr. and Clifford M. Lytle argue, "It is crucial to realize . . . that these have not been the forms of government that the Indian people themselves have demanded or appreciated and are certainly not the kind of government that most Indians, given a truly free choice in the matter, would have adopted by themselves."[90] While citizenship is widely seen as a primary indicator of political and cultural traditions, as in the examples of France and Germany, citizenship requirements in American Indian nations have been heavily affected by U.S. political investment in the disappearance of American Indian nations via the depoliticization and racialization of American Indian populations.[91]

Tribal citizenship requirements have changed dramatically over time. Federal officials encouraged tribes to use a blood-quantum minimum and/ or residence as criteria for citizenship. In her quantitative and qualitative study *Tribal Constitutionalism: States, Tribes, and the Governance of Membership*, Kirsty Gover examines the changes in tribal citizenship over time. Gover's data set included 322 historic and contemporary tribal constitutions, which represent 245 of the 344 federally recognized tribes from the lower forty-eight states.[92] She found that about 15 percent of the tribes in her study used lineal descent as a citizenship requirement before 1941, but today that number has increased to 44 percent.[93] She notes, "The rise in lineal descent rules therefore is primarily a function of the strong preference shown by tribes adopting constitutions *for the first time* after 1970."[94]

While a noteworthy number of Native nations populating the lower forty-eight states have rejected blood quantum as a means to define citizenship, some degree of blood quantum remains the most common way for Native nations to regulate citizenship.[95] Legal scholar Carol Goldberg suggests that blood quantum "may sometimes have a legitimate place in tribal governing documents."[96] Drawing upon historical evidence that the Department of the Interior strongly pushed the use of blood quantum for tribal citizenship, I argue that blood quantum is not the best way for either the MCT or the WEN to determine citizenship eligibility. In fact, as I will discuss at length in chapter 2, elected tribal leaders strongly resisted the implementation of a blood-quantum requirement for tribal citizenship for several decades.

Identity and citizenship requirements continue to be debated by many Native nations. Newspaper articles discussing identity as it relates to tribal citizenship abound. Enrollment/citizenship disputes are increasing.[97] In recent years, some tribes have disenrolled upwards of half of their citizens, causing many to argue that tribes are jeopardizing the future of their own nations. In 2006, Lumbee scholar David Wilkins explored the issue in an opinion piece entitled "Self-Determination or Self-Decimation? Banishment and Disenrollment in Indian Country" in *Indian Country Today*. Drawing upon the work of Vine Deloria Jr., Wilkins argues that "tribal nations were and should become again sacred bodies of related kinfolk. This is the essence of what it means to be a tribal citizen within a First Nation."[98] At a public lecture at the University of Minnesota-Duluth in the spring of 2009, Wilkins examined the issue in depth and argued that the striking increase in disenrollments and banishments that has occurred since the 1990s has largely been a response to crime rates, blood quantum, and financial circumstances. He noted that previously the expulsion of one's relatives was not common and was a last resort after a variety of reconciliation efforts were made. Wilkins asserted that tribes must consider whether they are engaging in self-decimation when disenrolling or banishing tribal citizens.[99]

CONCLUSION

My focus on citizenship is intended to emphasize political autonomy. While I contend that blood quantum is not an appropriate citizenship requirement for the White Earth Nation, there is no single "answer" to the way(s) in which tribal citizenship should be regulated. There is no one-size-fits-all answer; instead, it is critical to examine local histories, cultural practices, and stories to find guiding principles that can help guide individual nations as they answer questions about how citizenship should be determined today. Blood quantum has been used as a tool of dispossession and division. The Anishinaabeg have an important history of resistance to blood quantum and racialized conceptions of identity. Each Anishinaabe nation, and each Native nation, must decide for themselves what is the best way to regulate tribal citizenship. I hope that other nations will find it useful to examine how Anishinaabe conceptions and constructions of citizenship and identity compare and contrast with their own. In an increasingly global world with an ever-growing population of people who have a diversity of heritage and political affiliation, the Anishinaabe focus on family and fluidity might find a welcome audience.

CHAPTER ONE

No, No There Was No Mixed-Bloods

Mapping Anishinaabe Conceptions of Identity

IDENTITY HAS LONG BEEN ONE OF THE MOST CRITICAL AND CONTENTIOUS issues for American Indians, including Anishinaabeg. Identity pervades nearly all aspects of the lives of American Indians, and the American racialization of American Indian identity has not only proven to be counter to American Indian conceptions of identity, but has also served to erase and disenfranchise American Indians. For example, when the sale of allotments in the early twentieth century came into question at White Earth, the United States federal government used racial identity as the primary factor to determine the legality of the land sales. However, the Anishinaabeg of White Earth conceptualized and utilized identity in a variety of ways that differed from the simplistic racial identity pushed by the federal government. This chapter explores the varied ways in which the Anishinaabeg of White Earth conceptualized identity during the early twentieth century. I argue that the federal government used blood quantum as a way to disenfranchise the people of White Earth.

In the late nineteenth and early twentieth centuries, there were a myriad of complex systems and social regulations that Anishinaabeg used to determine who were and were not members of their tribe. It would be a mistake to think that these systems functioned without any conflict—undoubtedly, there were disagreements and power struggles. However, Anishinaabeg controlled these systems and they worked out conflicts or agreed to disagree, as was their sovereign right; they determined who was and who was not a member/citizen of the nation.

LANDING IDENTITY

In 1887, Congress passed the Dawes Act, also known as the General Allotment Act. This act authorized the President of the United States to allocate reservation land to individual American Indians and specified who should receive which amounts of land. The United States would hold the title to the land in trust for twenty-five years as a means of protection for the allottee while he or she learned to use the land to its fullest potential. It was presumed that after twenty-five years the individual would have the skills necessary to manage his or her own affairs, and a fee patent, which allowed unrestricted ownership of the land, would be issued. The paternalistic trust relationship between the federal government and American Indians established in treaties is clearly evident in the Dawes Act.[1]

In "The General Allotment Act 'Eligibility' Hoax," John P. LaVelle details the requirements of the General Allotment Act and the ways in which it has been misrepresented in scholarship. Contrary to popular belief and previous scholarship, the act did not require an individual to have one-half or more Indian blood. While the act did not define "Indians," the Code of Federal Regulations provided clarification on the qualifications of applicants. An individual wishing to apply for an allotment was

> required to show that he is a recognized member of an Indian tribe or is entitled
> to be so recognized. Such qualifications may be shown by the laws and usages
> of the tribe. The mere fact, however, that an Indian is a descendant of one
> whose name was at one time borne upon the rolls and who was recognized as
> a member of the tribe does not itself make such Indian a member of the tribe.[2]

LaVelle asserts: "Indeed, in enacting the 1887 General Allotment Act, Congress imposed no blood quantum–specific 'eligibility' requirement on Indians at all. Instead, Congress made eligibility for allotments under the act depend exclusively on the tribes' own independent membership determinations."[3] While the act required that those receiving allotments were members of Indian tribes, many tribes did not have official written membership/citizenship policies at this time, or complete lists of citizens.

Thus, the act signaled the most critical period in the evolution of United States involvement in citizenship among tribal nations because this new federal policy required an official census to determine who was a tribal citizen and, therefore, who would receive an allotment. The resulting "census," then, effectively became a primary source in determining who was a citizen of a band or nation. Individuals who for one reason or another were left off the list effectively lost their status within their tribe and with the federal government. Even though they were recognized as Indian in their communities, officially they were not counted as Indian.[4] As Goldberg has observed, "Once a roll is established as the basis for citizenship, it becomes politically difficult to expand citizenship beyond its confines."[5]

At White Earth, the Chippewa Commission was charged with enumerating individuals entitled to allotments but found this to be a difficult task. In their 1889 report, the Chippewa Commission concluded that more than the 8,304 people who were enumerated were entitled to be on the census.[6] The commission initially agreed to recognize individuals of mixed ancestry if the chiefs wanted them to be included on the list. However, members of the commission would soon begin to assert their own ideas and question the authority of tribal officials. The chairman of the commission wrote to the Indian Office, asserting that "there is a great deal of politics upon an Indian reservation. The chiefs in some instances have brought us names and asked us to place them upon the rolls of the Chippewas of Minnesota, and after inquiring into the matter, and questioning them closely, we have found in a number of instances that the parties were from Canada, or from out of the state, who were very evidently not entitled to be enrolled or to receive the benefits of the Act."[7] Thus the question arose: Who had the final authority to determine who should be listed—the Anishinaabe chiefs or the commission?

The Office of Indian Affairs instructed the commission that they were no longer to rely on the chiefs' opinions, and it would no longer be sufficient for individuals to prove they had Anishinaabe ancestry. Instead, applicants would have to have a parent who lived with Anishinaabeg and drew annuities prior to 1889, and they would also have to demonstrate an intention to live permanently on the reservation. These new procedures not only usurped the authority of the chiefs to determine who was Anishinaabe, they also were designed to allow as few people as possible to qualify as Anishinaabe.[8]

Meanwhile, the United States also wanted to consolidate all the Anishinaabeg in Minnesota onto one or two reservations. As a result, the population at White Earth expanded rapidly during the 1870s. In fact, the population increased from about 800 in 1875 to over 1,400 a year later, as the Pembina and Otter Tail Pillager Bands joined the Mississippi Band already at White Earth. In 1886, Congress appointed a commission to negotiate a formal agreement to move all Anishinaabeg to White Earth. The plan was for all Anishinaabeg in Minnesota to move to the White Earth Reservation and to eliminate the other reservations, but few Anishinaabeg were willing to agree to the arrangement. Despite little Anishinaabe support, in 1889 Congress passed the Nelson Act, which declared that the Anishinaabeg would cede all reservations except for White Earth and Red Lake. Red Lake Anishinaabeg were to take allotments on their own reservation, and everyone else would take theirs at White Earth.[9]

The Nelson Act also created the "Chippewa in Minnesota Fund," which would hold the profits from the sale of "surplus" agricultural lands and timber. The money was to be held for fifty years and earn 5 percent interest. Twenty-five percent of the interest was reserved for education and the remaining 75 percent was to be distributed on a per capita basis. After fifty years (in 1939) any remaining monies were to be distributed in equal shares to all Minnesota Anishinaabeg. The United States Chippewa Commission began negotiating the details of this act in June of 1889. White Earth leaders were not impressed with the plan and were wary of promises by the officials because so many other promised funds had never materialized. However, a majority of adult men were finally convinced once they were told that the act also allowed individuals to take allotments on their home reservations. Throughout the 1890s, about 1,200 of 4,000 individuals whom the Chippewa Commission attempted to relocate actually did move. Those who chose to move to White Earth increased the wide range of diversity already present there.[10]

Ultimately, the Dawes Act resulted in the loss of approximately 90 million acres of land previously held in common by American Indian nations.[11] The first allotments were made at White Earth in 1901, with 4,372 allotments being authorized that year. Eventually, over 12,000 allotments would be made.[12] Allotment tied identity directly with land, and there was conflict as to who was entitled to an allotment. For example, in 1907 Mrs. Stella Tourville of Fosston, Minnesota, requested enrollment at White Earth but was denied by the General Council of the White Earth Indians on June 1 of that year. The acting secretary of the Interior approved the action of the council rejecting the application.[13] Unfortunately, there is no other information in the file and no way of knowing why Tourville's application was denied.[14] In this case, the Anishinaabe government maintained control and determined that Tourville was not eligible for an allotment. The secretary of the Interior also had the authority to approve or reject decisions made by the Anishinaabe government. In fact, many individuals who did not live at White Earth but believed they were entitled to obtain an allotment there wrote directly to the secretary of the Interior or the commissioner of Indian Affairs and not tribal leaders to explain their circumstances and request an allotment. Both the United States as well as individual Anishinaabeg often circumvented tribal authority.

A barrage of legislation in the early 1900s made major changes to the governance of allotments, and White Earth would be the center of a national scandal. In the groundbreaking work *The White Earth Tragedy*, historian Melissa Meyer meticulously details the fraud and corruption at White Earth. She delineates questionable legislation and the resulting complex realities that would lead to the dispossession of thousands of Anishinaabeg and great wealth for a few. Meyer examines the complex and dynamic interactions between various political factions of Anishinaabeg at White Earth near the turn of the twentieth century. She defines two primary political and cultural factions at White Earth during the late nineteenth century as "conservative" and "progressive." She argues that "conservative Anishinaabe bands located at a distance from fur trade outposts maintained a more subsistence-oriented way of life," while progressives "participated more fully in the market economy."[15] Yet, she notes that "both groups had adapted to altered conditions from a foundation of continuity with past cultural constructs."[16] The conservative faction would eventually be known as "full-bloods" and the progressives as "mixed-bloods," but these labels were reflective of "culturally determined values" not biological or racial ancestry.[17] My work builds upon and expands the various determinants of identity utilized by the Anishinaabeg Meyer describes.

In 1904, the Clapp Rider passed Congress, which applied exclusively to the White Earth Reservation. Moses Clapp, a Minnesota senator, included the legislation at the end of the annual Indian Appropriations Act, where the "rider" inconspicuously slipped through. The Clapp Rider authorized the "Chippewa of Minnesota" to sell the timber on their allotments. In the spring and summer of 1906, Congress passed two more important pieces of legislation relating to the sale of allotted lands. In May, Congress passed the Burke Act, which allowed the Indian Office to issue fee patents to "competent" Indians before the end of the trust period prescribed in the Dawes Act. Competence was to be determined by individual agents and superintendents on a case-by-case basis.[18] Of course, "competence" was a term loaded with unspoken implications. Essentially, those Indians who were deemed competent by the federal government had adopted some European and American customs, spoke English, and often had European ancestry. In addition, the "mixed-bloods" were only considered "competent" to control their allotment. The United States continued to consider them "incompetent" for other purposes and remained in control of their trust funds.[19] An individual's "competence" effectively became the legal rationalization for deceitful land dealings.

Then, only a month and a half after the passage of the Burke Act, the second Clapp Rider passed Congress. Once again it was attached to the Indian Appropriations bill and garnered little attention. This Clapp Rider removed all restrictions on the sale of allotted land within the White Earth Reservation held by adult "mixed-bloods" as well as those "full-bloods" deemed "competent" by the secretary of the Interior, thus establishing blood quantum as a concept and concurrently correlating it with competence, which was to continue to be determined on an individual basis.[20] No definitions of "mixed-blood" or "full-blood" were given in the legislation, which would later lead to confusion and conflict. Congressman Moses Clapp and his co-collaborator Halvor Steenerson claimed to have had the best interests of the Anishinaabeg at heart.[21] This "rider" opened a watershed, and land offices at White Earth were nearly instantaneously flooded with paperwork for the sale of thousands of acres of land.

There would soon be many questions about this problematic and notable legislation. As noted, the legislation failed to define who exactly fell into the categories of "mixed-blood" or "full-blood," but there was an implicit understanding that these were scientific terms, which dealt with literal, biological measures of race. Essentially, an individual with only Anishinaabe ancestors was considered a "full-blood," an individual with one Anishinaabe parent and one non-Indian (generally European American) parent was defined as a half-blood, and so on. However, there were many questions about the legal definition of "mixed-blood." How much European blood did one need to be considered a "mixed-blood"? The U.S. District Court for the District of Minnesota, district 4, sixth division, ruled that an individual must possess a minimum of one-eighth "white blood" to be legally defined as a "mixed-blood."[22] The case was appealed and the United States Circuit Court of Appeals overruled the district court, finding that a "mixed-blood" was an individual with any amount of "white blood." The United States Supreme Court subsequently upheld this "one drop" rule on June 8, 1914. Under the law, an individual with any European ancestors was a "mixed-blood"; in this case the actual percentage of blood was irrelevant.[23] During this time, many European Americans thought that biological, racial ancestry played a significant role in determining intelligence.[24] Commissioner of Indian Affairs Francis Leupp opposed the Burke Act and both Clapp Riders because he thought the tasks of determining competence and racial blood quantum were complicated and problematic. He believed that most of the "mixed-blood" adults at White Earth were not "competent" to control their own resources, and feared that these Anishinaabeg would be taken advantage of by non-Indians and would lose their lands through fraudulent dealings.[25]

Indeed, only three years after the passage of the Clapp Rider, a full 80 percent of the White Earth Nation land had passed into private ownership.[26] In 1908, United States Indian Agent John R. Howard wrote to the Commissioner of Indian Affairs regarding how he should deal with the fraudulent land transactions at White Earth. He reported:

> Complaints are constantly being made to me by the Indians under my charge, that they are being robbed of their lands by certain white men, on or near the reservation, who are ostensibly engaged in business as lawyers, banks &c., but whose real business is, speculating in Reservation lands and systematically robbing the Indians.[27]

Howard went on to detail the fraud, writing:

> Numerous instances have been reported to me by the Indians, where they have been approached by these men, with a request to sign some paper, representing that it is an authority to probate the estate of a deceased relative, or an authority to sell an allotment, or some similar pretext; or the Indian borrows a small amount of money and signs what he is led to believe is a mortgage. In many instances the instrument signed, proves afterwards, to be a deed of the Indian's land.[28]

Howard requested permission to restrict access to the records of his office, which he claimed the men were using "for the sole purpose of robbing Indians."[29]

In 1909, Warren K. Moorehead, a scholar from Massachusetts and member of the Board of Indian Commissioners, arrived at White Earth to investigate the conditions there as he had heard rumors about the devastating circumstances. He found the rumors to be quite accurate and began to take affidavits from the individuals who claimed their land was illegally taken. Moorehead collected a plethora of evidence and delivered it to Commissioner of Indian Affairs R. G. Valentine. Meyer notes, "The results of Moorehead's probing horrified Commissioner of Indian Affairs Valentine and he authorized Moorehead and Edward B. Linnen, a regular experienced Indian Office inspector, to undertake another investigation in July of 1909."[30] Their final report fleshed out Moorehead's original findings and spurred further inquiry. In light of their extraordinary findings, the Indian Office sent several more officials to look into the land fraud. The fraud was so clear and rampant that, as Meyer has noted, "Nearly every Indian Office official sent to look into the matter was scandalized by the ways Indians had lost their lands."[31] Complaints of disenfranchised Anishinaabeg and the involvement of Indian Office officials soon caused those who had profited from the land sales to realize that their titles could possibly be revoked. With the cooperation of congressmen, including Clapp, these landholders were able to get a provision for the establishment of a commission to accurately determine the blood status of White Earth allottees in the annual Indian Appropriations bill in 1913 that would, in turn, resolve which land sales were legal in accordance with the Clapp Rider.[32] Although a blood classification roll, known as the Hinton Roll, was created in 1910, a new commission was appointed for the same purpose three years later because those who had profited from the land deals complained it was seriously flawed.[33] The primary difference between the rolls was, not surprisingly, that many individuals classified as "full-bloods" on the Hinton Roll were reclassified as "mixed-bloods" on the new roll.[34]

In 1913, Ransom Powell was chosen to head the new investigation. He was appointed by the United States to investigate the genealogy of two hundred Anishinaabe families (about five thousand individuals) and determine which were "mixed-blood," according to the legal definition established in the courts. Interior Secretary Franklin Lane did raise some questions about the appointment of Powell to this investigation because Powell served as attorney for a host of individuals and companies at White Earth. Indeed, the investigation of the roll commission would expedite the very cases Powell was serving as attorney for. While the conflict of interest was clear, Powell remained head of the investigation. As Meyer has observed, "Political and economic interests in northwestern Minnesota were obviously on quite cozy terms."[35]

MIXED TRANSLATIONS

Since no definition of "mixed-blood" was given in the Clapp Rider, one had to be established before the new investigators could officially begin the bulk of their work. As previously mentioned, the court did rule on this question and found that any fraction of white blood was enough to legally classify an individual as a "mixed-blood."[36] This legalized biological measure of race as the single determinant of United States definitions of Anishinaabe identity would result in the largest possible number of Anishinaabe being identified as "mixed-blood." It would soon become apparent that, at best, the conception of "mixed-blood" and "full-blood" as racial categories was new to the

Anishinaabeg of White Earth. It fact, it was likely that many people there had never used these terms or the metaphor of blood as an indication of a biological measure of race as a means to define identity within their own nation/community.

It is not entirely clear when the concepts of "full-blood" and "mixed-blood" were introduced among the Anishinaabeg, or how these terms might have been initially understood. While blood symbols and rituals are widely distributed throughout cultures, the meanings and metaphors attached to blood vary and change over time.[37] Meyer has observed that "The most widespread metaphorical trope attributes life-giving qualities to blood, both in terms of procreation and agricultural fertility."[38] In some cultures, blood is also associated with race. Anthropologist Brackette Williams asserts that ideologies that conflate race and culture produce "concepts which locate the source and meaning of cultural difference in the 'bloods' of different human populations."[39] Blood comes to be considered as the basis of culture, which is passed on from one generation to the next. There is evidence that beliefs Anishinaabeg held about blood during the late nineteenth and early twentieth centuries were complex, diverse, and evolving.

In addition, the term "half-breed" originated in English common law. It distinguished between siblings who shared a single, common parent. The term did not have any racial connotations. It gained popularity during the North American fur trade and was used to refer to people of mixed racial and cultural ancestry—usually French and American Indian, or English and American Indian.[40] As mentioned, in order to address confusion that resulted from the changing definitions of "half-breed" and "mixed-blood," United States courts eventually had to rule on the legal meanings.[41]

It is possible that the idea and/or belief that blood was directly associated with racial ancestry, as well as physical characteristics and mental abilities, was introduced among the Anishinaabeg during the treaty period. Some treaties include references to "mixed-bloods" or "half-breeds." For example, Article 4 of the Treaty of 1842 reads: "Whereas the Indians have expressed a strong desire to have some provision made for their half breed relatives, therefore it is agreed, that fifteen thousand (15,000) dollars shall be paid to said Indians, next year, as a present, to be disposed of, as they, together with their agent, shall determine in council."[42] This wording implies that it was the Anishinaabe leaders negotiating the treaty who asked for the special provision for the "half-breeds," and that the United States government was reluctant to comply with the request. Additionally, it implies that the "half-breeds" would determine how to spend the funds with the assistance of the agent. This raises a question: if the "half-breeds" were not considered

Indians, why would they be under the obligation to consult with an Indian agent? This example illustrates the ways in which the U.S. government defined individuals as Indian when it was convenient and advantageous.

Despite securing the special provision for the "half-breeds," several leaders were not satisfied with the agreement. La Pointe Chief Buffalo signed reluctantly, "expressing his disappointment for having secured so little for his relatives, the half-breeds."[43] A few months later, White Crow, principal chief of the Lac du Flambeau Bands, and Martin, chief of Lac Courte Oreilles, expressed their dissatisfaction with the recent treaty to subagent Reverend Alfred Brunson. They both complained that the mixed-bloods had not been adequately provided for. Martin asked that the half-breeds be provided for equally with the Indians.[44] Martin's request indicates that there was not a divide within the community based on ancestry, or that those with some European ancestry were treated differently.

Displeased with the terms of the 1842 Treaty, when negotiating the Treaty of 1847, Anishinaabe leaders made sure that "mixed-bloods" were included and considered "Chippewa Indians."[45] Article 4 of the Treaty with the Chippewa of the Mississippi and Lake Superior of 1847 states:

> It is stipulated that the half or mixed bloods of the Chippewas residing with them shall be considered Chippewa Indians, and shall, as such, be allowed to participate in all annuities which shall hereafter be paid to the Chippewas of the Mississippi and Lake Superior, due them by this treaty, and by the treaties heretofore made and ratified.[46]

In this case, those "mixed-bloods" residing with the Chippewa are explicitly included in annuities. Likewise, the Treaty of 1867, which established the White Earth Reservation, limits the inclusion of "half-breeds" and "mixed-bloods" to those who lived on a Chippewa reservation. Article 4 states: "No part of the annuities provided for in this or any former treaty with the Chippewas of the Mississippi Bands shall be paid to any half-breed or mixed-blood, except those who actually live with their people upon one of the reservations belonging to the Chippewa Indians."[47] Here, residence and "blood" are dovetailed in an effort to decide who is entitled to annuities. Residence is required for "mixed-bloods" to collect annuities, making it more important than "blood." However, the clause implies that "full-bloods" will get annuities regardless of residence.

Despite the use of the English terms "mixed-blood" and "half-breed," it is not clear how Anishinaabeg might have understood the terms, and what role they played in creating the special provisions for "mixed-bloods" in the treaties. Little information on translation of treaties is available. One document that provides some insight into terminology and translation is "A Bilingual Petition of the Chippewas of Lake Superior." The petition was recorded in 1864 and has been edited by John D. Nichols. The petition contains the phrase "your mixed-bloods."[48] In addition, White Earth scholar David Beaulieu has observed that the terms "mixed-blood" and "half-breed" were the same in the Anishinaabe language, and the terms were not used as either metaphoric or actual percentages of blood but as a reflection of lifestyle choices.[49] Indeed, as demonstrated in the examples above, the terms appear to have been used interchangeably. In the late 1800s, Bishop Baraga defined "half-breed" as *aibitawisid*.[50] During this period, "half-breed" was also often translated as "half burned piece of wood." The blood metaphor is absent from these translations.

QUESTIONABLE IDENTITIES

Due to his representation of a number of clients in land fraud cases, Powell had already begun extensive interviews as early as 1908 as part of his work for the defendants in these cases.[51] After the courts established a legal definition for "mixed-blood," Powell and those who worked under him officially began doing interviews for the investigation. During the course of the investigation, numerous Anishinaabeg were interviewed regarding each individual's ancestry, blood quantum, and physical characteristics. The investigators were to determine if the Anishinaabeg in question fit the standard for Anishinaabe identity, which had been created by lawyers and judges in courtrooms of the United States. This standard was highly influenced by popular simulations of the *indian*.[52] Gerald Vizenor argues, "The *indian* was a cultural concoction of bourgeois nostalgia and social sciences evidence."[53] In fact, the *indian* has no actual relation to Natives and tells us much more about European American conceptions of identity than it does about Anishinaabe identity. The *indian* is, in fact, a fantastic construction based on social and political motivations of European Americans.[54] The racialization of Anishinaabe identity and the broad definition of "mixed-blood" served as a means to ensure the dominance of the United States and to facilitate the fulfillment of manifest destiny. Regardless of the motivations of the investigators, the testimonies collected by this investigation provide rare, direct statements by Anishinaabeg of White Earth as to how they understood their identity.[55]

Ransom Powell and those who worked under him asked a variety of questions to determine who were "mixed-bloods" and who were "full-bloods." A number of important factors influenced the interviews. While the interviews were only recorded in English, language and translation were critical. The English and Anishinaabe skill level varied greatly at White Earth. Some individuals were fluent in both languages, while others possessed only partial understanding and still others spoke only one language. There is no information about the interviewees' skill levels in English or Anishinaabe; therefore, I can only speculate about when language and translation became an issue. However, there are cases in which translation appears to have influenced the answers of the interviewees.

Investigators most often inquired about the physical features and parentage of individuals to determine their racial ancestry. The investigators were well aware of the political stakes surrounding their investigation, and they were intent on establishing that a large portion of the people at White Earth were "mixed-bloods." Influenced by the pseudoscientific correlation between biological ancestry and physical characteristics, the investigators often insisted that physical features such as light hair and/or skin indicated that a person was a "mixed-blood." However, investigators also played the other side of the coin and, at opportune times, noted that dark-skinned and dark-haired individuals might have "one drop" of white blood and, therefore, might be "mixed-bloods," leaving little room for the possibility that an individual was a "full-blood." The questions were often asked in a leading and, at times, accusatory fashion, with the likely intent of agitating and/or confusing witnesses.

Despite the interests and tactics of Powell and his investigators, many Anishinaabeg insisted that they did not use the categories of "mixed-blood" and "full-blood" to define an individual's identity. The testimonies of this investigation illustrate that the racial categories of "mixed-blood" and "full-blood" were relatively new to the Anishinaabeg of White Earth. During questioning, some refused to use these categories and repeatedly asserted that this was not the way that they understood identity. Language and translation of the terms "full-blood" and "mixed-blood" likely influenced these responses.

In order to establish whether an individual in question was a "mixed-blood," an interviewee was often asked whether the person had any "white blood." The translation of this term would have been especially difficult, even for a skilled translator, because the root of the Anishinaabe word for blood, *miskwi*, is *miskw*. *Miskw* is the color red, and probably references the literal color of blood.[56] Consequently, red is inherently tied to the word blood.

Therefore, the term "white blood" was entirely nonsensical for Anishinaabe witnesses who did not understand blood as a metaphor for, or measure of, race used by the investigators. Lyons has observed, "The Ojibwe word for the color white is *waabishkaa*, but it has never been used to talk about people of European origin."[57] Furthermore he states, "There is nothing in Ojibwe language that evokes biological notions like blood quantum or other essentialist traffickers of identity."[58] In addition, in the recorded English transcripts, the terms "full-blood," "Chippewa Indian," and "Indian" are used interchangeably, which likely caused confusion because of the implication that "mixed-bloods" were not Indian.

A few interviewees did use the terms "mixed-blood" and "full-blood" in their testimony, but insisted on their own definition of the terms in which multiple factors were used to determine whether someone fell into those categories. Additionally, for the respondents, these categories were fluid and open to interpretation. The testimonies also show survivance. The fluidity of the categories allowed Anishinaabeg to account for the constant changes and evolutions that occur in a vibrant culture. The Anishinaabeg were not going to simply accept the racial biological definitions of "full-blood" and "mixed-blood" that the federal government desired. Even after the investigators explained the definitions of "mixed-blood" and "full-blood" they wanted to use, many Anishinaabeg continued to use their own definitions. In doing so, they asserted their right to define people in accordance with Anishinaabe values and beliefs. They resisted the dominance of terms and definitions provided by the investigators and, through their oral testimony, created a Native presence. Occasionally, in testimonies the Anishinaabeg of White Earth did use the terms "mixed-blood" and "full-blood" to distinguish among individual physical characteristics, but most often the terms denoted cultural characteristics and lifestyle choices.[59] The testimonies provided in the investigation give ample evidence that when individuals were identified as "mixed-blood" or "full-blood," biological percentages of blood were not a determining factor. There is considerable testimony that the people of White Earth did not consider biological ancestry to be a significant factor in an individual's identity. The oral testimonies create a conceptual map of Anishinaabeg views of identity.[60]

Several witnesses were baffled by the investigators' use of the terms "mixed-blood" and "full-blood" because, they claimed, these were not terms and designations with which they were familiar. The simplistic categories based on biology that the investigators insisted on were nonsensical for many of the Anishinaabe witnesses. The interview excerpt below demonstrates the nature of the exchanges between investigators and Anishinaabe witnesses.

Q. Do you know whether his father and mother were full blood Chippewa Indians or not?

A. They were Chippewa Indians, I know that.

Q. Do you know what we mean by a mixed blood Indian?

A. No. No, there was no mixed bloods.

Q. The question I asked was, do you know what we mean when we say a mixed blood Indian?

A. No; I just stated that I do not know that; I don't understand that word.

Q. When we say mixed blood Indian we mean that there has been some white blood or other blood mixed with the Chippewa blood?

A. Yes, sir.

Q. And when we say full blood Chippewa Indian we mean that the Chippewa has not been intermingled with the blood of any other race?

A. He is a full blood Indian; there is no mixed blood in him at all.[61]

First the witness indicates that the individuals in question are Chippewa Indians. Then he asserts that there are no "mixed-bloods," even though he admittedly doesn't know what the investigators mean by the word "mixed-blood." Both translation and lack of an understanding of blood as a metaphor for race and biological ancestry likely played a role in the witness's responses. After being informed about definitions of "full-blood" and "mixed-blood," the witness holds his ground that the individuals in question are not "mixed-bloods." There are several possibilities for the witness's reaction. Maybe he considered the definitions provided by the investigators to be inadequate or inappropriate, or he might not have understood them at all. Another possibility is that the individuals in question were "full-bloods" as the investigators defined it. His statement could also be a refusal to use the terms and definitions provided by the investigators. He might simply have been persistent in his claim that "there was no mixed-bloods" as a way to deny the terminology and definitions pushed by the investigators. The witnesses' responses may have arisen from some combination of these reasons or something else altogether.

Many witnesses essentially echoed the response of the individual cited above. In another case, a sixty-year-old woman from the Pine Point community was called as a witness. When she was asked if it was customary to distinguish "full-bloods" from "mixed-bloods," she replied that she had never heard of anything like that.[62] Likewise, another witness testified that it was not the practice of the tribal government to distinguish between "full-bloods" and "mixed-bloods."[63] Mah-ko-day testified that she did not know what a "mixed-blood" was and didn't know who would be known by that designation.[64] Taken together, these statements make a strong case that the concept of blood as a metaphor for racial ancestry, and the accompanying terms "mixed-blood" and "full-blood" were odd, illogical concepts to Anishinaabeg of White Earth. Many of them did not utilize these designations, and in some cases, they did not even understand the way the investigators defined "mixed-blood" and "full-blood."

During the investigation, many Anishinaabeg who were willing to use the terms "mixed-blood" and "full-blood" caused complications for the investigators because their conceptions of "full-bloods" and "mixed-bloods" were much more nuanced and diverse than a simple calculation of biological ancestry. They resisted the static definitions and told stories of the motion of survivance. For example, during an interview, George Morrison[65] argued that there was no designation of who was "full-blood" and who was "mixed-blood" among the Anishinaabeg until the question of land titles became tied to these identities. He asserted that all those who lived with the Anishinaabeg were considered "full-bloods" due to their way of living, not because of their actual biological ancestry.[66] He stated:

> In old times all who wore the breech cloth and blanket and also affiliated with the Indians, lived in wigwams and didn't live in houses, they were called "Indians"; they were considered the same as the full-bloods on account of their way of living; not on account of their blood, but on account of their—it was their way of living that regulated that.[67]

Morrison carefully noted that it was lifestyle, not blood, that determined who was an Indian. Morrison's use of the term Indian in place of "full-blood" furthers his point that racial/blood-quantum divisions were not in place "in the old times."

Likewise, Lizze McIntosh testified that "there was never no question about blood in them days, no sir, not until just within recent years,—talking about blood."[68] McIntosh's statement indicates that "blood" was not a topic of discussion and, possibly, that blood was not used as a metaphor for racial and/or biological ancestry. James Henry Van Nett stated that there was no distinction between "full-bloods" and "mixed-bloods" until the last few years. An investigator asked him, "Many of those—Isn't this true, that many of those who were known to have white fathers were living as Indians and considered in the tribe as Indians, just as though they had no white father?" And Van Nett replied, "Yes sir."[69] Van Nett's testimony indicates that an individual's racial ancestry was not what determined their acceptance into the community. These testimonies highlight the fact that the categories of "mixed-blood" and "full-blood" were relatively new and did not fit with the conceptions of identity utilized at that time by the Anishinaabeg. Clearly, during this period and before it, the Anishinaabeg did not normally use static measures of racial ancestry to determine who was Anishinaabe. While the investigators desperately searched for quantifiable identities to report back to Washington, blood was, in fact, absent from Anishinaabe understandings of identity.

Despite the fact that the Anishinaabeg did not utilize conceptions of "full-blood" and "mixed-blood" before the influence of the federal government, some savvy people found a way to take advantage of these categories to achieve their own purposes. Testimonies of the investigation provide evidence that some people were claiming to be "mixed-blood." For example, Nah-tah-wah-cumig-ish-kung was asked if he was a "mixed-blood" and he replied, "Yes, I am a mixed blood. I sold my land."[70] In this statement Nah-tah-wah-cumig-ish-kung connects blood quantum to land sale. He was then asked to define what a "mixed-blood" was and he testified that he understood it meant having some other blood. When he was asked if he had any white blood, he replied: "I can't tell. I must have some."[71] Nah-tah-wah-cumig-ish-kung's sarcastic claim that he couldn't tell whether he had any white blood was a challenge to the investigators. After all, if he couldn't "tell," how could they? It could also be a way of turning the tables on the investigators by asserting that because the Indian agent allowed him to sell his land then he must be a "mixed-blood" by way of government designation, and these were government designations, not Anishinaabe ones. In other words, he was essentially asking the investigators: how could he have been allowed to sell his land if he was a "full-blood?" The examiner then asked him what his mother had said on the issue of being "mixed-blood." Nah-tah-wah-cumig-ish-kung responded that she never said anything about being "mixed-blood" until they could sell their land.[72]

Nah-tah-wah-cumig-ish-kung's testimony illustrates that some Anishinaabeg were able to manipulate and employ the categories set forth by the federal government for their own purposes.[73] He was likely playing on the range of physiological characteristics available within the categories of "mixed-blood" and "full-blood" even as defined by the United States by questioning how exactly the United States expected to determine who fit into which category. The range of physiological characteristics was so great that observations of physical appearance alone could not be relied upon to determine whether an individual had one drop of white blood. Maybe Nah-tah-wah-cumig-ish-kung claimed to be a "mixed-blood" in order to avoid the revocation of his land sale, or maybe he felt frustrated with the categories and decided that if the Americans made up these categories, then they could regulate them. Nah-tah-wah-cumig-ish-kung may have run out of patience trying to establish his identity through such a peculiar system, and decided to let the American officials figure it out. His oral testimony is a story of survivance that renounces the simple classifications of "mixed-blood" and "full-blood" in favor of a "tricky sense of Native presence," which Gerald Vizenor describes as "transmotion."[74] By creating confusion and irony around the categories, Nah-tah-wah-cumig-ish-kung resists racial classification. As Vizenor has argued, "Natives have always been on one road of resistance or another, recreating postindian myths and tricky stories in the very ruins of representation and modernity."[75]

During the course of the investigation, several Anishinaabeg wrote to Powell to inquire about the findings of the investigation and their own status. For example, Sho-ne-yah-quay or Mrs. Jane Buckanaga wrote to Powell: "I have some land north of Mahnomen county and I can sell it but they do not think I am a mixed blood. Please tell me what I am . . . I think I am all right."[76] Powell replied that he thought she would be found to be a "mixed-blood." Eugene Bird also wrote to Powell with a similar question; however his status was not as clear. Powell replied that he could not tell if Bird was a "mixed-blood" or "full-blood" because there had been contradictory testimony on the issue.[77] Rather than trying to argue what their status was within the nonsensical categories of "mixed-blood" and "full-blood," or perhaps frustrated with the entire process, some chose to leave the findings up to Powell and wait out the investigation. With hundreds of land transactions hanging in the balance, many anticipated the findings of the investigation.

Others were unwilling to allow their identity to be established by a team of U.S. investigators and, instead, used the indistinctness of the categories to raise questions and offer their own answers. Well-respected Mississippi Band Chief Me-zhug-e-ge-shig[78] testified that Pud-e-goonce had no white blood despite the fact that Pud-e-goonce claimed he did. Me-zhug-e-ge-shig testified that if Pud-e-goonce claimed to be a mixed-blood he was lying, because he could recall Pud-e-goonce's ancestors and there were no "mixed-bloods" among them. Me-zhug-e-ge-shig said he understood the way that the investigators were using the terms "mixed-blood" and "full-blood."[79] It is unclear whether he had any personal motivation to claim that Pud-e-goonce was a "full-blood." Me-zhug-e-ge-shig might have been asserting his authority as a traditional chief; he might have wanted Pud-e-goonce to retain his allotment simply because he did not want it to be stripped of timber or for a person whom he did not have authority over to move in.

Individual land titles usurped the authority of Anishinaabe political leaders and Me-zhug-e-ge-shig might have been struggling to retain power over the nation. The Anishinaabeg had a lot riding on the outcome of these hearings, and quite possibly some people argued that they or people they knew were "full-bloods" because they wanted to get their land back. However, it is clear that regardless of their motivations, the Anishinaabeg testifying for this investigation did not have the same conceptions of identity that the federal government did.

Others also changed and/or manipulated their identities outside of the investigation. In 1914, Superintendent John R. Howard wrote to the White Earth Agency in response to complaints by Wah-we-yay-cum-ig that he had not received rations or supplies. At first Howard acknowledged that Wah-we-yay-cum-ig was a Mille Lacs chief, but then he went on to assert that Wah-we-yay-cum-ig was "unpopular with his people who refuse to recognize his authority."[80] Howard went on to claim that Wah-we-yay-cum-ig was "unreliable" because he had "represented to Mr. Hinton that he was mixed blood" when Hinton was making the blood status roll, but later testified in a United States district court that he was a "full-blood." Howard interpreted Wah-we-yay-cum-ig's changing identity as an illustration of his untrustworthiness, and failed to consider that Wah-we-yay-cum-ig might have conceptualized identity as fluid and dynamic, not fixed and "reliable." The letter offers no direct reason(s) why Wah-we-yay-cum-ig reported different identities. Howard lists the rations and supplies that Wah-we-yay-cum-ig was issued in previous years and states that he was no longer receiving rations because he was "well and strong and able to work for his living."[81] Finally, Howard asserts that since being denied rations, Wah-we-yay-cum-ig was "disgruntled and active in his efforts to create friction in the village of Elbow Lake."[82]

Howard's focus on Wah-we-yay-cum-ig hints at the political agendas behind the classifications of identity. Did Howard really stop the rations because Wah-we-yay-cum-ig was able to work, or was it a kind of retaliation for Wah-we-yay-cum-ig's new identity as a "full-blood"? Maybe Wah-we-yay-cum-ig had not understood the categories of "mixed-blood" and "full-blood" in his initial conversation with Hinton and mistakenly identified himself. It is also possible that Wah-we-yay-cum-ig understood the categories but did not believe they should be used, so he resisted them and even went so far as to purposely create confusion and difficulties for the investigators.

Several people testified that lifeways determined whether someone was designated as a "full-blood" or a "mixed-blood." Day-dah-bah-saush, a sixty-seven-year-old raised at Ottertail Lake, testified that he understood that a "full-blood" was a person with wholly Indian blood. But during further questioning, when asked if Min-o-ge-shig was a "full-blood Indian" he answered: "He was an Indian. He had a breech-cloth."[83] He stated that "mixed-bloods" were different because they wore pants and hats:

> Q. You said a while ago that O-sow-wah-kig in your best judgment was a person having only Indian blood. Did you say that because O-sow-wah-kig wore a breech-cloth and lived the Indian life?
>
> A. Yes sir, because he wore a breech-cloth, and he was a Grand Medicine man.[84]

Day-dah-bah-saush also stated that he did not know anything about O-sow-wah-kig's ancestors; therefore, Day-dah-bah-saush saw O-sow-wah-kig as a "full-blood" solely because of his lifestyle, which was, in part, reflected in his clothing choices. Likewise, he testified that Way-sho-wush-ko-gwan-ay-be-quay was an Indian because of her style of dress and hairstyle. Day-dah-bah-saush said that "mixed-bloods" dressed differently, suggesting that the motion of a change of clothing might alter an individual's identity.[85] Clothing contained possibilities of transformation, and individuals created their identity based on actions and decisions, including what they wore.

Clothing was likely related to economic status. Those with more money could afford to purchase expensive cloth or order ready-made clothing, while those who were less well off probably made their own clothes from cheaper cloth and hides they tanned themselves. Those with added income could afford the luxury of a store-bought hat, but those who just sought to subsist did not have such material items. Even though Day-dah-bah-saush understood that the investigators used biological ancestry to determine whether someone was a "full-blood" or a "mixed-blood," he refused to utilize their definitions and repeatedly testified that factors other than blood determined a person's status as a "mixed-blood" or "full-blood." This determination to employ Anishinaabe definitions and conceptions is an assertion of the sovereign right of the Anishinaabe to define their own people.

Likewise, Aysh-quay-gwon-ay-beak testified that O-dah-yah-je-o-quaince was a "full-blood" based on her lifestyle.

> Q. Your statement that she had nothing but Indian blood is based upon the fact that she looked and lived like an Indian, isn't that true?
>
> A. Yes, sir.

Q. If she had a small amount of white blood, coming from (her) grandfather or grandmother, you would not know anything about it, would you, unless it showed in her face?

A. No, I would not know anything about it.[86]

The interviewer first tries to discredit Aysh-quay-gwon-ay-beak's assertion that O-dah-yah-je-o-quaince was a "full-blood" based on physical characteristics. Then the investigator refocuses the question around physical characteristics and suggests that O-dah-yah-je-o-quaince's physical features might not reveal that she had a white ancestor(s). Aysh-quay-gwon-ay-beak was left little choice but to admit that if O-dah-yah-je-o-quaince's appearance did not reveal her ancestry, then she would not know for certain if O-dah-yah-je-o-quaince had any white ancestors or not.

Interviewers often played both sides when asked about the color of hair and skin people had to help establish whether they were a "full-blood" or "mixed-blood." Sometimes they would emphasize that an individual was light skinned as a way to assert that person was a "mixed-blood," but on other occasions they would hint that a person was a "mixed-blood" even though that individual had physical features, such as straight black hair, that fit popular European American conceptions of what Indians were supposed to look like. Anishinaabeg engaged in multiple acts of resistance. For example, Bay-bah-daung-ay-aush pushed the categories of "mixed-blood" and "full-blood" open by testifying that "though they were a little dark skinned . . . they were considered as mixed-bloods."[87] Just as those who were light-skinned could be "full-bloods," those with dark skin could be identified as "mixed-bloods." Clearly, for the Anishinaabeg, skin color alone was not enough to determine whether an individual was to be considered a "full-blood" or a "mixed-blood."

There was extensive questioning and testimony around skin color. Gay-bay-yah-bun-dung gave important testimony that he did not remember how Ah-she-gun-wae looked, but did consider him a "full-blood" regardless. Gay-bay-yah-bun-dung did not play the investigators' game. His refusal to remember the way Ah-she-gun-wae looked left no room for them to try and assert Ah-she-gun-wae was a "mixed-blood." However, the exchange continued:

Q. You mean by that that he lived in this community of Indians, just like the other Indians; isn't that true?

A. I just considered that he didn't have no other blood but the Indian blood. That is all.

Q. Why did you so consider him,—simply because he was living here with the other Indians, like the rest?

A. Yes, that is the only way I thought of;—I never thought of anything else.[88]

The testimonies of Aysh-quay-gwon-ay-beak, Day-dah-bah-saush, Gah-ge-zhe-gah-bow-e-quay, and Gay-bay-yah-bun-dung illustrate that multiple factors were used to determine whether someone was a "full-blood" or a "mixed-blood," and that these categories were fluid and open to interpretation, not the fixed racial definitions proposed by the investigators. They also show that the Anishinaabeg did not simply accept the definitions of "full-blood" and "mixed-blood" created by the federal government. Anishinaabeg continued to use their own definitions even though they demonstrated a clear awareness of U.S. federal application of these terms. In doing so, they asserted their right to define people in accordance with their Anishinaabe values and beliefs. Their oral testimonies created a Native sense of presence amid the racialized image of the *indian* that the investigators were attempting to measure them against.

The flexible nature of lifestyle had a significant impact on the adaptability of identity. In one case, Ke-zhe-waush was questioned about the blood status of her husband. She asserted, "He was a full-blood. He made himself a full-blood." The investigator asked, "You mean he made himself a full-blood by living like the Indians live?" She answered, "Yes, sir, he did not even take a paper to sign as a mixed-blood."[89] Ke-zhe-waush did not associate blood with racial and biological ancestry. Ke-zhe-waush's testimony is significant because it demonstrates that actual biological ancestry was not the primary factor for many Anishinaabeg in determining whether a person was a "full-blood" or "mixed-blood." She also directly correlates being a mixed-blood with "signing of paper," which is a reference to land sale and the idea that the United States was only supposed to allow "mixed-bloods" to sell their land. Her statement that her husband "made himself a full-blood" indicates that the categories of mixed-blood and full-blood were highly malleable for the Anishinaabeg and not dependent on the metaphor of blood as a measure of racial ancestry. For many Anishinaabeg, the motion of actions created identity, and individuals had the sovereign power to control their identity through the decisions they made.

Investigators also asked many questions about phenotype, especially skin color, and spent a considerable amount of time attempting to connect skin color with an individual's status as either a "full-blood" or a "mixed-blood." Gerald Vizenor has discussed the use of countenance to define identity, noting that

Native appearance, facial features, the walk, talk, manners, and other characteristics are traces of identities. Native countenance is a simulation, a pose that
is seen by others as the real score of native identities. For instance, the color of
skin, hair, and eyes, is seen as native countenance; however, few natives are born
with a "pure" countenance. There is no essential truth in the tone and hue of a
cheekbone.[90]

Likewise, many Anishinaabe witnesses in the 1910s resisted the use of phenotype and skin color to determine an individual's identity. Their experiences
and knowledge countered the arguments of the investigators.

Despite the attempts of the investigators to make skin color a primary
factor in determining whether a person was a "full-blood" or a "mixed-
blood," Anishinaabe witnesses frequently noted that skin color varied
and was not necessarily indicative of either an individual's racial ancestry
or their cultural status as a "full-blood" or a "mixed-blood." For example,
Bay-bah-daung-ay-yaush did not correlate the darkness of one's skin with
a specific degree of blood. An investigator asked, "Wasn't she light com-
plected?" And Bay-bah-daung-ay-yaush replied: "Yes, she was light. Some
Indians are light, but she was an Indian."[91] In this case, Bay-bah-daung-ay-
yaush's use of the term Indian, not "mixed-blood" or "full-blood," asserts
that the two categories of identity are Indian and non-Indian, thereby
undermining the definitions desired by the investigators. When asked a
similar question, May-zhue-sah-e-bun-dung replied, "Yes, he was light, but
he was a full-blooded Indian."[92] Nancy Taylor testified in a similar manner, saying, "Some of the Indians seem by nature to be light, even though
they are not mixed-bloods."[93] These Anishinaabeg turned the tables on the
investigators by asserting that skin color alone was not necessarily solid evidence of an individual's biological ancestry. They destabilized the idea that
all Indians look like the popular images the investigators were measuring
them against, and noted the diversity present within Anishinaabe identity.

During further questioning, Taylor again asserted that racial ancestry
alone should not be used by the investigators to determine whether a person was a "full-blood" or a "mixed-blood." The investigator then asked if
people with a small amount of white blood were called "full-bloods." She
responded that blood quantum or racial ancestry was not used, saying, "No,
sir, we call one another as Indians. We never call those as mixed-bloods and
nobody else calls them mixed-bloods." Taylor went on to directly question
the single factor of ancestry used by the investigators to determine who
was a "full-blood" and who was a "mixed-blood." When she was asked if
an individual was a "full-blood," she replied, "I will tell just what I think.

There are some have one drop of white blood and you call them mixed blood, but we call them as Indians."[94] Taylor's comments indicate that there were not distinctions based on racial ancestry. Her statements also show that the definition of "mixed-blood" and "full-blood" as defined by the investigators were not analogous to Anishinaabe conceptions of identity; racial categories based on the metaphor of blood were bizarre and meaningless. Like Bay-bah-daung-ay-yaush, Taylor's comment "we call one another as Indians" highlights a kind of unification—either a person was Indian or they weren't, and percentage of blood was irrelevant.[95]

Investigators continued to press the witnesses about the skin color of others, but the Anishinaabeg held firm that skin color alone was not a way to establish whether a person was a "full-blood" or a "mixed-blood." Several people testified that they did not take particular notice of the skin color of individuals. For example, when asked if an individual was "pretty white," Mak-ah-day-wub responded that he had "never taken particular notice."[96] When asked a similar question, Shin-ow-waince testified: "I could not say whether he was lighter than the others because it is so long ago. I cannot recollect. I used to see him swallow bones[97] about that long (indicating)[98] in his incantation for eliminating sickness among other fellow men. Is this the practice of a mixed blood?"[99] In this instance, not only could Shin-ow-waince not recall the "lightness" of the person in question, he asserted that it was the individual's practices that placed his identity firmly in the category of the "full-bloods." He even went so far as to question the investigator, a clear move indicating that although he understood the investigator wanted to know about actual ancestry, it was not the primary factor (maybe not one at all) in determining who was "full-blood" and who was "mixed-blood" from an Anishinaabe perspective.

These testimonies establish a pattern of resistance and refusal to accept the definitions of "full-blood" and "mixed-blood" that the investigators were pushing and are assertions of sovereignty. It is possible that the witnesses really did not recall the skin color of those they were being questioned about, showing that was not a primary factor in identity. However, it is also probable that witnesses purposefully refused to recall or describe the skin color of the individual in question as a calculated strategy to assert that it was not important. As Gerald Vizenor has observed, "Sovereignty as motion and transmotion is heard and seen in oral presentations."[100] These oral testimonies assert the sovereign right of Anishinaabeg to create and control their own identities.

Ain-due-e-geshig (or Andrew Daily) also attempted to evade the question of degree of Indian blood. In the following excerpt, Ain-due-e-geshig is pressed by investigators to define the skin color of an individual after they refused to accept his assertion that he couldn't recall.

Q. Was Ke-che-o-dah-num, the second wife of Mah-no-me-ne-kay-zhe, a full-blood Indian?

A. I do not know, because she was an elder person than I am, and even some of her children were older than I was; I could not tell who she was.

Q. You used to see her?

A. Yes sir, I did see her. You mean Ke-che-o-dah-num?

Q. Yes. Judging from her appearance, what would you say she was?

A. There are some Indians real dark and some not as the others, but she was a medium shade—she was not very dark. I do not say that she was light or dark.[101]

In this case, Ain-due-e-geshig refused to use the simple categories of light and dark set forth by the investigators. Like so many other Anishinaabeg who were questioned, he pushed opened the static categories to allow diversity, and testified that Ke-che-o-dah-num was "the medium shade." After this answer the investigator finally moved on to question him about the status of Ke-che-o-dah-num's sister, Ne-bah-min-de-moin. Ain-due-e-geshig stuck to his strategy and responded, "I would say the same thing, what I said about Ke-che-o-dah-num."[102] Ain-due-e-geshig's oral testimony is an example of how Anishinaabeg subverted the racist questions of the investigators and forced the borders of "full-blood" and "mixed-blood" open. In this case, by using transmotion to outwit the static categories of "light" and "dark" by creating "the medium shade," a new category that defied blood demonstrated the sovereign right of Anishinaabeg to determine their own identities and their own destinies, and was fashioned to assert the natural and inherent right of the Anishinaabeg to create their own identities.[103]

Some witnesses did employ the definition of "full-blood" and "mixed-blood" utilized by the federal government; nonetheless, they maintained that "mixed-bloods" were full members of Anishinaabe society. The witnesses emphasized that "mixed-bloods" were both members and leaders of the Midewiwin society.[104] I-ah-baince testified regarding the religious practices of "mixed-bloods." When asked, "Do you know some mixed-blood who did take part in the grand medicine?" by an investigator, I-ah-baince answered, "Yes, sir, all of them."[105] Nes-ke-gwon was asked about "half breeds" living among Indians in accordance with their customs. Nes-ke-gwon knew of such people and testified about a specific individual: "Yes, sir, he so practiced grand medicine, and he wore a breech-cloth. Then he had a medicine pouch where he carried his medicine. He was a mixed-blood."[106] I-ah-baince and Nes-ke-gwon appear to be using the biological definition of "mixed-blood" that the investigators advocated. Yet, their statements provide evidence that those with European ancestry did fully participate in Anishinaabe society.

Another aspect sometimes identified as a factor in classifying an individual as a "full-blood" or a "mixed-blood" was economic status, and "mixed-blood" status was frequently tied to the advent of annuity payments. Shin-ow-waince commented, "They (mixed-bloods) were existing, after the beginning of the payments."[107] The Anishinaabeg had a long relationship with the French and English during the fur trade, and consequently there were many Anishinaabeg who had French or English ancestors; the dramatic encroachment on Anishinaabeg lands did not occur until the 1800s.[108] There are several accounts of large numbers of people showing up for annuities who may not have been seen as community members because they no longer lived within the community, not necessarily because they had some non-Anishinaabeg ancestry. The people Shin-ow-waince identified as "mixed-blood" were those who only claimed an Anishinaabeg identity when it was economically advantageous. Shin-ow-waince further stated that s/he had not seen a "mixed-blood" until recently, saying, "It seems just like yesterday they came among us."[109] Shin-ow-waince's testimony shows that the categories of "mixed-blood" and "full-blood" were not noteworthy factors in defining people prior to treaty annuities and to the passage of the Clapp Rider, which made it the determining factor in a person's ability to have control over their individualized land allotments.

Bay-bah-daung-ay-aush's testimony reinforces the assertions of Shin-ow-waince. When asked, "If a person has only a small amount of white blood and lives as an Indian, would you call him as a mixed-blood?" Bay-bah-daung-ay-aush responded, "No, because he would be poor, and he just would look after what he wants to eat, or seeks after what he would to subsist."[110] Ah-nah-me-ay-gah-bow, an eighty-six-year-old from Leech Lake, stated that they had not paid any attention to the categories of "mixed-blood" and "full-blood" until very recently, saying: "We were foolish, didn't pay attention to things. I have heard said that there was a French mixed-blood,—an English mixed-blood—just lately heard that."[111] Ah-nah-me-ay-gah-bow's testimony shows that blood was not used as a metaphor for racial or national ancestry. The concepts of "mixed-blood" and "full-blood" simply did not exist as a means to define a person's identity prior to the federal legislation, which made it the determining factor in a person's ability to have control over their own resources. Bay-bah-daung-ay-aush defined some people as "full-bloods" "because they support themselves, like an Indian."[112] Bay-bah-daung-ay-aush's understandings of "full-blood" and "mixed-blood" had clear economic correlations. While it might seem surprising for the Anishinaabeg to relate economic status to an individual's classification as a "full-blood" or "mixed-blood," the widespread association between lifestyle choices and economic status is the likely impetus behind this connection.

MEASURED IDENTITIES

Investigators were looking for the simulation of the *indian*, the created image based on racial fictions, but were only able to find its absence in the oral testimonies of the White Earth Anishinaabeg.[113] The federal government ultimately refused to accept the multiple, fluid understandings of who was Anishinaabe, "mixed-blood" and "full-blood," and insisted that it was biological ancestry that determined which category an individual was placed in. Investigator Ransom Powell did not get the results he desired from his interviews, so he employed a new means to get answers regarding the racial ancestry of the people of White Earth. In May 1915, two nationally renowned anthropologists, Dr. Albert E. Jenks and Dr. Aleš Hrdlička, came to White Earth to administer a series of physical examinations as a way to determine the exact racial makeup of the individuals involved in the land fraud cases and create a blood roll detailing this information.[114] Dr. Albert E. Jenks founded the Department of Anthropology at the University of Minnesota and served as its chair for twenty years. He took a year of leave to complete his work at White Earth.[115] Dr. Aleš Hrdlička, curator of the Division of Physical Anthropology at the Smithsonian Institution, is the acknowledged "father of American physical anthropology."[116] Jenks adamantly claimed that he could indisputably determine "full-bloods" from "mixed-bloods" through various physical examinations, including a cross-section hair analysis.[117] Two major figures in early anthropology devoted a considerable amount of time to creating and administering various physical tests—despite the fact that the Anishinaabeg of White Earth did not consider percentages of white blood and Anishinaabe blood determining factors in who was considered a "full-blood" or "mixed-blood." Rather, as clearly demonstrated in the testimonies collected by Powell, for the Anishinaabeg, the distinction was cultural and reflective of lifeways. In addition, these categories were new and not widely used by Anishinaabeg.[118] As Meyer has noted, "The cross cultural faux pas would be humorous had it not, in reality, been so tragic."[119]

Using the findings from the examinations performed by Jenks and Hrdlička, Powell finally completed a blood roll in 1920. In a prime example of the ways in which "the simulations of the *indian* serve the manifest manners of unbidden dominance," less than 10 percent of the five thousand allottees listed on the roll were classified as "full-bloods."[120] Judge Page Morris, senior judge of the United States District Court for the District of Minnesota, approved the roll and it was considered final.[121] The blood quantum of allottees as listed on Powell's roll became the critical determinant in most of the allotment land fraud cases, while other significant evidence was ignored. Nearly all of the 142,000 acres of land in question were never returned to the original owners or their descendants.[122] As Beaulieu has astutely observed: "It is a rare moment in the historiography of the relationship of anthropology and the other social sciences to American Indians to find an example where the colonial nature and political purposes and the uses of academic enterprise seem so obvious and direct."[123] These cases raise many questions as to the ways in which "scientific" knowledge is created and used for social purposes. In the land fraud cases, anthropologists' understandings of "full-blood" and "mixed-blood" were considered scientific fact. The ways in which the Anishinaabeg classified themselves, on the other hand, were deemed unscientific and, ultimately, irrelevant. Racial simulations of the *indian* replaced Anishinaabeg and were employed as justification for fraudulent land transactions. This case highlights the political motivations behind the United States government's push for fixed racial identities among American Indians.[124]

Anishinaabeg at White Earth in the early twentieth century had complex identities tied to religion, economics, kinship, and lifestyle. There was no single system for determining who was a part of the community and who was not. These identities were malleable and dependent on the choices of individuals, not on static measures of racial ancestry. More importantly the Anishinaabeg maintained their identity as they adapted to new ways of life at White Earth. What was considered an Anishinaabe way of life was also in flux as more people adapted to new situations and found a way to maintain their cultural values. Many Anishinaabeg refused to employ the terms "mixed-blood" and "full-blood," insisting that they did not use those terms among themselves, nor did the tribal government use the designations. Many of them stated that they did not understand the terms, which was likely because blood was not used as a metaphor for racial and biological ancestry in Anishinaabe culture at that time. Yet, some interviewees did use the terms, but they insisted that these terms were flexible and did not necessarily follow ancestral lines. Ultimately, little was agreed upon except that designations of "mixed-blood" and "full-blood" in the simplistic and rigid biological understanding pushed by Powell and his investigators were unacceptable and in direct conflict with Anishinaabe understandings of identity. Anishinaabe identity could not be surveyed and divided the way the land had. There were no clear lines and neat allotments; rather, it was a varied and diverse landscape with a mix of lakes, birch, pine, and prairie.

Both during and after the investigation, the White Earth General Council and the Department of the Interior were bombarded with applications for citizenship. Many people waited years to find out about the acceptance or rejection of their applications. For example, Delia Gubbon, who lived in Minneapolis, wrote to request enrollment for herself and her nieces and nephews (the children of her brother Antoine "Tony" Lafond, who was already enrolled). Their petition was approved by the White Earth General Council in August 1909, but the Department of the Interior took four years to write to Gubbon to inform her of the decision and request additional information from her. Even though her petition had been approved, "the evidence submitted to said Council in [*sic*] your behalf is insufficient to form the basis for a report to the department." It is not clear what documents and/or evidence Gubbon provided to the White Earth General Council for their approval. It may have been enough to show that her brother was enrolled; however, for Gubbon to gain the approval of the Department of the Interior, she was asked to furnish

> a statement sworn and subscribed to before a Notary Public or Justice of the Peace, covering in detail the following points concerning yourself, your brothers and sisters, parents and grandparents, to-wit: 1. Family history. 2. Indian blood as to source and quantity. 3. Places of residence and length of time of residence in each place. 4. Affiliation with any tribe or band of Indians. 5. Recognition by the government of Indian rights, such as the payment of annuities and the granting of allotments. 6. Relatives on the White Earth rolls, if any. You should also furnish me with the affidavits of relatives or any other persons who have sufficient knowledge from which to make statements, covering the points included in your own affidavit.[125]

This request for a large amount of detailed information illustrates that getting the Department of the Interior to approve an enrollment was no easy task. No information from Gubbon is included in the record, but Antoine "Tony" Lafond took up the matter himself and had his attorney write to Powell, asking "if the facts stated in the affidavit are accepted by the

Department, that the children of Lafond will be enrolled and will receive an allotment of land."[126] Lafond detailed much of the information desired by the Department of the Interior. Lafond's father was "in blood, three-quarters French and one-quarter Chippewa."[127] He received an allotment on the White Earth Reservation and lived there until the time of his death. Lafond's mother was born in the Pembina region and was "one-quarter white and three-quarters Chippewa."[128] Lafond, who lived in the Mounds View Township in Ramsey County, had received annuities on several occasions and had several siblings who lived at White Earth.[129]

It is not clear if the secretary of the Interior ever approved Gubbon or the children of Lafond for tribal citizenship. However, their case illustrates the lengthy and complex process of becoming a tribal citizen. The time and resources needed to furnish the evidence required by the secretary of the Interior was likely simply unrealistic and unattainable for many Anishinaabeg. The Gubbon and Lafond case also shows the ways in which the secretary of the Interior exercised broad powers, engaging in paternalistic forms of oversight that undermined the authority of the White Earth government.

CONCLUSION

The statements made by the Anishinaabeg during this investigation are stories of survivance. They are visions of identity that resist static containment and insist upon the natural reason of transmotion. Gerald Vizenor has argued: "transmotion is motion and native memories."[130] The memories recounted in the oral testimonies of the White Earth Anishinaabeg included familial relationships and lifestyle choices but not pseudoscientific markers of phenotype. The oral testimonies demonstrate that White Earth Anishinaabeg did not use blood as a metaphor for ancestral/racial ancestry; to them, this association was illogical and senseless. In their understanding, the meanings of the terms "full-blood" and "mixed-blood" were not bound to notions of ancestry but were flexible terms generally tied to a variety of lifestyle choices, such as clothing and religious affiliation, as well as economic conditions. As Lyons has noted:

> Ojibwe recognized other Ojibwe by their proximity and the way they lived, including but not limited to their family relations. What they recognized as themselves—what they saw when they saw an Ojibwe—always had the potential to change and incorporate new ideas, and even incorporate new people, but this act of recognition did not rest entirely upon familial relationships.[131]

Several people testified that one's status as "full-blood" or "mixed-blood" could be manipulated by individuals to be advantageous. Some of those who wanted to sell their land allotments claimed to be "mixed-blood" in order to gain control over their newly individualized resources. The statements that the terms "full-blood" and "mixed-blood" were new to the Anishinaabeg are highly significant and likely played a role in the wide range of characteristics utilized by the Anishinaabeg to attempt to answer questions regarding the blood status of specific individuals. The relative newness of these categories and the complex view that blood was a metaphor for racial and biological ancestry could account for the variety of ways in which Anishinaabeg responded to the questions during the interviews. While difficult to ascertain, the linguistic skills of the interviewee and interpreter, if one was used, also impacted the responses. The Anishinaabeg were accustomed to intermarriage with other indigenous peoples, as well as European peoples, and continuously maintained their identity as Anishinaabeg through multifaceted cultural negotiations.

The federal government did not accept fluid Anishinaabe conceptions of identity and insisted upon fixed measures of race as the sole determinant of an individual's identity. This focus on race and biology resulted in the dispossession of thousands of acres of land. In addition, it legalized the conflation of "blood" with race and nationality. The racialization of Anishinaabe identity would have significant and lasting consequences, eventually leading to the dispossession of many individuals' legal status as Anishinaabeg, making them vanish just like so many politicians and academics predicted. Their construction of *indian* identity as racial served to fulfill manifest destiny.

As the White Earth General Council attempted to sort out the citizenship issues, there would soon be new issues to contend with. Shortly after the passage of the Indian Reorganization Act in 1934, a new government called the Minnesota Chippewa Tribe was formed by six Anishinaabe nations, including White Earth, and in the coming years they would face intense pressure from the U.S. government to use a specific degree of Indian "blood" as the sole determinant for tribal citizenship.

CHAPTER TWO

Consider the Relationship
Citizenship Regulations of the
Minnesota Chippewa Tribe

THIS CHAPTER WILL EXPLORE THE DECISION TO IMPLEMENT A MINI-
mum of one-quarter degree of blood for citizenship within the Minnesota
Chippewa Tribe (MCT). Officially formed in 1936, the MCT is an umbrella
government comprised of six Anishinaabeg bands/nations: White Earth,
Mille Lacs, Bois Fort (Nett Lake), Fond du Lac, Leech Lake, and Grand
Portage.[1] While enrollment within the Minnesota Chippewa Tribe is generally spoken of as membership, as discussed in the introduction, I use the
term citizenship with the intention of evoking the political status of the
MCT. In 1961, the elected leaders of the MCT instituted a one-quarter MCT
minimum degree of blood for citizenship (meaning that the "blood" from
each of the six nations participating would all count toward the one-quarter,
but "blood" from other Anishinaabe nations and other Native nations
would not). This created what were essentially two levels of citizenship: that
of their individual nation and of the MCT. Individuals were citizens of their
specific nation, often related to where they or their ancestors took allotments, and the MCT. This chapter examines the influences and motivations
that facilitated this dramatic shift from lineal descent to a specific quantum
of "blood" or race.

The MCT was formed in accordance with the Indian Reorganization Act
(IRA) of 1934, also known as the Indian New Deal. This federal legislation,
initiated by Commissioner of Indian Affairs John Collier, was intended to
recognize and strengthen tribal governments. Despite Collier's good inten-
tions, the paternalistic nature of the legislation has been critiqued by several
scholars and tribal leaders, including Vine Deloria Jr. and Clifford M. Lytle

in *The Nations Within*.[2] Indeed, the ways in which the Bureau of Indian Affairs (BIA), also known as the Indian Office, pressured the MCT to use blood quantum as a determiner for tribal citizenship are clear examples of paternalism. Several U.S. officials did not believe that the elected leaders of the MCT knew what they were doing when they decided that lineal descent was the best way to determine tribal citizenship, and/or these officials thought they knew what would be "best."

Identity was a significant aspect of the IRA. Congress debated who should qualify as American Indian under the IRA. Collier proposed that candidates should include persons of American Indian descent who were members of recognized tribes, their descendants who resided on a reservation, as well as those who had one-quarter or more Indian blood. Reflecting a racialized perception of Native identity, several members of Congress objected to the inclusion of those who were not of one-quarter or more Indian blood. Senator Burton K. Wheeler of Montana advocated for a 50 percent blood requirement, stating:

> I do not think that the government of the United States should go out there and take a lot of Indians in that are quarter bloods and take them in under this act. If they are Indians in the half blood then the government should perhaps take them in, but not unless they are. If you pass it to where they are quarter blood Indians you are going to have all kinds of people coming out and claiming they are quarter blood Indians and want to be put on the government rolls, and in my judgment it should not be done. *What we are trying to do is get rid of the Indian problem rather than add to it.*[3]

Wheeler's statement shows a clear concern about the potential of increasing the number of people who were defined as American Indian. He seems frustrated that there are any Indians at all and wishes to fulfill manifest destiny and the final vanishing of Natives. In addition, he asserted that Indians with less than one-half Indian blood were really "white people" who were "just as capable of handling their affairs as any white man."[4] Due to the concerns of Wheeler and others, Collier's proposed definition of American Indian was amended to raise the blood quantum from one-quarter to one-half or more. Therefore, in order to be defined as American Indian under the IRA, an individual could be a citizen of a tribe, a descendant of citizens living on a reservation, or an individual possessing one-half or more Indian blood.[5] Legal scholar Paul Spruhan has observed, "The increase of the blood quantum threshold from one-quarter to one-half perpetuated the notion of Indian as biological ward, as powerful congressmen successfully objected to the extension of benefits to allegedly competent mixed-bloods."[6] Thus the same rationale of "competency" and blood quantum that were used to dispossess hundreds of Anishinaabeg of their land allotments was now being used to erase their very status as American Indians.

After the IRA became law, tribes had to decide by popular vote whether to accept or reject it in a special referendum. Those that accepted the IRA could then draw up a constitution and create a governing structure. In addition, tribes that created and adopted IRA constitutions became eligible to incorporate for tribal business purposes and apply for loans from the revolving credit fund established in the IRA.[7] With the IRA came the rejection of allotment and the creation of new provisions for land purchase and loan programs designed to foster economic development.[8] Two hundred and fifty-two tribes participated in referenda, with 174 voting to accept and 78 to reject, yet more than 80 of the tribes that accepted the IRA neglected to adopt a constitution.[9]

The standard constitution supplied to tribes for their use and adaptation was very simplistic, with no separation of powers and few checks or balances. In addition, one provision allowed the secretary of the Interior broad powers for approving contracts and constitutional changes.[10] The IRA would become an important crossroads for tribal citizenship. While the BIA officially recognized the inherent sovereignty of American Indian nations to define and regulate citizenship, in practice the Bureau would push tribes to enact racial requirements. Legal scholar L. Scott Gould has argued that the IRA "helped entrench race as an essential requirement for tribal membership."[11]

On October 29, 1934, the White Earth Anishinaabeg voted to accept the IRA by a vote of 1,222 for and 245 against. White Earth, Mille Lacs, Bois Fort, Fond du Lac, Leech Lake, and Grand Portage decided to create a confederation and spent the next couple of years working out details for nation level government and inter-nation-level powers. The resulting constitution was ratified in a general election at each nation on June 30, 1936.[12] On July 24, 1936, the constitution and bylaws of the MCT were approved by Secretary of the Interior Harold L. Ickes.[13] Each nation retained the right to manage its own affairs through locally elected Reservation Councils, which would later be known as Reservation Business Committees, Reservation Tribal Councils, and Tribal Councils.[14] The councils were created by separate charters and were approved by each nation in a majority-vote election on February 22, 1939.[15]

The original MCT constitution states that "the governing body of the tribe shall have power to make rules governing the qualifications required for enrollment in the tribe and descendants of members of the tribe."[16] Initially, all Anishinaabeg who had registered on any of the approved annuity rolls of the six nations participating in the MCT were members of the MCT, and children of these individuals were subsequently qualified to enroll as citizens.[17] However, there were no definite policies or procedures governing the citizenship process. It seems as though a system of lineal descent was used as the method for determining citizenship, but there is some indication that residency might have been required.[18] While the MCT did enroll citizens under this loose system of lineal descent, the BIA felt that the language of the constitution was not explicit enough, and wanted the MCT to pass an amendment relating to the exact requirements for tribal citizenship.

The governing body of the MCT is known as the Tribal Executive Committee (TEC). Today it is comprised of twelve members: the chairman and secretary/treasurer from each of the six nations.[19] Within this group, a president, vice president, secretary, and treasurer are elected. Each nation has their own Tribal Council or Reservation Business Committee, which is comprised of a chairman, secretary/treasurer, and district representatives. Originally, tribal delegates played an important role in the governance of the MCT. Article IV, Section 1 of the original MCT constitution states that "Tribal Delegates, numbering not more than two from any designated district or community, shall be chosen by each community at an annual election."[20] In 1936, there was a total of twenty-eight districts among all the nations. White Earth had fourteen districts, which was more than other nations and included the Mille Lac Trading Post. At this time, the Mille Lacs Nation was included as part of White Earth; thus, the TEC was comprised of ten individuals.[21] Tribal delegates chose the members of the TEC. Section 2 of the MCT constitution reads: "Tribal Delegates shall select from the tribal membership two persons from each reservation . . . who shall compose the Tribal Executive Committee."[22] In addition, delegates selected the officers of the TEC. Districts changed over time; for example, in 1950 there was a total of thirty-one districts. The White Earth Nation (WEN) continued to have the largest number of districts, but was reduced to eleven. Mille Lacs was no longer considered part of White Earth and had four districts.[23] With a large proportion of the MCT population and, therefore, a large number of districts and tribal delegates, the WEN played a major role in the MCT. In fact, John L. Pemberton and A. C. Beaulieu, the first president and secretary of the TEC, were both from White Earth.[24]

In 1963, several major constitutional changes were approved by the secretary of the Interior. The practice of electing tribal delegates ceased, and the TEC was from that time on composed of the chairman and secretary/treasurer of each nation. In addition, the drastic change in tribal citizenship requirements that mandated a minimum of one-quarter Minnesota Chippewa blood quantum was also approved.

WHO SHALL BE AMONG US?

Shortly after the MCT was created, fear arose that Congress would repeal the IRA, a development that would have rendered the MCT defunct. MCT elected leaders registered their zealous protest against the possible repeal of the IRA and passed a resolution indicating their support for the act. The MCT elected officials saw the IRA as the vehicle that would allow them to develop a permanent program designed to help restore economic self-sufficiency to the nation.[25] Despite this enthusiastic support for the IRA, there were complaints about the blood-quantum requirement used by the federal government to designate who was legally American Indian. White Earth Anishinaabeg Joe Morrison and Scott Porter addressed the TEC, relaying how many Anishinaabeg of White Earth did not support the IRA. They attributed this to the blood-quantum requirement that had been instituted by the BIA for certain programs and services.[26] During this time, the BIA was primarily using one-quarter blood quantum as a qualification for specific programs and services, as established by Congress.[27] However, as Spruhan has noted, "Inconsistency is the main theme in federal applications of blood quantum."[28] Superintendent Scott explained that laws that discriminated on the basis of blood quantum went beyond the IRA; therefore, doing away with the IRA and/or the MCT would not resolve the issue. He agreed that "the quantum of Indian blood shouldn't enter the picture at all when it comes to credit loans or educational loans or those things where tribal funds are used. If you have one drop of Indian blood—enough to get on the rolls—you are as much entitled to a credit loan as a full-blood because you are on the rolls and there is no reason why you should be discriminated against because you don't have a quarter degree Indian blood, but the law is there and we must obey it and we can't do otherwise until you—an organized group—get the law change."[29] Scott's response to the fact that many citizens of the MCT did not approve of blood quantum and those with less "blood" than the one-quarter required by the BIA were still full members of their communities and the MCT shows respect. He even encouraged the elected leaders to challenge the racist divisions set in place by the United States.

Tribal citizenship was discussed on several occasions during TEC meetings, and frequently the minutes of these meetings contain an excellent level of detail. Tribal citizenship and U.S. blood-quantum requirements were discussed at great length at a TEC meeting held on May 17–20, 1940. Mr. Broker noted that the United States government had set the standard of a minimum of one-fourth Indian blood for their services. According to Broker, the MCT often approved loans that were later denied by the Indian Office because the person did not meet the blood-quantum minimum.[30] The MCT's approval of loans for tribal citizens regardless of blood quantum shows resistance as well as determination to exercise their sovereign right to decide who was and was not a citizen of the MCT and, therefore, who was eligible for federal Indian programs. During the meeting, Pete Smith of Nett Lake told how they did not have the idea of fractions/degrees of blood at Nett Lake; they called anyone with any amount of white blood a "mixed-blood."[31] He does not, however, say that "mixed-bloods" are less a part of the community, and his statement that fractions of blood were not tracked is an indication that they were not significant. Possibly reflecting shifting views of identity, Smith's definition of "mixed-blood" is identical to that of federal law used to strip Anishinaabeg of their land allotments during the early twentieth century.

Many at the meeting spoke out about the impact that using blood quantum for tribal citizenship would have on their children and grandchildren. For example, William "Bill" Anywaush from the White Earth Nation declared that he did not approve of the use of blood quantum and felt it would be a great harm to institute it because it would deprive their children of participation in the MCT. William Nickabonie, delegate for Mille Lacs, began his statement by noting, "Where I come from the percentage of mixed-bloods is so small that we know they won't be stricken from the rolls." However, he went on to state, "I personally wouldn't want to be a party to this striking off of our youths for the reason that my children in the future time may have these little mixed bloods and I don't want them to say I have done that—restricting them from the rolls."[32] Nickabonie's statements reflect concern for his family and his responsibility to ensure that they will be eligible for tribal citizenship. Anywaush and Nickabonie's resistance to blood quantum was based on concern for the survivance of the MCT. They recognized that the MCT would need a robust body of citizens—not only to exist, but to thrive in the future.

Likewise, Bill Morrell, delegate from the Leech Lake Nation, spoke out against blood quantum. Morrell reversed the one-drop rule to be inclusive by insisting that everyone with any amount of Indian blood should have the same privileges, and he spoke at length on the issue. He stated:

I feel this way. The only way we can ever reach a settlement is that no matter how small quantity of Indian blood a man has, he should have the privileges of a Chippewa Indian. We are all human, just like any other people in this world. Why should you deprive your own grandson of the rights of a Chippewa Indian? We aren't like dogs, who forget their pups as soon as they are big enough to go off by themselves.[33]

Morrell used family as leverage to call for the TEC to follow Anishinaabe values and practices. His assertion that Anishinaabeg should take care of their families connects traditional values and practices. Morrell went on to advise the TEC to be "guided by the love of children, your little grandchildren, even if they are mixed-bloods."[34] He continued:

The movement is already going on. There will be another little mixed-blood born tomorrow. We won't have any people left, because every day the new-born Indians have less and less Indian blood in them. You can't tell your own relatives to get out because they aren't full-bloods. If you are a loving people, consider the people you are going to hurt by making that demarcation. Think how bad that poor old Indian woman (or man) is going to feel when she hears that her little grandson is not a member of the Chippewa Tribe.[35]

Morrell's comments are reflective of a communal focus and the attention to the future of the nation. He recognized the reality that a growing portion of the younger generations were of racially "mixed-blood," and was aware that many of them would be ineligible for tribal citizenship if a blood-quantum requirement were instituted. Morrell's comments figure the MCT as family, with the elected leaders of the TEC fulfilling a parental role, making familial love a real influence on the issue of blood quantum. He calls on Anishinaabe cultural values and practices to guide political decisions, illustrating the connections between these two realms. His emphasis on children implies that the TEC had a responsibility toward all future MCT citizens.

Concern for future generations was expressed at the meeting, and past generations were mentioned as well. Mr. Savage from Fond du Lac noted that their forefathers had included "mixed-bloods" in treaties made with the United States. He asked, "Why should we go on record as opposing the mixed bloods when they were approved of by our forefathers so many years ago?"[36] Asking this question forced those at the meeting to think about the ways in which their ancestors had addressed the question of including or excluding "mixed-bloods."[37] The question of tribal citizenship was not only about the inclusion of future generations but also about honoring the wishes of their ancestors and continuing Anishinaabe practices of inclusion and caring for relatives, which were well established.

The lengthy and passionate discussion continued at the meeting, with several others joining in to give their views. Mr. Fairbanks, from the WEN, noted that the majority of MCT citizens were enrolled at White Earth, and slightly more than 32 percent of White Earth enrolled citizens would be impacted by a one-quarter rule, according to the Cass Lake Indian Office.[38] Fairbanks was concerned about the large number of people who would be excluded should the one-quarter rule be enacted. He emphasized that this would have a significant impact on the MCT since the majority of citizens were enrolled at White Earth. What was in store for the future of the MCT if the number of Anishinaabeg eligible for citizenship declined? The specific statistic Fairbanks provided indicates that the Indian Office had spent a considerable amount of time figuring out how many people would be impacted by a one-quarter blood-quantum rule. With about one-third of the population estimated to be excluded, Morrell's worries about younger generations being affected by a one-quarter requirement were clearly justified. In fact, not only were future generations a concern, a significant portion of the then-current population would have been ineligible for citizenship under a one-quarter blood-quantum rule. Additionally, John Pemberton from the Twin Lakes community at White Earth stated that he had discussed the issue with his community members, and they had instructed him to vote against imposing any blood-quantum requirement.[39] These statements reflect a significant concern about the consequences of implementing a one-quarter requirement for tribal citizenship. Furthermore, they demonstrate survivance through a strong objection and resistance to the use of blood quantum by the BIA.

As the discussion continued, there was some question about who had or should have the authority to decide the issue of tribal citizenship. Mr. Sanders, employee of the Indian Office, noted that the BIA held that, under the constitution, the MCT had the authority to make its own regulations regarding tribal citizenship. Sanders stated: "Whenever the Executive Committee is ready, we have about 3,000 cases that they can consider. In the meantime, the Washington Office says to follow the old rule as the enrollment; enroll them if they are born on the reservation, otherwise not."[40] Sanders's comments show that there was a pressing need to settle the matter as soon as possible, but there was no decision made at the meeting.

One year later, at TEC meetings in May and July 1941, tribal citizenship was again a prominent issue. A resolution that only required descent from the 1889 rolls was passed, but BIA authorities questioned whether the

MCT understood the ramifications of their decision. In a lengthy memorandum to Mr. Flanery (chief, Indian Division, Office of the Solicitor), the assistant commissioner details the discussion of tribal citizenship at the May 1941 meeting, using numerous quotations from the minutes.[41] The assistant commissioner argues, "[That] the tribal authorities fully appreciate the far-reaching scope of their proposed action is, we believe, conclusively shown by the excerpts from the minutes of meetings of the Tribal Executive Committee of May 15–18 and July 25–26, 1941."[42] Yet Flanery was unable to move beyond popular notions of Natives as simple or inept to conceive of the elected leaders of the MCT as smart, capable, and competent. He thought it impossible that the elected leaders of the MCT knew what they were doing, even though the meeting minutes show that they exercised great caution and were careful and deliberate in their actions.

Mr. Rogers began the discussion on citizenship at the meeting in May 1941. He said that he felt that during their previous discussion in May 1940, it had been agreed that everyone who was a descendant from the "Treaty of 1889"—known as the Chippewa in Minnesota Fund as established under the Nelson Act—should be able to enroll "regardless of blood degree, place of residence, etc."[43] He noted that the question of how citizenship should be regulated had come up for the last five years, and that the MCT had received a large number of applications with which nothing could be done until the council passed clear regulations. Rogers worked with Sanders to draft some regulations and presented them to the TEC. The two men based proposed regulations on previous meeting discussions. Rogers explained:

> These rules throw the gate wide open. Any descendents of the original members who were entitled to enrollment under the treaty or agreement of 1889 are entitled to enrollment. These rules provide that any descendent, no matter what degree of blood he possesses or where he lives, or where he is born, so long as he can prove that he is a descendent or issue of one of the original families, is entitled to enrollment under these regulations. . . . We want to enroll everybody who is entitled to enrollment. We didn't consider the quantum of Indian blood, nor we didn't consider the place where they were born or where they lived. . . . The present policy of the Department is to enroll only those who were born or are born in the Indian country. We felt there are a great number of members of the tribe who are rightfully entitled to enrollment that are not on the rolls because they were born just outside the reservation. . . . That seemed to be the sentiment of the delegates a year ago and when this matter was discussed I made some notes of what the different speakers said.[44]

Rogers and Sanders were attentive and deliberate with the citizenship regulation they created. Their suggestion was for generous inclusion based on family relationships and Anishinaabe values. Rogers noted repeatedly that they did not want to exclude anyone who was "entitled" to citizenship, indicating that restrictions such as blood quantum and place of birth were considered forms of disenfranchisement. Rogers and Sanders were confident that their suggestion reflected the wider sentiment among the TEC, but left their recommendation open for debate.

After the presentation of Rogers's and Sanders's suggestions, the discussion of blood quantum continued. William "Bill" Anywaush, of the WEN, shared his perspective on the issue. He spoke in Anishinaabe, which was translated by Shingobe and recorded in English. Anywaush began, "Friends and Relatives—The reason I say 'relative' is that you are Indian and so am I."[45] By noting that Anishinaabeg are all friends as well as relatives, Anywaush was highlighting their unity and responsibility to each other. His use of the Anishinaabe language was likely a choice he made as another way to draw people together, to remind them of their common heritage and culture.[46] He believed they were dealing with a "very dangerous" issue because of the impact it would have on future generations. He went on, stressing:

> There was never in the past any mention of drawing any line; relationship was the only thing that was considered in the past. Even though the child had very little Indian blood, in considering relationship, he was still an Indian. One thing that these old folks over there urged me to do was to have mercy on my Indian people. Don't ever, as long as you live, discriminate against your fellow Indians.[47]

Anywaush appealed to the TEC to use kinship/family as the way to determine whether an individual should be able to become a tribal citizen, noting that this is what the "old folks" wanted. He reminded TEC members of their responsibilities both to children and to elders. In addition, he declared that they had never used blood quantum before, implying discordance with Anishinaabe values, and that using it would discriminate against "fellow Indians." Blood quantum was not only absent from Anishinaabe culture, it went against the long-standing importance of and regard for family relationships.

At the July meeting, Anywaush spoke in English but was equally vocal and "earnestly requested the delegates . . . to seriously, carefully and fully consider the matter before them considering its seriousness to them and their children, not be hasty in anything they did concerning it."[48] He went on to say, "The White Earth people felt that the Indian people would be endangered unless extreme care were exercised in passing these rules."[49] Again Anywaush emphasized that the issue required a great deal of caution because their children would be impacted. His use of the word "endangered" is powerful because it describes well the effects of a blood-quantum requirement: fewer and fewer Anishinaabeg would likely be eligible for tribal citizenship under this system. The word "endangered" also implies that one day there might not be anyone with enough "blood" and the MCT would be, so to speak, "extinct."[50] Later in the meeting, Anywaush spoke up to repeat that "all due caution should be taken for the sake of the children who would live after the delegates."[51] According to the minutes, he also "begged the delegates to be careful that they did not tie a knot which their children and grandchildren could not untie."[52] Anywaush's strong conviction that future generations must be taken into consideration was unwavering and demonstrates a commitment to survivance. Several others noted that this was a decision deserving serious attention.

RESOLUTIONS AND REJECTIONS

Finally, after years of discussions, a resolution on tribal citizenship was passed on July 26, 1941. It required only lineal descent from the Act of January 14, 1889, requiring that those wishing to apply for citizenship "file a birth certificate or other supporting evidence which will make it possible for the Minnesota Chippewa Tribe and the Consolidated Chippewa Agency to definitely establish the fact that said issue is rightfully eligible for said enrollment."[53] In Section 5, the policy of requiring residence was explicitly terminated: "The present policy now existing of enrolling only Indians who are residents of the recognized Indian country, or their issue, shall by these acts be forever abrogated."[54] The resolution passed easily, 10 to 0, among the TEC, and 35 to 12 among the tribal delegates.[55] The objection to the use of residence is likely the result of a combination of factors. First, Anishinaabeg at White Earth had long been accustomed to seasonal mobility, and while that mobility had decreased with reservations and allotment, a new kind of mobility with regard to urbanization was emerging; increasing numbers of Anishinaabeg were moving to Minneapolis, St. Paul, and Duluth in search of work.[56] With the onset of World War II, many Anishinaabeg were leaving their reservations and entering the armed services.[57] Also, as many delegates had carefully and articulately emphasized, kinship should be the primary factor in determining tribal citizenship. It was important to consider relationships, which could and did transcend physical location. After the passage of the resolution, superintendent of the Consolidated Chippewa Agency Francis J. Scott wrote to the commissioner of Indian Affairs, submitting the resolution for approval. He took care to note that it was the result of five years of thoughtful discussion. Superintendent Scott wrote, "It is hoped that the rules governing enrollment as adopted by the governing body of the Minnesota Chippewas be given approval and I so recommend."[58]

Despite Superintendent Scott's recommendation for the approval of the resolution and the length of time spent discussing the important issue, the Office of Indian Affairs was strongly against it. At first, some thought it was so outlandish that the MCT could not have possibly understood the ramifications of their decision. In an overt display of paternalism, Mr. Flanery wrote to the commissioner of Indian Affairs, suggesting that the resolution be returned to the MCT because it was "questionable whether the tribal authorities appreciate the far-reaching scope of the proposed action."[59] He suggested that a letter be sent to the MCT explaining the results of their resolution and to ask them to consider alternatives suggested by the Department of the Interior, presumably either a blood-quantum minimum and/or residency requirement. The assistant commissioner wrote back to Flanery, indicating that it was already quite clear that the MCT knew what the results of the proposed citizenship requirements would be. The assistant commissioner went on to suggest that the MCT should be informed that "if the Minnesota Chippewa Indians persist in their demands for such all-inclusive enrollment rules," the Department of the Interior would ask "that the matter be made the subject of an Act of Congress."[60] This thinly veiled threat was an attempt to pressure the MCT into adopting restrictive citizenship requirements, which would conform to racialized perceptions of identity and eventually result in the disappearance of the MCT.

Meanwhile, concern arose within the Department of the Interior about the increase in MCT citizenship that was likely to occur. On February 25, 1942, John Holst.[61] sent a memorandum to the Indian Office indicating that if the secretary of the Interior approved the 1941 MCT resolution on citizenship, the tribe would increase by the "some 4,000 names now awaiting a decision."[62] But that was not all, as "several thousand more may be eligible under the rule, thus creating a desperate situation for the Agency and without real service to the Indians."[63] Due to the circumstances, Holst. recommended that they "discontinue the present Agency as of 1940 [*sic*] and allow the tribe to maintain whatever roll it desires."[64] It is unclear whether the MCT was ever informed about the possibility of this extreme action, but if it was, it would have undoubtedly been cause for trepidation by the TEC and all tribal citizens.

A few days later, in a memorandum to Mr. McCaskill, George E. Fox voiced his concern that if the MCT only required an individual to prove descent from an ancestor listed on the 1889 rolls for tribal citizenship, that "it is distinctly possible that the tribal membership will in the next few years increase from its present 14,000 to around 18,000 to 20,000."[65] Fox went on to note that while the MCT had the right to determine its own citizenship, he wondered "just what should be the course of the Indian Service in a case of this sort. Is the function of the Indian Service to continue extending to the tribe all the services ordinarily rendered an Indian tribe when the tribal membership is composed of many individuals who no longer affiliate with the tribe, no longer reside upon the reservation, and have no intention of returning to it?"[66] Like Holst., Fox's first reaction was to consider the retraction of services from the MCT. He did not have the long-term welfare of the tribe in mind; instead, he focused on the amount of services that would be required for a growing population. In addition, Fox assumed that an inclusive citizenship policy would result in individuals who did not affiliate with the tribe becoming citizens. This is a curious interpretation, because enrolling as a tribal citizen would itself be an affiliation with the tribe. Fox also falsely presumed that individuals could not maintain tribal loyalties while living outside reservation boundaries. In the memoranda written by Holst. and Fox, the primary concern is regarding the possibility of an expanding body of citizens, rather than the vanishing population he, and other federal officials, expected. Federal officials simply did not want to extend services to an increased population; in fact, they wanted Natives to finally vanish along with all U.S. fiscal obligations. This external pressure would come to play a very important role in the MCT's eventual acceptance of one-quarter blood quantum as the sole determinant for tribal citizenship, but before that happened, the MCT would put up a long, hard fight.

Finally, in December 1942, Oscar Chapman, assistant secretary of the Department of the Interior, wrote to the MCT rejecting the resolution they had passed in 1941. Chapman noted that increased membership would not result in increased funding from Congress, stating:

> If the Minnesota Chippewa Indians desire to share their property with a large number of persons who are Indians neither by name, residence or attachment but merely by the accident of a small portion of Indian blood. . . . the Minnesota Chippewa Tribe must realize that every new name which they add to the membership roll will by that much decrease the share every member now has in the limited assets of the Minnesota Chippewa Tribe.[67]

Here, Chapman's direct implication is that the fewer citizens there were, the more resources there would be for each individual, using economics in an attempt to sway the MCT into passing a citizenship resolution that would be more restrictive. Chapman presumed that MCT elected leaders and citizens would be more concerned with monetary compensation than with the inclusion of their own family members as citizens in the tribe.[68]

The MCT again considered the question of citizenship in the spring of 1943. It was noted that their resolution on citizenship had been rejected, in part, because they did set a minimum of "Indian blood." Superintendent Scott advised the TEC that some degree of Indian blood should be established, and that it would impact new citizens but not current members. The TEC could not come to any agreement, and the meeting was adjourned with no resolution on the issue.[69]

In April 1944, William Zimmerman, assistant to the commissioner, wrote to superintendent Scott, regarding his concerns about getting the MCT to pass a citizenship resolution that would be approved by the Department of the Interior. Zimmerman began by referencing a recent visit to his office by Scott and a delegation from the MCT with their attorney to request that the citizenship resolution denied by the assistant secretary of the Interior in 1942 be reconsidered and the decision disapproving it be rescinded. Zimmerman agreed to ask the department to reconsider the decision if "there were new facts or circumstances which warranted its reconsideration."[70] The letter does not indicate that any such circumstances presented themselves and went on to detail why the MCT should pass a more restrictive citizenship resolution. Zimmerman writes that while "the Indians believe themselves to be morally, if not legally, bound to provide for the enrollment of the descendants of the Indians who appeared on the 1889 rolls without taking into consideration any other factor," this was not the case.[71] Furthermore, he suggested that one of the motivations for the inclusive citizenship requirement was the erroneous belief that a division and distribution of tribal funds might soon be at hand. Zimmerman asserted that such a distribution was likely never to occur, but that if it did, MCT citizenship rolls would not be used, and a new roll for that explicit purpose would be created. Consequently, "the Indians' desire to protect any supposed future rights of the descendants of the 1889 enrollees by burdening the present membership rolls of the tribal organization" was unnecessary.[72] Zimmerman went on to detail more restrictive citizenship requirements that were likely to gain approval, including requiring residence with a provision for the adoption of those who had left the reservation but later returned, but he noted that "if the conferring of membership by adoption is applied indiscriminately to all persons who are remote descendants of the 1889 enrollees, without regard to any other factor, any tribal legislation embodying such principles again will be disapproved."[73] Clearly, broadly inclusive citizenship requirements were not going to be approved by the department.

Meanwhile, thousands of Anishinaabeg waited to become citizens, and both the MCT and the commissioner of Indian Affairs saw new requests flowing in on a regular basis. Mr. Youngdahl sent an inquiry for tribal citizenship to Commissioner of Indian Affairs John Collier in May 1940. Assistant to the Commissioner John Herrick responded to Youngdahl, telling him he should send his request to the MCT because "the tribal authorities have practically full power of deciding the membership of the tribe."[74] As evidence of this, he noted that the MCT constitution stated "that the governing body of the tribe may make necessary corrections in the rolls subject to the approval of the Secretary of the Interior."[75] Herrick also noted that Section 3 of the constitution "provides that the governing body of the tribe shall have the power to make all necessary rules and regulations governing qualifications required for enrollment."[76]

The MCT continued to deal with questions and issues related to blood quantum throughout this time. For example, in 1940, Ruth Marie Fairbanks wished to have her blood quantum changed from 1/16 to 5/16, and on July 19, 1940, the TEC unanimously approved Resolution No. 5, which changed Fairbanks's blood quantum.[77] Even though the TEC approved the change, the matter was not closed—according to Article II, Section 2 of the MCT constitution, the resolution was subject to the approval of the secretary of the Interior. Superintendent Scott wrote to the commissioner shortly after the resolution was approved: "It is my understanding that the Tribal organization has the power and authority to determine its own membership but I question its power to have authority to determine quantum of Indian blood. Please let me have your views on this matter."[78]

The resolution was submitted for approval, but the Department of the Interior wanted more information before they would decide approval.[79] On August 16, 1940, Assistant to the Commissioner Fred H. Daiker wrote to superintendent Scott requesting copies of all the evidence upon which the TEC based its decision. He wrote: "These cases are decided not alone upon oral evidence and affidavits, depositions, etc., but upon agency and office records dealing with allotments, sales of land, certificates of competency, etc., which have transpired in connection with the applicant himself or his ancestors."[80] Daiker does not say whether the MCT had the power to determine blood quantum, but his request to see the evidence upon which the TEC made their decision to change Fairbanks's blood quantum indicates that he did not consider the TEC to have such authority. Daiker ends his letter by informing Scott that "the resolution will be held in this Office until compliance with the requirements herein."[81] It is unclear whether Fairbanks's blood quantum was ever officially changed or not.

Superintendent Scott wrote to the commissioner of Indian Affairs on December 14, 1940, regarding the request of Henry Lufkins to have his two children enrolled at White Earth. Lufkins was born in 1895 and took an allotment at White Earth. He married a woman enrolled with the Sisseton Indian Agency, and their two children were enrolled there as well. Scott felt that "in view of the fact that the two children referred to above are now duly enrolled with the mother at Sisseton we can see no reason for their transfer to the rolls of this Agency where the father is enrolled. Kindly advise what the Office would suggest in this case."[82] No response to the letter is included in the file.

While many requests dealt with people who wanted to enroll, there were those who wished to be taken off the rolls and cease being MCT citizens. For example, in 1944, Levi J. Dence of Mahnomen requested that he and his five children be removed as citizens of the MCT. Dence had received an allotment as well as several annuity payments. He made the request because his wife was non-Indian, and their children were attending a public school in which they were the only Indians and had, as a result, experienced "many embarrassing situations" that "[affected] the children in both mind and spirit . . . hinder[ing] their scholastic achievement."[83] Consequently, Dence argued, "it would be an aid to their well being socially and personally to have their names thus stricken from the rolls."[84] In a surprising recognition of tribal authority, the Office of Indian Affairs advised Dence that his application for the removal of himself and his children from the tribal rolls be submitted to the Tribal Executive Committee of the MCT, as it was the right of the tribe to determine matters of citizenship.[85]

As individuals and families sought to clarify their citizenship status, the elected officials of the Minnesota Chippewa Tribe continued to work to create a resolution on tribal citizenship that would gain the approval of the secretary of the Interior. In the spring of 1945, a resolution requiring one-quarter or more Indian blood was drawn up, but the matter was tabled by a vote of 39 to 0 by the tribal delegates and no action was taken.[86] Apparently, the MCT was not quite ready to bow to the pressure of the BIA and enact a resolution that would, undoubtedly, gain the approval of the secretary of the Interior.

STAUNCH RESISTANCE

Despite pressure from the BIA and the rejection of several resolutions requiring lineal descent for tribal citizenship, the MCT seemed to have no intention of limiting tribal citizenship based on a racial requirement. In June 1948, the MCT stood up against the Consolidated Chippewa Agency's use of blood quantum, passing a resolution insisting that all "Chippewa Indians" be treated as such by the Consolidated Chippewa Agency:

> NOW THEREFORE BE IT RESOLVED, that we insist that all Chippewa Indians entitled to enrollment under the provisions of the Act of 1889 and their issue, regardless of marital status, degree of blood or place of birth be entitled to and be given all the rights, benefits and privileges incident to and given to all regular enrolled Indians now on such rolls of the Consolidated Chippewa Agency at Cass Lake, Minnesota and that in particular this policy be applied and followed with respect to medical and hospital care under the jurisdiction of this Agency, and
> BE IT FURTHER RESOLVED, that all such persons referred to herein be considered Chippewa Indians and entitled to all benefits as such.[87]

The MCT was careful to explicitly incorporate clauses that would ensure wide inclusion; neither blood status, residence, nor marital status were to be cause for exclusion from tribal citizenship or any services provided by the Consolidated Chippewa Agency. While the resolution makes it clear that the individuals are "entitled to all benefits," it makes specific reference to medical care, implying that health and medical care were of prominent concern. The MCT took a bold stand against the use of blood quantum to define who was and who was not Indian when they passed this resolution. The MCT was also asserting its right to determine tribal citizenship over that of the Consolidated Chippewa Agency and, more importantly, the secretary of the Interior.

During this same period, Congress began considering ways to reduce spending on American Indian tribes. In 1947, Commissioner of Indian Affairs William Zimmerman was asked to create a list of tribes from which monetary federal support could be withdrawn. Zimmerman's list was divided into three groups: those who were "predominantly acculturated" and ready for the withdrawal of federal support, those who were "semi-acculturated" and would be ready in ten years, and those who were "predominantly Indian" and would need more than ten years of continued support before all federal support could be ended. The new rhetoric was that American Indians should be "freed" from their status as wards of the government and become fully American.[88]

The TEC continued to search for an answer to the question of tribal citizenship that would both enact Anishinaabe values and satisfy the BIA. On December 9, 1948, TEC minutes note a "lengthy discussion of enrollment" that seems to have gone on for at least a couple of hours, but unfortunately, in this case, no details were recorded.[89] The meeting continued, and two days later the TEC unanimously passed a new resolution relating to tribal citizenship. The resolution stated, "Indians not now enrolled as members of the Minnesota Chippewa Tribe, if able to so prove shall be enrolled if he or she is a descendant of a member of the Tribe" provided both the tribal delegates and the secretary of the Interior approved the resolution.[90]

Despite the resolution requesting that all MCT citizens be treated the same by the Consolidated Chippewa Agency, the discrimination continued. The issue was addressed again at the December 1948 meeting when the TEC passed Resolution No. 6, by a vote of 8 to 2. This resolution addressed the "injustice . . . perpetrated against members of the Minnesota Chippewa Tribe by reason of the marital status" or "their degree of Indian blood and place of birth," insisting that all MCT citizens be treated equally by the agency, especially with regard to medical and hospital care.[91] This resolution implies that MCT citizens who did not have one-quarter blood quantum or did not reside on their reservation were being denied services by the Consolidated Chippewa Agency as Holst. and Fox had threatened just a few years earlier. The TEC's insistence that the agency treat all MCT citizens the same illustrates their resolve and commitment to all MCT citizens, with no preference for those who were born on a reservation or had a higher degree of "blood." They asserted the authority of the tribe to decide matters of citizenship and to do so in a way that followed Anishinaabe values.

The tribal delegates ratified the inclusive resolution on citizenship on May 21, 1949, passing it unanimously. However, once again, the resolution only required individuals to prove descent from a citizen of the tribe in order to become a citizen.[92] The MCT anxiously awaited approval of the resolution, writing to Commissioner of Indian Affairs John R. Nichols in August, indicating their desire to have the matter settled as soon as possible so as to begin the process of creating a new approved roll for the tribe.[93] Secretary of the Interior William Warne rejected the resolution on December 9, 1949. He felt the resolution was too similar to the 1941 resolution in that it allowed all descendants to enroll with no blood quantum or residence restrictions. The secretary noted that the new resolution was "for all practical purposes almost identical" to the previous resolution and "will accomplish the same purposes."[94]

During this period of flux, questions about enrollment requirements remained an issue. On May 20, 1950, the tribal delegates unanimously passed a resolution that "ordered that the tribal enrollment roll be brought up to date under such rules and regulations as are now prescribed by the rules and regulations of the Bureau of Indian Affairs."[95] However, there were many uncertainties regarding BIA rules. On June 20, 1950, Lyzeme Savage, MCT tribal manager, wrote to Commissioner of Indian Affairs D. S. Myer, asking for "your interpretation of the rules and regulations governing enrollment with the Minnesota Chippewa Tribe" because the MCT was working on a new tribal roll. The MCT was especially concerned about citizens who were living off the reservation.[96] Savage further noted, "There are a number of families where one or more children are enrolled and the rest of the children are not. We wish to have these cases clarified."[97] When a quick response to the inquiry was not received, Savage wrote again on July 19, 1950, because the tribe was "anxious to know what steps should be taken in governing enrollment with the Minnesota Chippewa Tribe," and requested an "immediate reply."[98] Commissioner Myer responded to the letter on August 2, 1950. In the letter, Myer quoted the MCT at length, noting that the MCT had the authority to establish citizenship requirements, but that the tribe had not done so because the secretary of the Interior had rejected the resolutions regarding citizenship on several occasions. Myer advised that the MCT constitution had no provision applying to the loss of citizenship; therefore, "it would appear . . . that those persons who are members of the tribe but have removed from the reservation retain their membership."[99] The MCT proceeded with efforts to bring their citizenship rolls up to date and appointed Bernard Morrison "Supervisor to make such a corrected roll."[100] It is unclear what specific criteria were used.

Getting the MCT to pass a resolution on tribal citizenship that would be approved by the secretary of the Interior was of increasing concern to federal officials. On September 19, 1951, the commissioner of Indian Affairs wrote to Don Foster, area director of Minneapolis, about the problem. The commissioner noted that the resolutions passed by the MCT were "in conflict with the policy expressed by Congress and followed by the Department of the Interior to the effect that the application of Indian benefits should be limited to those persons who are Indians by virtue of actual tribal affiliation or by virtue of possessing one-half or more Indian blood."[101] The commissioner said that the MCT should be urged to pass a more restrictive resolution offering ideas such as requiring that "both parents are recognized members of the tribe, or that the residence of the parents is within the reservation, or that the child is of a certain degree of Indian blood."[102] It appears that the commissioner tried to get the area director to place pressure on the MCT to pass a resolution that would be approved.

Meanwhile Congress pursued more aggressively what would come to be known as the "termination" policy. Under this policy, American Indian governments were to be phased out and eliminated, and important federal programs such as health care and education would also end. In the summer of 1953, Congress passed House Concurrent Resolution 108, which made termination the official policy of the United States. Both Secretary of the Interior Douglas McKay and BIA Commissioner Glenn Emmons were ardent supporters of the new policy. Freedom continued as the rhetoric behind the policy. Senator Arthur V. Watkins was a key player in the establishment of the policy. He is famous for announcing that termination would have a special place in American history: "Following the footsteps of the Emancipation Proclamation ninety-four years ago, I see the following words emblazoned in letters of fire above the heads of the Indians—THESE PEOPLE SHALL BE FREE!"[103] However, termination was not really about freedom for American Indians; rather, it was about assimilation and a final end to the "Indian problem." It seems clear that termination policy was designed to give the United States "freedom" from fiscal responsibilities toward American Indians.[104]

Despite the TEC's efforts to secure access to health services for all tribal citizens, provided by the Consolidated Chippewa Agency in the late 1940s, the issue arose again in 1956 because the agency continued to deny health care to some MCT citizens. A resolution was passed to address the issue where certain tribal citizens were being denied access to health services. The resolution states:

> It has come to the attention of this body that any Indian who is married to a white person is not entitled to hospitalization because of such marriage. NOW, THEREFORE, BE IT RESOLVED, that such procedure be terminated and those Indians be granted the same privilege as the other Indians, such as hospitalization, as long as they are on the tribal rolls.[105]

The resolution passed unanimously (10 to 0), demonstrating the TEC's desire for all tribal citizens to be allowed equal access to health services. The resolution also illustrates the TEC's assertion of sovereignty; they wanted political status as an enrolled citizen—not blood quantum—to determine an individual's legal identity as American Indian.

Overall, the records of the MCT are much less detailed in the 1950s than in other historical periods. There is some evidence that conflict was prominent within the MCT for several years. While it has been challenging to ascertain the underlying issues, there were times when conflict was unconcealed. For example, at a TEC meeting in August 1957, Secretary John Buckanaga walked out because he felt the chairman was not conducting the meeting in a businesslike manner. Meeting minutes indicate that the TEC president and another member of the TEC repeatedly interrupted Buckanaga. After being asked to take his seat, Buckanaga told one of the TEC members to "go to hell."[106] Prior to leaving, Buckanaga stated: "I absolutely refuse to turn over any records to an unbonded officer for the simple reason that the meeting is improperly conducted and completely out of order due to domination of our chairman and his underhanded committee men."[107] It is unclear what exactly Buckanaga was referring to or whether he had good reason to withhold records from the president of the TEC. The explicit conflict in this meeting likely prevented the TEC from operating in an effective manner.[108]

Even during this tumultuous period, the MCT continued to resist the adoption of a blood-quantum requirement for tribal citizenship. By 1959, elected leaders of the MCT were again working together to fight the use of blood quantum, even going so far as to attempt to get the BIA to stop using it. At a meeting on March 23, 1959, the TEC unanimously passed a resolution that noted the one-quarter degree policy had "created much confusion, hardship, and conflict" and requested that the "¼ degree policy set forth by the Bureau of Indian Affairs be eliminated in order that the Indians may increase their economic and social stature."[109] The resolution also stated "that the congressmen, state officials and other agencies interested in Indian welfare be requested to assist in the elimination of the ¼ degree Indian blood requirement and policy set for [sic] by the Bureau of Indian Affairs."[110] In this case, the TEC went beyond its own regulations to encourage change in BIA practices. The TEC went so far as to request that U.S. elected officials and other agencies join with them in their effort. In requesting the elimination of the one-quarter degree policy, the MCT reinforced its commitment to families and future citizens, showing no signs of willingness to accept blood quantum as a requirement for tribal citizenship.

Considering the atmosphere of the time, the MCT's actions were bold and surprising. Termination had become a reality for several tribes, including the nearby Menominee. James Officer observes that "Many Indians by the late 1950s were convinced that the federal government intended to set them adrift without regard for the consequences."[111] Despite the risk of termination, elected officials continually insisted that blood quantum not be used as a criterion by the Consolidated Chippewa Agency or the BIA as a means to determine who was and was not Indian; instead, they insisted it was an individual's political status as a citizen of the MCT that made them American

Indian. When discussing the requirements for tribal citizenship, family was often the primary focus. Many voiced concerns about current relatives and future generations who might be excluded if an arbitrary amount of "blood" was used as a means to determine tribal citizenship.

A REVERSAL AND A LIMITED ACCEPTANCE

After years of attempting to get a resolution on tribal citizenship, which only required lineal descent, approved by the secretary of the Interior, the TEC finally bowed to the pressure and, as mentioned previously, passed an ordinance relating to tribal citizenship that required a minimum of one-quarter MCT blood in 1961. The ordinance stated:

> After the approval of this ordinance by the Secretary of the Interior, all children born to a parent or parents whose names appear on the basic membership roll shall be eligible for membership, provided they possess at least one-quarter (¼) degree Minnesota Chippewa Indian blood, and provided further that an application for enrollment is filed with the Secretary of the Tribal Delegates within one year after date of birth.[112]

The ordinance also allowed individuals who met the citizenship requirement but were not enrolled due to error to be admitted into the MCT by adoption. Individuals who did not have one-quarter Minnesota Chippewa Indian blood were made citizens of the tribe provided they were born before May 12, 1961.[113] Two days later, at the delegates meeting, MCT president John L. Pemberton was called upon to explain the ordinance to all the tribal delegates. Pemberton explained that "it was necessary to set the ¼ degree blood quantum in the ordinance in order to receive approval of the Department of the Interior which defines an Indian as being ¼ or more degree Indian blood."[114] He went on to defend the ordinance, stating that "if the MCT does not set up enrollment rules, than [sic] the Department will make their own rules."[115] Pemberton implied that the TEC had little choice in passing the ordinance because if they did not do so, the department would. Delegates would have been very familiar with the ways in which the department had attempted to restrict services to those individuals with one-quarter or more Indian blood. Despite Pemberton's rationale for the ordinance, about one-third of the tribal delegates continued their opposition to the use of blood quantum to determine tribal citizenship and voted against it. The ordinance passed among the tribal delegates, 29 for and 15 opposed.[116] MCT citizens voted 1,761 for and 1,295 against the constitutional amendments proposed in 1963.[117] The secretary of the Interior approved it along with other constitutional changes in 1963. Article 2 of the MCT constitution now reads:

Section 1. The membership of the Minnesota Chippewa Tribe shall consist of the following:

(a) Basic Membership Roll. All persons of Minnesota Chippewa Indian blood whose names appear on the annuity roll of April 14, 1941, prepared pursuant to the Treaty with said Indians as enacted by Congress in the Act of January 14, 1889 (25 Stat. 642) and Acts amendatory thereof, and as corrected by the Tribal Executive Committee and ratified by the Tribal Delegates, which roll shall be known as the basic membership roll of the Tribe.

(b) All children of Minnesota Chippewa Indian blood born between April 14, 1941, the date of the annuity roll, and July 3, 1961, the date of approval of the membership ordinance by the Area Director, to a parent or parents, either or both of whose names appear on the basic membership roll, provided an application for enrollment was filed with the Secretary or Tribal Delegates by July 4, 1962, one year after the date of approval of the ordinance by the Area Director.

(c) All children of at least one quarter (¼) degree Minnesota Chippewa Indian blood born after July 3, 1962, to a member, provided that an application for enrollment was or is filed with the Secretary of the Tribal Delegates of the Tribal Executive Committee within one year after the date of birth of such children.

Section 2. No person born after July 3, 1961, shall be eligible for enrollment if enrolled as a member of another tribe, or if not an American citizen.

Section 3. Any person of Minnesota Chippewa Indian blood who meets the membership requirements of the Tribe, but who because of an error has not been enrolled, may be admitted to membership privileges from the date the adoption is approved.

Section 4. Any person who has been rejected for enrollment as a member of the Minnesota Chippewa Tribe shall have the right of appeal within sixty days from the date of written notice of rejection from the decision of the Tribal Executive Committee to the Secretary of the Interior and the decision of the Secretary of the Interior shall be final.

Section 5. Nothing contained in this article shall be construed to deprive any descendant of a Minnesota Chippewa Indian of the right to participate in any benefits derived from claims against the U.S. Government when awards are made for and on behalf and for the benefit of descendants of members of said tribe.[118]

The new citizenship requirement makes it clear that one-quarter MCT blood is the primary requirement; place of birth and residence are not factors. Individuals may not be enrolled with another tribe, which is a common clause in IRA-style constitutions, and they must be U.S. citizens. After years of asserting their right to determine citizenship, the MCT gives the secretary of the Interior final decision-making authority for enrollment challenges in the amendment. The new requirement divided families and bowed to federal authority while eschewing Anishinaabe values and practices that so many emphasized in previous years.

CONTINUED RESISTANCE

Even after the one-quarter MCT blood-quantum requirement went into effect, it remained a prominent matter of discussion. For example, at a TEC meeting on October 1, 1965, Mr. Savage noted that Indians who were less than one-quarter blood were not eligible for scholarships through the BIA, and he felt they should be included. Mr. Martin stated: "The one-quarter degree should be changed to enable any Indian to be eligible for all benefits."[119] Like some of his predecessors, Martin believed that some Indians were being excluded and discriminated against based on racial requirements that did not reflect or determine identity. While the minutes of this meeting do not contain much detail, some support for equal treatment regardless of blood quantum remained. For example, at a TEC meeting in 1967, delegate(s) moved to abolish the one-quarter requirement because several felt it was wrong to deny community members citizenship because of blood quantum. Once again, either there was not a lengthy discussion or it was not recorded in the minutes. The motion passed 8 for, 2 against.[120] After having a one-quarter blood-quantum requirement for only four years, the TEC decided to abolish it. This action raises several questions: Were people protesting because they could not enroll their children? Or did the specific situation that caused the MCT to implement the blood-quantum requirement change? Despite this retraction of blood quantum, the MCT continued to use the one-quarter requirement. It is probable that—like the resolutions of the 1940s, which did not require a specific degree of blood—the secretary of the Interior rejected the resolution, and so it was never enforced.

Federal Indian policy would shift dramatically in the next few decades. The 1960s were primarily a transition period retaining some termination characteristics, but as the decade progressed, a new policy involving the support of American Indian self-determination would be introduced. During the mid-1960s, the Johnson administration was able to push the Economic Opportunity Act through Congress. This legislation was markedly different than past legislation because it actually gave control to tribal governments. This legislation allowed tribal governments to create their own programs to cope with poverty. Although these programs were subject to approval, this was the first time that American Indian nations had the opportunity to assume full responsibility for the management and use of funds for their programs.[121]

More new legislation during the 1970s had a significant impact as well. On January 4, 1975, the Indian Self-Determination and Education Assistance Act (ISDEAA) became law. This act allowed American Indian nations the chance to administer programs previously overseen by the Department of the Interior and the Health Education and Welfare Programs (HEW).[122] Under this act, the secretary of the Interior could approve grants to provide funds for the planning of the takeover of federally operated programs, for training for managerial and technical positions once the tribe had assumed control of the program, and for financing through evaluation of performance.[123]

In accordance with the ISDEAA, both the MCT and the Reservation Tribal Councils began to contract for a wide variety of programs and services, including several that provide educational assistance, employment, health care, and legal services. Many of the programs and services are supported by grants from the United States government and thus are subject to change due to funding. The MCT had a strong commitment to education, as demonstrated through their educational assistance programs. In the 1970s, the MCT began contracting with the BIA for several programs. The MCT administered the Higher Education Scholarship Grants Program, which provided grants to Anishinaabe students who met several requirements, including the possession of at least one-quarter blood quantum.[124] The MCT also contracted to administer the Johnson O'Malley Program. The goals of this program included reducing the dropout rate and increasing the attendance rate of Anishinaabe students, improving the grades of Anishinaabe students, improving communication between schools and communities, and developing Native studies curricula.[125] A Head Start Training and Technical Assistance Program, a program for preschool children, was also administered by the MCT. In addition to education programs, the MCT, in conjunction with the Reservation Tribal Councils, began to administer several social programs, including the Elderly Nutrition Program and Health Planning Program. The MCT also managed housing programs such as the Planning and Development Program, the Housing and Urban Development Department, and a Home Loan Program.[126]

In the early 1970s, the elected leaders of the MCT raised the issue of constitutional reform. The constitutional changes went to the Anishinaabeg for a vote in 1972, when the MCT was granted authorization for a constitutional election by the BIA. One amendment required that elected Reservation Business Committee members be enrolled members of the band/nation they were elected to represent.[127] The MCT leaders felt that by requiring a person to be enrolled at the band/nation they represented, "outsiders" would not have the chance to take control. Simon Howard said that at Leech Lake more White Earth enrollees controlled governance, and White Earth enrollees were the source of most of the dissident groups at Leech Lake. He felt that eventually the "genuine enrollees" and "true residents of Leech Lake" would lose control of their nation without the protection afforded by the amendment. Yet, not everyone agreed. Mr. Isham was an enrollee of White Earth but had never been to White Earth. He grew up at Nett Lake and considered it his home. He thought that the new requirement would "drive a wedge into our Tribal unity, will split us more."[128] Clearly opinions regarding residence and citizenship differed. Was it where an individual was raised that made him or her a member of that community, or was it more significant where they were enrolled? Isham's concern that the amendment would divide the tribe "more" indicates that he felt there were already other issues dividing the MCT. This is possibly a reference to the blood-quantum requirement, which by this point had excluded many people from citizenship and divided them from the nation.

Indeed, when discussing amendments to the MCT constitution, the issue of the required one-quarter blood quantum was raised. Illustrating continued resistance to blood quantum, Mr. Clark asked if the MCT could get rid of the one-quarter degree rule. However some Anishinaabeg had internalized the concept of racial identity and, in the ultimate reversal, now supported it. Mr. Howard responded:

> Once again, our dark people would be left out. In the long run, we would lose control of all that we have worked for. It is common knowledge that our genuine, dark Indian people are always left out of everything now. Most of us feel that we should hold tight to the one-quarter degree rule.[129]

In this statement, Howard equated a physical feature—the darkness of one's skin—with the degree of "Indian" an individual is, believing that to be a "genuine" Indian one must possess dark skin. His conception of what a "real" Indian is, is reflective of the racial conceptions present in dominant society and is an internalization of the external divisions created by the colonial society. Howard also stated that most people now agree with him, indicating a possible shift in the ways in which MCT citizens thought of identity; the focus on the darkness of one's skin is dramatically different from the familial focus on children that was called for at earlier meetings, or when concern was focused on the external power of the BIA to deny citizens with less than one-quarter blood quantum loans, heath care, and other services.

A CALL FOR CHANGE

The shift to blood quantum as the single determinant for citizenship has had a significant impact on the MCT. As feared by Anishinaabe leaders, many Anishinaabeg have been excluded as a result of this requirement, especially impacting current and future generations. In fact, research conducted by the Wilder Research Center in the 2010s found that "the overall population of MCT and each of the Bands is declining significantly under the current enrollment criteria (¼ MCT blood quantum)."[130] The clear influence and pressure of the BIA that pushed the MCT to adopt a blood-quantum provision raises questions about its appropriateness. In fact, the BIA refused to approve citizenship regulations based on lineal descent, ultimately compelling the elected leaders of the MCT to implement a blood-quantum requirement.

In the late 1990s, at White Earth, there was a strong effort for constitution reform, including an examination of the requirement of one-quarter blood quantum for citizenship. The reform effort was spurred, in part, by issues that arose due to rampant corruption that resulted in the conviction of three of the five members of the White Earth Tribal Council on various charges of embezzlement, bid rigging, and election fraud in 1996.[131] United States District Court Judge Michael J. Davis sentenced longtime tribal chairman Darrell "Chip" Wadena to fifty-one months in prison for his participation in a variety of illegal activities. Reservation Tribal Council councilman Rick Clark was sentenced to forty-six months, and then former secretary-treasurer Jerry Joseph Rawley Jr. received a thirty-three-month sentence.[132] Journalist Gary Blair wrote: "The Nov. 21 sentencing of the trio concluded one of the darkest eras for the White Earth people. Not since the land was stolen by whites during the turn of the last century has the reservation known such corruption."[133]

With a newly elected Tribal Council in place, the WEN moved forward and seriously considered the need for constitutional reform.[134] Then White Earth Secretary/Treasurer Dr. Erma Vizenor told *The Circle* in 1996 that she believed the problems with corruption, which had been rampant at White Earth for several decades, stemmed from a despotic BIA governance structure, which does not have a separation of powers or checks and balances. "We need to go after the system," said Vizenor.[135] As the constitutional-reform effort gained momentum, White Earth citizen Leah Carpenter was chosen as the director. She graduated from the University of Wisconsin Law School in 1989 and worked tirelessly on the project, holding community meetings and drafting ideas for change.[136] In March 1997, Carpenter wrote an article for the *Ojibwe News* about a Constitutional Reform Panel presentation held at White Earth earlier that month. While Carpenter did not go into detail, she wrote about her disappointment because of negativity at the presentation, noting, "I am saddened and disheartened at the level of anger, hatred and confusion amongst our tribal membership."[137] Apparently there was a wide diversity of opinions on constitutional reform and tribal citizenship at the meeting. Instead of respectful dialogue, the meeting was dominated by arguments and accusations. In an attempt to guide the group through the process of reform, Margaret "Peggy" Treuer, member of the Constitutional Reform Committee, shared the Anishinaabe word *shawanima*, which means "to keep the people together and make decisions on what is best for all."[138] Carpenter went on to call for Anishinaabeg to "reclaim some of the basic Anishinaabe values of Respect, Honor, Dignity and Pride."[139] She also encouraged everyone to participate in the process of constitutional reform. While some may have been negative at the meeting, Treuer's appeal for the group to consider what was best for everyone, and Carpenter's call for the employment of basic Anishinaabe values are reflective of an inclusive process that many were trying to facilitate.

In July 1997, the White Earth Tribal Council held an urban council meeting in Minneapolis. The meeting generally centered on the challenges that faced the tribe in light of the previous fraud and corruption; however, constitutional reform and the issue of the use of one-quarter blood quantum for tribal citizenship was also discussed. Then newly elected tribal chairman Eugene "Bugger" McArthur said, "We are throwing away our grandchildren the way it is now."[140] In this statement, McArthur references those who are excluded from tribal citizenship because they lack the required amount of "blood." His statement is reminiscent of those made by MCT elected officials in the 1940s. In fact, Morrell's worry that children and grandchildren would be excluded under a one-quarter degree of blood rule had become reality.

McArthur's intense comment speaks beyond mere exclusion and reminds White Earth Anishinaabeg that tribal citizenship is a family issue.

After much hard work and thoughtful discussion, the White Earth Constitutional Drafting Committee completed a proposed constitution on February 21, 1998.[141] Article III deals with "Membership" and says that "The membership of the White Earth Ojibwe Nation shall consist of all persons *descended from the Anishinaabe Ojibwe who were signators* [sic] *to treaties and agreements with the United States government*," and those already enrolled or who have applied for enrollment (emphasis original).[142] The article goes on to provide four options for the regulation of citizenship for the future for White Earth citizens to consider.

Option A. Lineal descendants of enrolled members of the White Earth Ojibwe Nation;

Option B. Lineal descendants of enrolled members of the White Earth Ojibwe Nation and who are at least ¼ degree Anishinaabe blood;

Option C. Lineal descendants of enrolled members of the White Earth Ojibwe Nation who are at least ¼ degree Indian blood, with at least ⅛ degree White Earth Ojibwe Nation blood;

Option D. Children of enrolled members of the White Earth Ojibwe Nation who are at least ¼ degree Minnesota Chippewa Tribe (Bois Fort/Nett Lake, Fond du Lac, Grand Portage, Mille Lacs, Leech Lake, White Earth) blood.

Option E. *Deleted.*[143]

The variety of citizenship options reflect the diversity of opinions regarding the regulation of tribal citizenship. While the first option eliminates blood quantum in favor of lineal descent, several of the options would require very precise calculations of "blood."

Attendees at a Constitutional Reform Committee meeting on May 12, 2001, held at the Shooting Star Casino in Mahnomen, Minnesota, discussed the fact that some action needed to be taken by either the White Earth Tribal Council or the TEC because the committee had essentially completed its work. The list was designed as a quick introduction to the complex options and ideas for change. Among the suggestions was "Reject 'Blood Quantum' as a membership requirement," illustrating that it was one of the most important and fundamental issues that the committee wished to address.[144]

At a regular quarterly meeting of the White Earth Tribal Council held at the Shooting Star Casino on July 7, 2001, tribal historian and member of the Constitutional Reform Committee Andrew "Andy" Favorite reminded the council that a draft constitution had been finished for several years. The proposed constitution has suggestions for constitutional reform at the MCT level. He asked Chairman Doyle Turner and Secretary/Treasurer Erma Vizenor to present the suggestions at the next TEC meeting. Turner responded that he would be proud to do so. Favorite inquired about the possibility of having a constitutional reform meeting in Minneapolis. Vizenor responded that September would be a good time to do so and that the council would pay mileage and an honorarium to those who attend.[145] Despite these efforts and gestures of support, this effort for constitutional reform would fade for a few years before a renewed effort began in 2007.

CONCLUSION

While the MCT did finally bow to federal pressure to use blood quantum as the determinant for tribal citizenship in 1961, they put up a long, hard fight. Time and again, discussions centered on family as the proper method of determining citizenship. Elected leaders took the issue of tribal citizenship seriously, understanding that their decisions would impact future generations of Anishinaabeg. They resisted the application of blood quantum by passing several resolutions on tribal citizenship that only required lineal descent, emphasizing that family superseded blood quantum as the primary determinant of an individual's identity. The elected leadership of the MCT wanted to be inclusive and worried that using blood quantum would discriminate against their fellow Anishinaabeg. In addition, the MCT recommended that BIA end its use of blood quantum as a determinant for defining who was Indian. Anishinaabeg continued to raise concerns about the one-quarter MCT blood-quantum requirement even after it was implemented. WEN began its own effort for constitutional reform, including addressing membership/citizenship requirements, in the late 1990s. That effort laid the groundwork for the 2007–2013 effort, which is the focus of the next chapter.

CHAPTER THREE

It is Time to Take Our Own Leadership

The Constitution of the White Earth Nation

On March 1, 2007, Dr. Erma Vizenor, Chairwoman of the White Earth Tribal Council, gave the annual State of the Nation address at the Shooting Star Casino in Mahnomen, Minnesota. She spoke of the accomplishments of the tribe as well as the work that still needed to be done. Among the issues she wanted to address in the upcoming year was constitutional reform. As a beginning point, she announced that it was her goal to hold a constitutional convention in September. Vizenor noted that a clear separation of powers of the tribal government should be considered as well as the requirements for citizenship, stating, "As tribal membership continues to decline under the present one-fourth blood quantum requirement, we must decide eligibility for enrollment."[1] She went on to note, "White Earth members must decide these issues by referendum vote."[2]

I was elated. I had been studying tribal citizenship for several years and was preparing to defend my dissertation, "Fictions and Fractions: Reconciling Citizenship Regulation with Cultural Values among the White Earth Anishinaabeg."[3] I immediately contacted Joe LaGarde in Vizenor's office and asked how I could be of assistance. We agreed that I would write a series of newspaper articles for the tribal newspaper, *Anishinaabeg Today*, based upon my dissertation research.[4] I set to work and wrote eight articles before the first Constitutional Convention was held on October 19–20, 2007.[5] In the articles, I delineated the ways in which Anishinaabeg at White Earth conceptualized identity during the early 1900s, shared the history of blood quantum, and discussed changes in tribal citizenship requirements. I also hoped that the articles would encourage White Earth citizens to get involved in the constitutional reform process.

Throughout the reform process my focus was on citizenship. I was deeply inspired by what I had learned in my research, but I knew that citizenship would be one of the most difficult issues addressed during the process of constitutional reform. As Goldberg has observed: "Indian nations' constitutional reform efforts encounter some of their most paralyzing conflicts over criteria for membership."[6] Yet, Lyons has argued, "It is absolutely essential that Indian nations devise their own criteria, and it is just as crucial that they do so in ways that do not violate universal human rights."[7] It was my goal to help White Earth citizens make informed decisions as they constructed a requirement for tribal citizenship that enacted Anishinaabe values.

Prior to the first Constitutional Convention in 2007, an open call to all White Earth citizens went out in the tribal newspaper inviting them to apply to be constitutional delegates. Additionally, Community Councils were asked to select two delegates and one alternate. The sole requirement for becoming a delegate was enrollment as a White Earth citizen. In an effort to encourage as much participation as possible, everyone who applied was accepted.[8] I consulted with LaGarde often during the months leading up to the first convention, offering to be of assistance. It was decided that I would be one of two individuals taking notes and helping with other tasks as needed. I was also asked to give presentations on my research regarding the history of blood quantum and tribal citizenship.

CONSTITUTIONAL REFORM IN INDIAN COUNTRY

As noted in the previous chapter, many scholars have critiqued Indian Reorganization Act (IRA) constitutions and governance structures. White Earth is far from alone in its desire and effort for change. Many tribes have had IRA-style governments for over half a century and found them to be ineffective. As a result, constitutional reform has become increasingly common in Indian Country. Scholar Eric Lemont argues that "the wave of constitutional reform sweeping Indian Country will represent a critical starting point in American Indian nations' journey to retake ownership of their governments."[9] Indeed, the White Earth Nation (WEN) has found the Minnesota Chippewa Tribe (MCT) constitution to be restrictive and impractical. The constitution lists a mere nine powers, some of which are "subject to the review of the Secretary of the Interior," of the Tribal Executive Committee (TEC), and six powers of Reservation Business Committees (now called Reservation Tribal Councils).[10] In addition, as many Native nations with IRA constitutions have found, the constitution is overly focused on economics and does not reflect Anishinaabe values or practices.

Emerging scholarship examines recent and current efforts for reform, beginning to theorize the "best practices" that result in positive change. Much of this scholarship focuses on connections between economic development and successful governance reform. For example, the Harvard Project on American Indian Economic Development (HPAIED), founded by Stephen Cornell and Joseph P. Kalt in 1987, has focused significant attention on these issues. The primary goal of HPAIED is "to understand and foster the conditions under which sustained, self-determined social and economic development is achieved among American Indian nations through applied research and service."[11] Additionally, the University of Arizona's Native Nations Institute for Leadership, Management, and Policy (NNI) works directly with American Indian nations to create and implement plans for development. NNI's mission is to "assist in the building of capable Native nations that can effectively pursue and ultimately realize their own political, economic, and community development objectives." The NNI "sponsors training sessions in Native nation building designed for tribal leaders" and "works with Native nations and organizations on strategic and organizational issues ranging from constitutional reform to government design, intergovernmental relations, and economic and community development."[12] HPAIED and NNI have collaborated on several projects, including the publication of *Rebuilding Native Nations: Strategies for Governance and Development*, edited by Miriam Jorgensen.[13] During the reform process at White Earth, it was acknowledged that research indicates that a clear separation of powers correlates with strong economies, but little time was spent discussing specific economic-development issues.

Native nations currently amending their constitutions and/or making other changes to their governing documents are motivated by a variety of issues. Distinguished Lumbee scholar David E. Wilkins identifies four primary factors that motivate the desire for change(s) in tribal governance:

(1) structural and philosophical inadequacies (for many tribes) of the Western-style constitutional systems established in the 1930s and beyond; (2) state and societal developments in the last four decades that have spurred tribal governmental changes; (3) a resurgence of traditionalism among some tribes; and (4) internal political, economic, and moral crises that compel governmental change.[14]

Wilkins also notes that a "set of innovative and deeply committed individuals" is crucial for reform to be carried out.[15] The factors identified by Wilkins influenced and motivated efforts for reform at White Earth. In fact, the 2007 call for reform was not the first attempt to change the governing structure. As discussed in the previous chapter, in the late 1990s an internal political and moral crisis created an impetus for change at White Earth, but the effort never resulted in any changes to the governance structure. As a result, there was some skepticism that the 2007 effort for reform would accomplish anything, but a significant number of people were still motivated to participate in the process and work toward the creation of a new governance structure that would reflect Anishinaabe traditions and aid in the creation of a vibrant future for the whole nation.

WE WANT CHANGE

Chairwoman Vizenor realized her goal of holding what would be the first of four Constitutional Conventions on Friday, October 19, 2007.[16] She began by thanking the constitutional delegates for their willingness to serve and participate in the historic process of writing the White Earth constitution. The convention was open to all interested observers and Vizenor also welcomed them, noting that constitutional reform would be an open, public process. She went on to discuss the need for reform and gave a brief history of previous attempts at change. White Earth citizen and then Chief White Earth Tribal Court Judge Anita Fineday swore in forty constitutional delegates.[17] The delegates were provided copies of the draft constitution generated by the late 1990s effort for reform, another draft/model constitution, and the MCT constitution. Extra copies were distributed to nondelegates in attendance. There was an open comment period during which both delegates and nondelegates voiced a variety of opinions and ideas.[18]

There was an air of both excitement and nervousness the next day when the work of the convention began. Delegates were numbered off into eight small groups, and the agenda included discussion of four key issues. The delegate groups were first asked to discuss the questions "Should White Earth have its own constitution?" and "What should White Earth's relationship with the Minnesota Tribe be?" While all the groups agreed that White Earth should have its own constitution as opposed to continuing to operate under the MCT constitution, there were many questions about what White Earth's relationship with the MCT would be. Delegates noted that White Earth does not have equitable representation in the MCT. White Earth has nearly one half the population, but each nation has two votes at the MCT. They expressed a desire to have White Earth exercise increased independence with the creation and implementation of a separate constitution, but did not want to fully withdraw from the MCT. Many saw a degree of strength and solidarity with the MCT. The discussion continued, but there were no clear answers to how White Earth's relationship with the MCT would change with the implementation of a new constitution. Indeed, these questions remain unanswered and continued to be a source of anxiety for some.

The next topic on the agenda was tribal citizenship. Throughout the reform process, citizenship would prove to be an emotional issue that caused strong feelings in many delegates. Other tribes who have engaged in constitutional reform have also found citizenship to be a difficult issue. Defining citizenship requirements is one of the most fundamental activities a nation must engage in. This is a difficult task for any nation, but colonization and the U.S. government's use of blood quantum to define American Indian identity makes this an especially difficult question for Native nations. For example, Martha Berry, delegate to the 1999 Cherokee Nation Constitution Convention, has noted: "Of all the cruel and subtle gifts bestowed upon the Cherokee by colonization, this [blood quantum] is perhaps the cruelest and most subtle of them all."[19] Based on a study of 322 current and historic tribal constitutions, legal scholar Kirsty Gover found that blood-quantum requirements for tribal citizenship peaked between 1960 and 1970.[20] She argues that citizenship decisions made after 1970 are "influenced not just by the new opportunities and resources provided by federal and self-determination policy, but also by the legacy of termination-era policies and migrations."[21] Scholars argue that the implementation of blood quantum for tribal citizenship in the mid-twentieth century was a form of termination because it was designed to eventually eliminate American Indian nations.[22] As discussed in the previous chapter, the elected leaders of the MCT only approved a minimum of one-quarter MCT blood for tribal citizenship in the 1960s after letters containing thinly veiled termination threats were sent from the Bureau of Indian Affairs (BIA).[23] Grover notes that in response to termination-era policies, Native nations are electing to employ a genealogical approach to citizenship requirements and are increasingly likely to use lineal descent as a requirement for tribal citizenship because lineal descent is often seen as a way to repair or reconstitute nations that have been split under blood-quantum requirements.[24]

The requirement of one-quarter MCT blood has been in effect for nearly half a century, and in that time it has divided families, friends, and neighbors.

As a means to begin a discussion on citizenship, I gave a presentation about the importance of tribal citizenship and shared some of my dissertation research, which had already been published in my newspaper article series. I reminded delegates that during the mid-twentieth century, when the MCT was under heavy pressure to implement a blood-quantum requirement for citizenship, White Earth citizen William "Bill" Anywaush had made some of the most compelling arguments against the use of blood quantum. While many elected leaders had carefully and articulately emphasized that kinship should be the primary factor in determining tribal citizenship, few spoke as eloquently as Anywaush did on the issue. He appealed to MCT leaders to consider their future generations and "earnestly requested the Delegates . . . to seriously, carefully and fully consider the matter before them considering its seriousness to them and their children, not be hasty in anything they did concerning it."[25] Perhaps most importantly, the MCT passed several resolutions that did not contain a blood-quantum requirement and, instead, used lineal descent as the requirement for tribal citizenship. The U.S. secretary of the Interior rejected these resolutions. If it were not for the U.S. government's desire to erase and eliminate MCT, blood quantum would never have become a requirement for tribal citizenship. It was important for the delegates to know the history of tribal citizenship so that it could inform their decision-making.

The concept of *mino-bimaadiziwin* was also discussed as it related to the issue of citizenship. *Mino-bimaadiziwin* translates as "live well, have good health, lead a good life" and is not about mere physical survival but a world-view in which individuals and groups actively work to create a rewarding, ethical, and nourishing life. It is a time-honored Anishinaabe concept that involves spiritual, mental, emotional, and physical health; it is a holistic concept that recognizes that all these things must be in balance. In fact, the word "Anishinaabe" carries many meanings and is considered by some to be related to *mino-bimaadiziwin*. Louis Councillor, a spiritual leader from the Nagaaji-wanaag First Nation in Canada, believes the word comes from *anishin*, a short form of *onizhishi*, which means "he or she is good," and *aabe*, which means "human" or "being."[26] Dennis Jones notes: "Councillor went on to say that a good being in the eyes of an Ojibwe is one who follows all the spiritual principles of living a good life. These include being charitable, honest, humble, forgiving, generous, loving, caring, and respectful."[27] The White Earth Tribal Council's vision statement includes *mino-bimaadiziwin* and reads:

> The White Earth Tribal Council will be a proactive organization that makes sound decisions promoting mino-bimahdiziwin (the good life). The White Earth Reservation will be a safe place where all people have access to quality

employment, housing, education, health, and human services. While we protect our inherent right to self-governance and identity, we are a community of
respect where cultural, historical, and environmental assets are treasured and
conserved for future generations.[28]

The vision statement draws upon Anishinaabe values and includes actively
supporting *mino-bimaadiziwin* as a primary goal. The White Earth Tribal
Council pledges that all people will have access to the various services they
provide. The statement ends with a promise to conserve cultural, historical,
and environmental resources for future generations. The vision statement is
reflective of the same Anishinaabe values that were seen at TEC meetings
during the 1940s. Requiring a minimum of one-quarter blood quantum for
tribal citizenship contradicts the vision statement. The use of blood quantum defies the goal of "protect[ing] our inherent right to self-governance
and identity" because it creates a nation based on racial requirements and
will actually result in the demise of our nation. Reclaiming the right to
define tribal citizenship requirements in a way that draws upon Anishinaabe
values would be a way of living *mino-bimaadiziwin* and simultaneously
practicing self-governance. In addition, it would ensure that the nation
would have future generations of citizens to sustain it.

The issue of citizenship was just as serious in the early years of the
twenty-first century as it had been fifty years earlier. For example, William
Anywaush's plea to "consider the relationship," as discussed in the previous
chapter, remained equally relevant. The Constitution of the White Earth
Nation and the requirements for tribal citizenship therein should reflect
Anishinaabe values and cultural practices. During the discussion, I asked
the delegates to consider two questions: "Should tribal citizenship be based
on blood quantum—an idea that will eventually eliminate all Anishinaabeg?
Or do we have the courage to create a new requirement?" These overt and
provocative questions were designed to compel delegates to consider the
context and history of blood quantum and to imagine what a new requirement might look like. I also suggested that White Earth should work to
restore *mino-bimaadiziwin* in our families, communities, and nation.

Delegates were then allotted time to share their thoughts and ideas
about the question "Who shall be eligible for membership?" in their small
groups. The groups had lively discussions and a wide variety of opinions
were expressed. The small groups then reported back to the whole group.
One delegate noted that there was not an "easy answer" to the question of
what the requirement for tribal citizenship should be. Several of the groups
agreed that blood quantum was not an effective or appropriate way to

regulate tribal citizenship. Many noted that they had at least some children or grandchildren who could not enroll because they lacked the required blood quantum. One group stated that they were confident that a strong effort to maintain our culture and language would ensure that using lineal descent as the requirement for tribal citizenship would not "water us down." In addition, they noted the political importance of using the word "citizen" rather than "member."

A few delegates voiced their desire to continue to use blood quantum. Having internalized pseudoscientific racial constructs due, in part, to nearly half a century of the one-quarter MCT blood requirement for tribal citizenship, they were unwilling or unable to conceptualize citizenship as a political state. One delegate went so far as to say, "It is dangerous to lower blood quantum and let everyone in." S/he argued that by having children with non-Indians "we are destroying ourselves." These comments reflect ideas of racial purity and they disregard traditional cultural values and practices. The delegate especially emphasized the danger of having children with African Americans due to the risk of "becoming black." A short discussion about the possible use of DNA as a more advanced "scientific" replacement for blood quantum followed. Another delegate insisted, "We are so unique that we have our own unique DNA." S/he told of DNA testing kits advertised online, which s/he thought could indisputably calculate blood quantum.[29] It was agreed that the issue of tribal citizenship would require further consideration, and delegates were encouraged to discuss the issue with their families and communities.

After a lunch break, delegates moved on to discuss the third key issue, "Separation of powers, courts, and referendum vote." Chairwoman Vizenor asked them to consider: "Do we need separation of powers? If so what kind of court system?" The discussion of these issues was not contentious. There was unanimous agreement that separation of powers was important and that power should be decentralized; some suggested that three branches of government (judicial, legislative, and executive) that balanced powers be created. Delegates also felt that there should be different types of courts to deal with different offenses (family, criminal, and civil). One group noted that there should be a process for the removal of elected officials, and other groups were quick to note their agreement. These desires were likely a response to the illegal actions and conviction of several elected leaders during the 1990s. It was clear that deeper discussions about specific details would need to take place, but a strong majority of delegates agreed upon the foundational elements.

Finally, Chairwoman Vizenor asked the constitutional delegates to discuss how they wanted to proceed. After a short consultation, all groups reported that they wanted to meet again and to move forward with the creation of a White Earth constitution. There was a clear feeling of excitement and hope in the room. One delegate summarized the feelings of many delegates well when s/he succinctly stated: "We want change." The convention ended with optimism for positive change.

THESE ARE HARD DECISIONS

Chairwoman Vizenor called the second Constitutional Convention to order on January 4, 2008, and discussed the schedule for the evening, which included a presentation by Natalie McArthur on values as well as my presentation on citizenship. Time was allotted for open comments, and several people spoke about land and the need for more education on treaties. The issue of the timber settlement from the Nelson Act was discussed at length.[30]

Constitutional delegates had expressed a desire for the White Earth constitution to reflect Anishinaabe values. White Earth citizen Natalie McArthur gave a presentation on ways in which values could be applied to, and implemented within, the constitution. She stressed that a constitution must reflect a society's values if it is to be its highest law. McArthur explained that core values represent the core priorities in an individual's life and shape how a person truly acts and participates in the world. As a starting point, she asked the delegates to write down four of their own personal core values and a correlating belief statement. Delegates then discussed their personal values in small groups. The groups then reported back the common values they had identified in their groups. A variety of different values ranging from sobriety to hard work were mentioned. Many of the values related to respect, love, truth/honesty, family, and compassion. One delegate noted, "Everything we do—all the hard work, love, respect, etc.—should be pointed toward future generations. Core values should be used to take care of future generations." The core values and sentiments discussed closely parallel the Anishinaabe Seven Grandfather Teachings, which emphasize the importance of courage/bravery, truth/sincerity, respect, love/loving, honesty, wisdom, and humility in guiding Anishinaabe life.[31]

Next I gave a presentation on the history of tribal citizenship and reviewed a definition of blood quantum. I also summarized the Indian Reorganization Act of 1934 and how the MCT was created. Like other nations, the MCT regulates citizenship within the constitution. Blood quantum was not required for tribal citizenship until 1961; before that, the requirement was somewhat flexible, but generally a person could be enrolled if one or both of their parents were. The BIA was not happy with this and pressured the MCT to use either blood quantum or residency instead. I used a variety of examples from my research, which are now part of chapter 2 of this book, to show that the elected leaders of the MCT fought very hard against blood quantum because they knew that someday their descendants would not qualify to become tribal citizens. For example, I recounted information about William "Bill" Anywaush, of White Earth, who was vocal on the issue of citizenship on several occasions. At one meeting Anywaush began by saying, "Friends and Relatives—The reason I say 'relative' is that you are Indian and so am I." By noting that Anishinaabeg are all friends as well as relatives, Anywaush was highlighting their unity and responsibility to each other.[32] He believed they were dealing with a "very dangerous" issue because of the impact it would have on future generations. He called for an inclusive citizenship requirement:

> There was never in the past any mention of drawing any line; relationship was the only thing that was considered in the past. Even though the child had very little Indian blood, in considering relationship, he was still an Indian. One thing that these old folks over there urged me to do was to have mercy on my Indian people. Don't ever, as long as you live, discriminate against your fellow Indians.[33]

In this example, Anywaush urged the TEC to use family as the way to determine if an individual should be able to become a tribal citizen. He noted that blood quantum had not been used in the past and that the "old folks" did not want it to be used. He implied that blood quantum is contrary to Anishinaabe values and practices and asserted that using blood quantum would be a form of discrimination. This information empowered the delegates to redefine citizenship in a way that enacted Anishinaabe values and emphasized relationships.

I shared information about how the MCT came to use one-quarter MCT blood as the sole requirement for citizenship, including resolutions passed by the MCT in the 1930s and 1940s that required lineal descent for tribal citizenship. Those resolutions were rejected by the secretary of the Interior and, therefore, were not made part of the constitution. In 1942, the MCT was warned that "if the Minnesota Chippewa Indians persist in their demands for such all-inclusive enrollment rules," the Department of the Interior would ask "that the matter be made the subject of an Act of Congress."[34] This thinly veiled threat was an attempt to pressure the MCT into adopting restrictive citizenship requirements.

The TEC passed a resolution that required one-quarter degree MCT blood for tribal citizenship in 1961. Two days later at the delegates meeting, the president of the MCT was called upon to explain the ordinance to all the tribal delegates. He explained, "It was necessary to set the ¼ degree blood quantum in the ordinance in order to receive approval of the Department of the Interior which defines an Indian as being ¼ or more degree Indian blood." He rationalized the ordinance, stating that "if the MCT does not set up enrollment rules, than [*sic*] the Department will make their own rules."[35] This statement demonstrates that it was pressure from the BIA that influenced the TEC to finally pass a resolution on citizenship that employed blood quantum. It was important for the delegates to know that MCT leaders strongly resisted blood quantum for several decades before they were pressured into accepting it. The MCT's acceptance of blood quantum as the sole requirement for tribal citizenship coincides with the decade in which the most tribes accepted this same requirement.[36] The question of the requirement(s) for tribal citizenship was a difficult and controversial issue for some of the delegates, but I emphasized that it was an opportunity to put Anishinaabe values into action. The core values discussed earlier that evening provided a starting point for creating a new citizenship requirement(s). In addition, the wishes and wisdom of the leaders of the twentieth century were also a source of guidance.

The convention reopened on January 5 with a lengthy discussion about the possibility of seating new delegates. This question was brought to Chairwoman Vizenor, and she, in turn, brought the question back to the delegates who were seated at the first convention. Delegates discussed the issue within their groups. The motion to seat new delegates was defeated with 19 "no" votes and 7 "yes." Chairwoman Vizenor announced the results and assured everyone that nondelegates would still be allowed to share their thoughts and opinions during open comment periods and that the conventions were open and public.

The next topic to be addressed was a judicial system. In recent years, many Native nations have amended their constitutions to create new judicial systems or reform inadequate judicial systems common in IRA constitutions. These systems often blend Indigenous systems, values, and ideas with Western legal systems.[37] Chairwoman Vizenor instructed delegate groups to start drafting language on the court system and noted the importance of separation of powers. After the group discussion period, many delegates voiced their support for restorative justice, peacemaking circles, and other forms of justice that directly involve the community and focus on healing as opposed to punishment. The establishment or reestablishment of restorative justice is a trend across tribal judicial systems Many see it as a way to implement cultural values into governance structures and reflect a holistic approach to the concept of justice.[38] Delegates also wanted to see several different levels of courts created (i.e., a supreme court, lower courts, etc.). In addition, they asked that a Council of Elders and/or a review board be created. Overall, delegates felt that these so-called "alternative" forms of justice fit with the values discussed the previous day. They thought that a focus on healing would be positive not only for individuals and families but for the nation as a whole.

After a break for lunch, the convention turned again to the contentious topic of citizenship. Delegates were asked to examine the citizenship options listed in the draft constitution created during the effort for reform during the late 1990s. The options included:

Option A. Lineal descendants of enrolled members of the White Earth Ojibwe Nation;

Option B. Lineal descendants of enrolled members of the White Earth Ojibwe Nation and who are at least ¼ degree Anishinaabe blood;

Option C. Lineal descendants of enrolled members of the White Earth Ojibwe Nation who are at least ¼ degree Indian blood, with at least ⅛ degree White Earth Ojibwe Nation blood;

Option D. Children of enrolled members of the White Earth Ojibwe Nation who are at least ¼ degree Minnesota Chippewa Tribe (Bois Fort/Nett Lake, Fond du Lac, Grand Portage, Mille Lacs, Leech Lake, White Earth) blood.

Option E. *Deleted.*[39]

Chairwoman Vizenor instructed the delegates to narrow down the list to one or two options. During the discussion time there was a question about terminology. It was explained that the term "citizen" is a legal and political term used by nations, and "member" is a term used by clubs and other social organizations. One group noted that they created an additional option not listed in the draft constitution: "All those who are currently enrolled members be made full bloods." This option came to be referred to as the "4/4 band-aid" because it would be a temporary fix. Groups continued to discuss the wide range of options identified for some time.

When the delegate groups reported back, there was a strong feeling that citizenship was a difficult issue, and they expressed a range of concerns. For example, a delegate stated, "No one really knows how much Indian blood they have and the only way to know would be to go back to the beginning." Many in the room nodded in agreement. The history of how the different blood rolls were created in the early 1900s was discussed, including the fact that siblings often had different blood quanta listed on the final roll. Consequently, there are families today who go through a process to have their blood quantum "corrected," which often results in new generations qualifying for enrollment under the one-quarter MCT blood-quantum rule. This comment expressed a frustration that several delegates had with blood quantum. Even though this delegate wasn't fully challenging the validity of blood quantum, s/he was highlighting what s/he saw as inaccuracy, which rendered blood quantum moot.

Others felt that it was possible to continue to use blood quantum but to do so in a new way. For example, one delegate argued that blood quantum was created by the U.S. government to "get rid of us" and instead it could be used to "strengthen us." S/he favored the "4/4 band-aid" because it would mean that everyone who was currently enrolled would have his or her grandchildren enrolled. Another delegate spoke in agreement of making everyone currently enrolled 4/4 and said it was the only compromise that most people in her/his group could agree on. S/he acknowledged that it would only be a temporary solution, but argued that when the blood of future generations is "watered down farther and farther it will be up to them what they want to do." Clearly, some delegates were uncomfortable making a perpetual decision regarding citizenship, and even though they desired change, they were unwilling or unable to completely let go of blood quantum.

As the discussion continued, the issue of family surfaced in many of the delegates' comments. One delegate noted that s/he favored the use of lineal descent because it includes all family members and is also a way of taking care of our families. It was also noted that lineal descendants would go on forever, and that if blood quantum were to continue, White Earth's sovereignty would be in jeopardy because the day would come when no one would have the required one-quarter blood quantum. Other delegates struggled to connect values including family with actions. A delegate argued, "Our job is to take care of one another. This is one of our true traditional values." S/he went on to discuss that it was his or her opinion that the tribe cannot "take care of those already on the doorstep" because of limited resources. The delegate asked, "How can we cut this pie any smaller? It scares me." This delegate wanted to practice traditional values, but instead of seeing "taking care of one another" as a family or community responsibility s/he saw it as one of the government's responsibilities. The delegate was apprehensive that more citizens would put an increased strain on already limited resources. The comments imply that "taking care of one another" is about providing services as opposed to sharing cultural teachings or engaging in other activities that do not require monetary resources. The delegate's fears of an increased population reflect a view of citizens as liabilities, not assets. S/he did not consider that citizens might make positive contributions to the nation, only that they would deplete resources. Another delegate stated that "no one is happy with blood quantum" but was unsure how White Earth should regulate citizenship.

Delegates grappled with the concepts of blood quantum and race and the various ways in which they have been used. A spokesperson for one of the small groups began her or his comments with an observation that during the days of slavery, a person with "black, black skin" was considered to be black, but a person who had white skin but a tiny, tiny fraction of black blood, so to speak, was still black. S/he stated: "Any fraction of black blood made you less than a citizen, made you second-class, and unable to marry into the white race. Then the U.S. government decided that reservations were costing too much money and the promises that they made in those treaties were costing too much money. So they wanted to find a way to cut down on the number of Indians. All of a sudden a fraction means the opposite—all of a sudden one drop of white blood and you are white." This delegate's astute observation reminded other delegates about the ways in which the United States has used blood for opposing political purposes over time. S/he asserted that if the tribe wants to treat people fairly, then fractions should be eliminated. The group agreed that lineal descent was the best option.

The wide diversity of comments and opinions reflects both a desire for change as well as trepidation about what change might really mean. Even though delegates could easily identify core values, some had a difficult time conceptualizing how to practice those values in the contemporary context. Concerns about the ways in which a larger population might put an increased strain on resources directly parallels arguments made by the BIA in their efforts to get the MCT to implement restrictive citizenship requirements. The idea of the "4/4 band-aid" simultaneously reinforces and dismantles the power of blood quantum. It exemplifies how arbitrary the calculation of blood is, and yet by "restarting the clock," so to speak, it maintains the status of the importance of blood. Delegates were unable to come to a clear conclusion about what the best requirement(s) for citizenship within the WEN would be. Once again, it was agreed that the topic would be revisited at a later date.

Chairwoman Vizenor thanked the constitutional delegates for their hard work and comments on issues of tribal citizenship. She noted that there was a lot of work to be done and that it was time to move on to the next issue on the agenda, which was land. She invited Robert "Buzzy" Howard forward to talk about the current land situation. Howard noted that land is a constitutional issue because some of "our land is MCT land," meaning that White Earth holds the title to some land, but the MCT holds the title to some land within the reservation borders too. He went on to give a lengthy, detailed presentation on the importance of land, efforts to get land returned to trust status, and land development. Delegate groups were then asked to consider land and jurisdictional issues using both Howard's presentation and the draft constitutions as starting points. The groups felt that the language in the draft constitution was acceptable. A few questions regarding jurisdiction were asked, and most delegates supported the assertion of jurisdiction. The convention was adjourned.

PERSEVERANCE AND PROGRESS

The third Constitutional Convention began on October 24, 2008, at 4 P.M. Many delegates were frustrated by the long hiatus since the second convention. In fact, some delegates chose not to attend the convention and never completed their duties. Chairwoman Vizenor acknowledged the lengthy lapse since the last convention ten months earlier and mitigated fears that this would be another failed effort for reform by insisting that the process would continue and would result in a new constitution for White Earth. She asked delegates to brainstorm and refresh their memories with regard to issues that had been discussed at past conventions. A long list of items including citizenship, land and jurisdiction, separation of powers, traditional values, and separation from the MCT was generated. This activity helped to reinvigorate the delegates and inspire movement forward.

Initially, I was supposed to facilitate a discussion of *American Indian Constitutional Reform and the Rebuilding of Native Nations*, edited by Eric Lemont; however, delegates did not receive their copies of the book in advance as originally planned. Consequently, I decided to present some basic strategies covered in the book, explore how delegates might want to apply them to White Earth, and present some more of my research. I began my presentation by acknowledging my sincere humility and honor to be part of the historic process of constitutional reform. A quote from Hassen Ebrahim on the first page of the book states that a constitution "must be a reflection of a people's history, fears, concerns, aspirations, vision, and, indeed, the soul of that nation."[40] This quote provided constitutional delegates with guidance and inspiration as they worked to implement a vision for the future of the nation within the constitution.

Constitutional reform was both a challenge and an opportunity for the delegates. This was an exceptional chance because constitutions are seldom written or revised. Making the White Earth Constitution a reflection of Anishinaabe culture was one of the great challenges and opportunities facing the delegates. Finding ways of practicing and enacting Anishinaabe cultural values not as artifacts in need of preservation but as vital to the people today was essential. In "Remaking Tribal Constitutions," Anishinaabe scholar Duane Champagne writes: "The opportunity to remake a constitution is a great chance to incorporate community traditions, organization, and values directly into the constitution."[41] The quote effectively connected the challenges of the reform effort at White Earth with other reform efforts and helped motivate delegates to continue their work.

Delegates had discussed values at the last convention, and I suggested that a good way to think about fundamental or core values was to think about the things we were taught as children or the kinds of things we emphasize to our children, grandchildren, nieces, nephews, and cousins today. Stories are one of the primary ways that we teach children place in the family, community, nation, and world. Stories also delineate both proper and improper behavior. Anishinaabe scholar John Borrows argues that stories contain core Anishinaabe legal principles and traditions that continue to be important as Anishinaabe nations create legal codes and judicial systems today.[42] I wanted to tie constitutional reform to cultural revitalization in a very concrete way and thought that story would be an excellent way to make this connection. The story of Shingebiss offers several valuable possibilities for interpretation with regard to core values and governance.

The story goes that Shingebiss (a grebe or helldiver bird) was living alone on the shores of a deep bay of a lake. He remained there always, even in the harshest cold of winter. Shingebiss was hardy and fearless. He would go during even the coldest of days and pluck out rushes that came through the ice on the lake to create openings to dive through and catch fish. One day Kabebonica (the winter-maker) felt a bit annoyed at Shingebiss's perseverance and ability to live such a good life in spite of the severe weather he created. So Kabebonica created even fiercer winds, colder temperatures, and deeper snow; but Shingebiss continued on just as before, plucking out rushes and diving into the icy waters to catch fish. Kabebonica decided to visit Shingebiss—he was near the door when he could hear Shingebiss singing.[43]

Henry Rowe Schoolcraft translates Shingebiss's song literally as "Spirit of the North West—you are but my fellow man," but then goes on to give a more creative interpretation in which he seems to be trying to relate what is implicit in the song; so the longer version is:

> Windy god, I know your plan,
> You are but my fellow man,
> Blow you may your coldest breeze,
> Shingebiss you cannot freeze,
> Sweep the strongest wind you can,
> Shingebiss is still your man,
> Heigh! for life—and ho! for bliss,
> Who so free as Shingebiss?

Shingebiss knew that Kabebonica was at his door, but he kept on singing his songs of survivance, acting indifferently to his presence. Kabebonica left with even more resolve to break Shingebiss. However, Shingebiss continued on as he had, and finally Kabebonica was compelled to give up the contest and leave Shingebiss alone.[44]

Above all, the story of Shingebiss is about perseverance and sovereignty, and correlates with the core values delegates had previously identified and discussed. There are many different ways to interpret and apply this story.[45] I went on to explore the ways in which principles contained within the story could be applied to the work with the constitution.[46] I asked delegates to imagine Shingebiss as a representation of the WEN and Kabebonica as illustrative of the BIA/United States. The story provides an opportunity to understand the relationship between these two nations as well as to provide a model for correct actions for the WEN. In the story, Kabebonica dislikes Shingebiss because he is independent and Kabebonica wants control over him. This can be interpreted to parallel the relationship between the United States and White Earth (as well as the MCT).

Shingebiss's reaction, or lack thereof, to Kabebonica's efforts to make his life more difficult can serve as a model for the WEN. Race and blood quantum have been used as a way to erase and eliminate those legally recognized as Anishinaabe—as White Earth citizens. What if, in the face of U.S. efforts to employ race as a means to eliminate Anishinaabeg, the WEN "keeps singing"? Singing represents a positive action. Shingebiss's song highlights his sovereignty, resiliency, and persistence in *mino-bimaadiziwin* (living a good life).[47] Shingebiss refuses to become a victim and engages in inspirational acts of survivance.

The concept of *mino-bimaadiziwin* can be seen in the story of Shingebiss. In both versions of Shingebiss's song, he refers to Kabebonica as

his friend or his fellow man. In doing so, Shingebiss refuses to acknowledge that Kabebonica is more powerful than he is; Shingebiss emphasizes
his own sovereignty by insisting they are equals. Finally, at the end of the
story Shingebiss's perseverance is rewarded when Kabebonica recognizes his
autonomy. White Earth can relate to the circumstances faced by Shingebiss
and can follow his actions as a model. The United States has made many
attempts to control the MCT/WEN, including limiting sovereign authority by
requiring secretary of Interior approval for some decisions and improperly
pressuring elected officials to employ blood quantum as the single requirement for tribal citizenship.

An allegorical interpretation of the fish in the story is that they represent citizens. Despite Kabebonica's efforts to thwart Shingebiss, Shingebiss
persistently works to obtain the fish. The BIA/United States has tried to
make it impossible to "get any more fish" (citizens) by using racialization
as a way to erase Anishinaabeg. In the story, "pulling up new rushes" creates the opportunity for Shingebiss to "dive under for fish." He must clear
away the rushes every time he wishes to obtain more fish. In this scenario,
WEN must make a concentrated effort to find the strength to "pull up new
rushes, and dive under for fish." The rushes can be seen as a metaphor for
blood quantum/race because they are what must be pulled out of the way to
allow for Shingebiss or the WEN to enroll new citizens and to live the good
life. The fish are food, sustenance for Shingebiss just as citizens nourish and
uphold the nation. I argued that White Earth must "pull up" the blood-
quantum requirement for tribal citizenship to clear the way for new citizens
to enroll.

In the story, Shingebiss acts alone; he is self-reliant and sovereign. Yet
he relies on the fish for *mino-bimaadiziwin*; they enable him to be sovereign. Like Shingebiss, WEN is sovereign but it needs citizens. White Earth
cannot have *mino-bimaadiziwin* without the sustenance a strong body of
citizens provides. I invited the delegates to consider how to create a citizenship requirement that is based on the positive values expressed both at
the convention in January and in the story about Shingebiss. The story of
Shingebiss provided delegates with a model for action. The themes of sovereignty, resiliency, persistence, respect, and *mino-bimaadiziwin* were all
useful points of consideration as constitutional reform moved forward.[48]

The Constitutional Convention reconvened the next morning. Chairwoman Vizenor began by introducing special guest and consultant
Dr. David E. Wilkins. Dr. Wilkins (Lumbee), professor of American
Indian studies at the University of Minnesota, has published extensively
in the area of tribal governance and politics. He gave a presentation on

tribal governments, including a detailed history of the Indian Reorganization Act (1934), and an overview of constitutions. Wilkins defined a constitution as the basic legal and political document that governs a nation, describing different types of constitutions and their core elements. He noted that several other tribes had written new constitutions or significantly revised their constitutions, and informed the delegates that many tribes were removing the provision for "approval by the secretary of the interior."

Wilkins acknowledged that the concept of kinship had come up several times the previous evening, and argued that tribes can and should use their traditions as the basis for government. He asserted that using kinship or relationship as the core of nation creates a culture of responsibility, because if a person views themselves as related, it will inform their actions. He further explained that "rights" are often emphasized with regard to citizenship, but this is the result of a culture of distrust. Delegates appreciated his expertise and outsider perspective.

My presentation, "Evaluating the Options for Tribal Citizenship," was next on the agenda. I began the presentation by noting that writing a constitution is a challenging task, but with hard work the result would be a document that was both meaningful and effective. I echoed Wilkins's assertion that Anishinaabe values could be implemented throughout the constitution, including the citizenship requirement(s). Like other nations, Native nations have the right to determine the requirements for citizenship and, in addition, U.S. courts have consistently recognized this right. As further evidence of this point, Felix S. Cohen has noted: "The courts have consistently recognized that one of an Indian tribe's most basic powers is the authority to determine questions of its own membership. A tribe has power to grant, deny, revoke, and qualify membership."[49] I moved on to pose a variety of answers to the question: "What is tribal citizenship?" Goldberg has argued: "Citizenship is intimately entangled with fundamental cultural, social, economic, and political dimensions of tribal life, which vary from tribe to tribe."[50] Citizenship is a key component of nationhood because citizens form the very foundation of a nation, and it carries rights to political participation but is also about responsibilities. For example, the concept of active citizenship includes an acknowledgment of responsibilities such as obeying the criminal laws, paying taxes, serving on a jury, and participating in the improvement of political and civic life.

Delegates then took a closer look at each of the citizenship options listed on the draft constitution. Goldberg argues that "As citizenship is a key constituent of individual identity and tribal cultures, the only appropriate decision-maker is each tribal community."[51] I posed a set of questions to help delegates effectively evaluate each of the options and decide which one would best fit the needs and goals of White Earth. The questions were:

- What kind of citizenship requirement will put our beliefs, values, and culture into motion?
- How might our values of love and family be expressed in citizenship regulations?
- Which citizenship requirement will strengthen our nation?
- What do we want to teach our children and grandchildren?
- Who are we in our hearts?

We began to go through the list and discussed the options. Option A was "Lineal descendants of enrolled members of the White Earth Ojibwe Nation."[52] This option was the most inclusive on the list and uses family as the base. Several delegates had questions about the meaning of the term "lineal" during previous conventions, and there was an explanation and discussion in detail regarding the term. Option A was a family-based system and would prioritize family, indicating its importance to the WEN. This requirement enacts the core values of love and respect identified at the previous convention. Lineal descent eliminates the hierarchy inherently embedded with blood quantum. This option would also be a way to ensure that the WEN would exist in perpetuity. Delegates considered the following questions when evaluating this option:

- What kind of future for our nation and for our families would this option create?
- What would it teach our children and grandchildren?
- What kind of answer does it provide for the fundamental question: Who are we in our hearts?

The next option listed on the model constitution was "Lineal descendants of enrolled members of the Minnesota Chippewa Tribe–White Earth Band who are at least ¼ degree Anishinaabe blood." In addition to requiring lineal descent from the WEN of the Minnesota Chippewa Tribe, this option requires a minimum blood quantum and is similar to the requirement for citizenship in the MCT Constitution. The primary difference between this option and the MCT requirement is that this option requires "Anishinaabe blood" generally, not Anishinaabe blood from a specific nation, band, or reservation.[53] This option privileges blood quantum and supports the idea that "Anishinaabe blood" both exists and can be measured. This option would not include all family members. Under this option there would be fewer and fewer Anishinaabeg who could enroll, and eventually the WEN would cease to exist. Delegates considered the following questions when evaluating the option:

- What kind of future would this option create?
- Does it incorporate our values?
- What would it teach our children?
- Who are we in our hearts?

While most delegates were listening intently and appeared to be weighing the information, I could also feel tensions beginning to rise in the room. It seemed to me that some people did not want to engage in discussion of the questions. A few people began talking loudly to each other, which was disruptive. Some delegates found it difficult to hear and appeared to become irritated. Clearly frustrated, a delegate took action. S/he stood up and interrupted to ask if a motion could be made. Chairwoman Vizenor agreed, and a motion requesting that no options for tribal citizenship that required blood quantum be discussed any further was made. The motion passed.[54] There was only one option on the list that did not include blood quantum: "Lineal descendants of enrolled members of the White Earth Ojibwe Nation." Consequently, the issue of citizenship was decided. I was surprised by what seemed, in some ways, like a quick decision; however, the decision was a culmination of the numerous discussions of citizenship that had occurred at previous conventions. Additionally, because this was such an important issue, delegates had carefully considered the options and discussed them with their families and communities outside of the conventions. The constitutional delegates demonstrated their support for lineal descent and organizing the nation around family and relationships. They were willing to resist the imposition of colonial measures of blood and reimagine the nation as a political body that does not rely on race as a foundation. The delegates' elimination of the use of blood quantum for tribal citizenship was an act of survivance.[55]

After a break for lunch, Chairwoman Vizenor called the delegates back together. They got into groups and began drafting the preamble. Delegates presented back to the group and to nondelegates who were present. The drafts were written in English, but they requested that the final preamble be translated into the Anishinaabe language. They felt that it would be an important expression of support for language revitalization efforts and also a demonstration of sovereignty. After the discussion of the various preambles, a nondelegate White Earth citizen stood up and spoke at length regarding the "crooked council" and the importance of traditions. S/he spoke in favor of utilizing the clan system as the basis for tribal citizenship and criticized the delegates for considering what s/he identified as the U.S. system of separation of powers as a possible model. S/he did not provide any concrete details for implementing his or her ideas. Other concerns were raised, questions were addressed, and the meeting was adjourned.

THE CONSTITUTION OF THE WHITE EARTH NATION

After the October meeting, Chairwoman Vizenor designated a Constitutional Proposal Team to draft a constitution based on the three Constitutional Conventions. She asked constitutional delegate Gerald Vizenor[56] to be the principal writer and to draft the document. Other members of the team included Erma Vizenor, Jo Anne E. Stately, Anita Fineday, and me. David E. Wilkins served as a special consultant. Gerald Vizenor drafted the constitution and circulated it to the team in January 2009; a meeting was held later that month in Minneapolis to discuss the document. The main issue that the writing team dealt with was how much detail to include in the constitution. The constitution was completed in late January and is organized into twenty chapters. While it is beyond the scope of this work to analyze the constitution in depth, I do want to briefly summarize the highlights.[57] See appendix 1 for the full document.

The constitution begins with a preamble, which introduces and establishes the constitution. It also describes some of the values embedded in the constitution, including the desire to promote traditions of liberty, justice, and peace. The preamble reads:

> The Anishinaabeg of the White Earth Nation are the successors of a great tradition of continental liberty, a native constitution of families, totemic associations. The Anishinaabeg create stories of natural reason, of courage, loyalty, humor, spiritual inspiration, survivance, reciprocal altruism, and native cultural sovereignty.
>
> We the Anishinaabeg of the White Earth Nation in order to secure an inherent and essential sovereignty, to promote traditions of liberty, justice, peace, and reserve common resources, and to ensure the inalienable right of native governance for our posterity, do constitute, ordain and establish this Constitution of the White Earth Nation.[58]

This preamble honors the past and envisions a strong nation with a commitment to broad rights, freedoms, and responsibilities.[59] It acknowledges the importance of the past and the succession of Anishinaabe peoples into the future. The preamble emphasizes continuance by centering family relationships as the core of the nation by naming "a native constitution of families" and acknowledging our "totemic associations," which are relationships that connect Anishinaabeg both within and beyond the borders of the WEN. The preamble also recognizes the importance of Anishinaabe stories, including stories of survivance, which evade victimization and affirm values such as courage, loyalty, humor, and reciprocal altruism. There is an assertion of the importance of stories of "native cultural sovereignty," which defy the ways in which dominant society and the U.S. legal system have attempted to control the parameters of both what native culture is and what degree of sovereignty native nations can exercise. This assertion reclaims the power to define our dynamic and vibrant culture.

Chapter 2, "Citizens of the White Earth Nation," regulates citizenship in a way that demonstrates and promotes family as the base of the nation. Tribal citizenship provides at least part of an answer to the fundamental question "Who are we?" In *X-Marks,* Anishinaabe scholar Scott Lyons suggests that citizenship criteria be chosen because they promote traditional values.[60] As noted, after several lengthy discussions, constitutional delegates decided that blood quantum was not an appropriate means to define citizenship and that instead family relationships should take precedence. The first article states:

> Citizens of the White Earth Nation shall be descendants of Anishinaabeg families and related by linear descent to enrolled members of the White Earth Reservation and Nation, according to genealogical documents, treaties and other agreements with the government of the United States.[61]

This inclusive vision of citizenship reflects the core values identified by many delegates as well as the motion and vote that ended any consideration of citizenship requirements that included any form of blood quantum. The term "blood quantum" does not appear in this chapter; instead family relationships create the body of the nation. The requirement bears significant resemblance to the requirement that the TEC tried to officially implement on several occasions during the mid-twentieth century.

The second article deals with services and entitlements provided by government agencies to citizens. This article notes that services and entitlements "shall be defined according to treaties, trusts, and diplomatic agreements, state and federal laws, rules and regulations, and in policies and procedures established by the government of the White Earth Nation."[62] Gerald Vizenor recognized that it was necessary to clearly state that not all citizens will receive entitlements and/or services to address the concerns about resources that were raised by delegates. All nations have to be responsible in their management of resources and prioritization of services. Simply being a citizen does not mean that an individual "gets" anything except the right to vote and the protections provided in the constitution. A citizen must meet the various qualifications for any of the numerous social service programs that the WEN operates. Each of those programs has a range of qualifications, including things like income and residence. Programs that experience increased pressure may add new qualifications to ensure that those most in need are served. In addition, the WEN could consider weaving cultural requirements into service qualifications. For example, to receive a scholarship a student could be required to take a course on White Earth/ Anishinaabe history, or to volunteer a specific number of hours at one of the Head Start programs. The requirement for housing assistance could be attending language classes or, for those who are already fluent, volunteering a certain number of hours teaching the language. Requirements like these would create reciprocity, one of our fundamental Anishinaabe values. As Anishinaabeg we all carry a responsibility to give back to our families, communities, and nation. These classes and volunteer requirements would facilitate relationships among citizens. These activities are also empowering. They give people an opportunity to find their place and to feel good about helping others. There are endless ways that the WEN can work to build a strong nation with citizens who practice Anishinaabe culture and know our history.[63]

Chapter 3, "Rights and Duties," contains seventeen articles, which define many important civil liberties and human rights guaranteed to the citizens of the WEN. Freedom of religion, speech, and expression are all protected. Article 6 guarantees that the government may not practice censorship. Several articles ensure due process of law and protect privacy against search and seizure by requiring a warrant. Article 10 guarantees citizens the right to own firearms. Article 16 prohibits the practice of banishment. These rights go largely unprotected in the MCT constitution and provide transparency for citizens.

Throughout the reform process, constitutional delegates expressed a desire for a larger and more representative governance structure. Chapter 6, "Governance," consists of seventeen articles, which describe the basic governance structure of the WEN. It creates a representative and elected governing body: the Legislative Council. The Legislative Council consists of the secretary treasurer, the elected representatives of acknowledged communities of the WEN, and the president, who presides over the meetings and casts a vote in the case of a tie. Each "acknowledged community" will have one representative on the Legislative Council; Article 4 explains how communities will be established. There is neither a fixed number of representatives nor fixed borders or definition of communities; not providing this level of detail in the constitution allows for change and adaptation to population shifts over time. The president and secretary treasurer will be elected at large. Term limits were also important to delegates; Article 6 establishes a limit of two four-year terms (eight years) in any single position. Due to the illegal activities of past elected officials, delegates wanted to do as much as possible to enforce ethical standards. Consequently, Article 10 establishes that citizens who have been convicted of a felony may vote but cannot hold elected office. As a means to hold leaders accountable, which was emphasized as necessary on several occasions by delegates, Articles 13 and 14 institute two distinct processes for impeachment.

Fulfilling the desire expressed by many constitutional delegates for citizens to have multiple ways in which to both participate in governance and engage with elected leaders, three separate councils were created. Chapter 7, "Community Councils," Chapter 8, "Council of Elders," and Chapter 9, "Youth Council," each formally establishes and recognizes a council. As the constitution prescribes, Community Councils are to be geographically based but the Council of Elders and the Youth Council are to be at-large bodies. The constitution provides a basic framework for these councils, but the first people to hold seats on them will need to create bylaws and other governing documents. These formal councils are a way for citizens to organize and make recommendations to both members of the Legislative Council and the president. The constitution states that Community Councils will promote the philosophy of *mino-bimaadiziwin* and work to demonstrate, teach, and encourage the Seven Grandfather Teachings of courage/bravery, truth, respect, love, honesty, wisdom, and humility for all citizens. The Council of Elders will provide guidance and recommendations on traditional knowledge and cultural and spiritual practices. The Youth Council shall provide information about matters that affect young people, and advise the president and Legislative Council. All councils provide opportunities for citizens to speak with, and listen to, the ideas and perspectives of other citizens. Councils can work together to come to a consensus on what is best for all.

When the effort for reform began, separation of powers was one of the primary issues that Chairwoman Vizenor wanted to address; delegates unanimously supported separation of powers. Chapter 10 of the constitution, "Separation of Powers," creates three branches of government: Executive, Legislative, and Judicial. The separation of powers balances power between different branches of government. Each branch has powers that it can exercise to balance the other branches.[64] Chapter 11, "The President," outlines the powers and duties of the president, who is the head of the government. The powers and duties of the president are balanced. The president is responsible for the administration and management of the government. The president is obligated to promote, protect, and defend cultural and political sovereignty and the Constitution of the White Earth Nation. The president does not have the authority to create laws, ordinances, or resolutions, but does have the responsibility to execute them.

Chapter 12, "The Legislative Council," establishes the Legislative Council and outlines its powers and duties. The Legislative Council forms the primary governing body of the WEN. One of the primary duties of the Legislative Council is to propose and enact laws, codes, ordinances, resolutions, and statutes. The Legislative Council has a wide range of responsibilities, including the proper management of government programs, land, waterways, resources, commerce, public housing, transportation, casino operations, business enterprises, and other assets of the WEN. The citizens retain any powers of the government not specifically expressed or entrusted to the Legislative Council.[65]

Chapter 13, "The Secretary Treasurer," outlines the duties and responsibilities of the secretary treasurer, who is elected at large. The primary duties of the secretary treasurer are all related to the financial matters of the WEN. The secretary treasurer is required to make certain financial documents available for public viewing. This ensures an open, transparent process and allows White Earth citizens to hold elected leaders accountable for the financial dealings of the nation.

Chapters 14, 15, and 16 all deal with judicial issues. Chapter 14, "The Judiciary," creates the framework for the Judiciary of the White Earth Nation. As described in the chapter, the main role of the Judiciary is to interpret and apply laws, statutes, ordinances, and other regulations. Another role of the Judiciary is to resolve disputes. The Judiciary cannot make laws, but the Court may invalidate laws that conflict with the constitution. The Judiciary does not enforce laws. Chapter 15, "Powers of the White Earth Courts," also deals with judicial matters. It establishes the White Earth Court and Court of Appeals, but also allows the Legislative Council to establish other courts. The Courts have the authority to interpret and construe the laws, ordinances, and regulations of the Legislative Council and the

Constitution of the White Earth Nation. The Courts will practice restorative justice whenever appropriate to resolve complaints and disputes of the WEN. Chapter 16, "The White Earth Judges," lists the requirements of White Earth judges and describes the appointment process. Judges must be at least twenty-five years old, be a graduate of a law school accredited by the American Bar Association, and have knowledge of Anishinaabe culture, traditions, and general history. The chief judge is elected to a lifetime appointment and must be a citizen of the WEN and a resident of the reservation. Associate judges will have five-year terms and be appointed by the chief judge, with the consent of the Legislative Council. The Legislative Council has the authority to impeach and remove judges for abuses of impartiality, bribery, political impropriety, or felony conviction.

Chapters 18, 19, and 20 all respond to concerns about potential abuses of power. Delegates requested procedures both to hold elected leaders accountable and to remove leaders who commit crimes while in office. Chapter 18, "Ethics and Impeachment," provides ways to hold elected leaders to ethical standards and, if those standards are not met, to impeach them. Article 1 provides for impeachment and removal from office with a two-thirds majority vote by the Legislative Council. An elected official may be impeached or removed from office for a felony conviction or two misdemeanor convictions, including driving while intoxicated, but not including ordinary traffic violations. In addition, Article 6 ensures that citizens can initiate a petition to recall an elected official.[66] Chapter 19, "Petitions and Referenda," explains the process for petitions and referendum votes. The chapter states that citizens retain the power to initiate a referendum by petition. There was wide support for processes by which citizens could initiate change and have a direct voice. Finally, Chapter 20, "Amendments to the Constitution," establishes that neither the Legislative Council nor the president has the authority to amend the constitution; only citizens have the power to amend the constitution through a referendum vote. This chapter protects citizen interests and ensures that a small number of elected leaders do not have broad authority to make dramatic changes in governance such as amending the constitution.

The Constitution of the White Earth Nation was created through a grassroots process of open discussion and compromise. Delegate Gerald Vizenor did an incredible job writing the document; he astutely balanced a wide range of viewpoints. His attention to detail was crucial for the mechanics of the constitution. The constitution is a unique reflection of the WEN. It is a vast improvement over the IRA-style Minnesota Chippewa Tribe constitution, which provides little protection for citizens and gives a significant amount of authority to the U.S. secretary of the Interior. The White Earth

Constitution creates a framework that does not compromise sovereignty and retains the degree of adaptability necessary to ensure that the document has lasting staying power. Most importantly, the document both reflects and enacts Anishinaabe values; it incorporates enduring cultural traditions while envisioning a certain future.

RATIFICATION OF THE CONSTITUTION

The Constitutional Proposal Team was satisfied with the document and prepared to present it to the constitutional delegates. The fourth and final Constitutional Convention was held April 3–4, 2009. After a welcome by Chairwoman Vizenor and an opening prayer, Gerald Vizenor gave a presentation on the history of constitutions and introduced the draft constitution. He discussed traditional forms of governance and Native practices of reciprocity and specifically noted that the draft constitution would allow citizens to know their rights. Chairwoman Vizenor reviewed the constitutional reform process. She clearly explained that if the delegates ratified the constitution it would then go to all citizens for a referendum vote. Some delegates were uncomfortable with their position of leadership and were concerned that they should not be making such an important decision. The assurance of a referendum vote satisfied most concerns. She concluded the evening session by commending the delegates who had continued through the entire eighteen-month process, noting that it was not easy but that it was important. She thanked delegates for giving their time to the conventions. Delegates received a copy of the draft constitution; copies were also provided to nondelegates who requested them.

The next day the task at hand was to read through and explain the constitution. Delegates were given a comment form and asked to note comments and questions during the review process. Comment forms were anonymous and designed to allow delegates to address any aspect of the constitution. Gerald Vizenor and I had agreed that we would each read some of the chapters. We began the process and took care to draw connections to previous conventions and highlight the ways in which the wishes of the delegates had been incorporated into the document.

We read through the constitution chapter by chapter and answered questions as they arose. There were moments of tension when a small number of nondelegates yelled objections, questions, and personal attacks, but the majority were committed to the process and it was not derailed. All questions were addressed in a calm and constructive manner.[67] Upon completion of the review of the constitution, delegates were given time to discuss the document among themselves and to complete the comment form. Comment forms were then submitted. One delegate wrote an especially encouraging message at the bottom of the form: "It is time to take our own leadership—we can embrace our responsibility to lead the White Earth Nation." Gerald Vizenor and I addressed questions and comments from the forms with the delegates. Delegates voted to increase the number of individuals on both the Council of Elders and the Youth Council from five to twenty. They also voted to lower the age requirement from sixty to fifty-five for the Council of Elders. On the comment form, several delegates questioned why there were no seats designated for off-reservation representatives on the Legislative Council. In fact, the writing team had considered the issue but was not confident that there was enough support for the provision. There was a discussion about how many off-reservation representatives would be appropriate. Ultimately, the delegates decided to include two representatives for White Earth citizens who live in Minnesota but outside the reservation boundaries. Approximately two-thirds of White Earth citizens live off the reservation; delegates wanted to give citizens living off the reservation an increased role in government and direct representation.[68]

We were then ready to move forward with a vote to ratify the document. Everyone had made compromises during both the writing process and the decisions made earlier in the day. Constitutional delegates were invited forward to sign in and collect their ballot.[69] A small number of nondelegate White Earth citizens yelled objections during the ballot-counting process because they wanted a roll-call vote instead of the secret ballot provided. Completed ballots were collected in a box at the front of the room; in an effort to maintain transparency, they were counted out in the open and all present were invited to watch.[70] Delegates voted 16 to 8 in favor of ratifying the draft constitution as amended.[71] Many clapped and cheered while a few voiced their opposition. Chairwoman Vizenor reminded everyone present that the document would still have to be voted on by all White Earth citizens in a referendum vote. She thanked the delegates for their hard work and perseverance with the process. The convention was adjourned.

LOOKING FORWARD

White Earth spent several years exploring options for a referendum vote and navigating the politics of the Minnesota Chippewa Tribe. Since the ratification of the White Earth Constitution, I have written a number of newspaper articles explaining details of the document and addressing concerns and issues relating to citizenship.[72] In December 2012, the WEN was awarded a substantial grant from the Bush Foundation[73] to move ahead with a citizen education and engagement effort that would culminate in a referendum on the proposed constitution. A range of educational materials were created to provide critical information for voters to make their decision. During the summer and fall of 2013, more than fifty community-education sessions were held at various locations on and off the reservation. The referendum was held on November 19, 2013. The citizens of the WEN voted by a margin of nearly 80 percent to approve the proposed constitution. There was a total of 3,492 accepted ballots, with 2,780 approving the new constitution and 712 rejecting it.[74] "I am very gratified that the people of White Earth have spoken," said White Earth Tribal Chairwoman Erma Vizenor.[75] The WEN is currently in the process of transition and implementation.

The process of reform has not been easy, but it has been rewarding. I am thrilled to have been part of the historic process of writing the Constitution of the White Earth Nation. We encountered some of the same challenges that other nations face when creating such a foundational document, but worked through the difficult tasks and questions by keeping a focus on family and the future of the nation. Joseph Thomas Flies-Away, Carrie Garrow, and Miriam Jorgensen argue, "The best approaches to Native nation constitutional reform are thoughtful, deliberate, and squarely focused on strengthening the nation's self-determination well into the future."[76] As Gerald Vizenor has observed:

> The Constitution of the White Earth Nation is not a document of revolution, and it is not a document prepared by supreme military officers or federal bureaucrats. The Constitution was created in the spirit of resistance and independent governance, by the sentiments of native survivance, and by the inspiration and vision of the delegates and Erma Vizenor. There is no other constitution in the world that contains the profound sentiments of survivance, and native continental liberty.[77]

The ratified Constitution of the White Earth Nation echoes Anishinaabe traditions and envisions a perpetual future of promise. It is a governing document of which the people can be proud.

Conclusion

"The muskrat said, 'I'll try,' and he dived down."

—GERALD VIZENOR, *EARTHDIVERS*

CITIZENSHIP IS ONE COMPONENT OF ANISHINAABE IDENTITY. IT IS the official, legal recognition of one's identity. It brings legal responsibilities and protections. For many, being Anishinaabe goes beyond legal status and also includes a myriad of other aspects, including kinship relationships, clan identity, actions, cultural values, language, spiritual beliefs, residency, and worldview. There is no single fixed meaning; we define and create our own identity in unique ways. The new Constitution of the White Earth Nation brings a major shift in citizenship requirements from blood quantum to lineal descent. There were many, like me, who occupied a space between—recognized as a "first-degree descendant" by the nation but lacking citizenship for many years. So while many of us considered ourselves Anishinaabe, legally we were left in the margin. The day has come, and we can now tell the story about how we were recognized and welcomed into the nation as citizens. We see how this pattern has played out across time. Our ancestors consistently resisted blood quantum/racialization, setting an example for us to follow.

Anishinaabeg strongly resisted racialization during the 1910s. They asserted diverse views of identity based on action, and challenged simplistic notions of static identities based on pseudoscientific notions of biological race, which the U.S. government insisted upon. For many Anishinaabeg, people created their identity through their actions. They also insisted that identity wasn't fixed but could change over time. Additionally, Anishinaabe definitions of identity were diverse; there was not one universal way in which identity was created. Anishinaabeg respected that individuals could create and control their own identity. Anishinaabe conceptions of identity were dramatic contrasts to the ways in which the U.S. government wished

91

to define Anishinaabe and American Indian identity. The U.S. government employed race as a means to justify the disenfranchisement of thousands of Anishinaabeg. The impact of the dramatic land loss during the early twentieth century continues to shape and influence the White Earth Nation (WEN) one hundred years later.

Anishinaabeg showed determination to maintain lineal descent as the sole requirement for citizenship within the Minnesota Chippewa Tribe (MCT). Several elected leaders have warned of the dangerous consequences of using blood quantum for citizenship and asserted that family relationships should continue to be a deciding factor in citizenship just as they had been since time immemorial. The Tribal Executive Committee of the MCT passed several resolutions that required only lineal descent for tribal citizenship. If the U.S. secretary of the Interior had not rejected these resolutions, the MCT would not have created and implemented the one-quarter MCT blood-quantum requirement. One-quarter Minnesota Chippewa Tribe blood was the sole requirement for tribal citizenship for more than fifty years and had a dramatic impact on the WEN.

During the 2007–present effort for constitutional reform at White Earth, with a particular focus on citizenship, I was closely involved in the process and worked to share knowledge about both Anishinaabe identity and MCT citizenship regulations. I helped the constitutional delegates work through the difficult issues related to citizenship to create a citizenship requirement that enacts core Anishinaabe values. The decision to use lineal descent as the sole requirement for citizenship was not easy for some of the delegates. They debated several other options and carefully considered what would be best for their families and for future generations. Ultimately, the majority of delegates agreed that blood quantum contrasts starkly with Anishinaabe values and, therefore, was unsuitable. In addition, they noted that it is also unsustainable, and the population would continue to decline if it remained in place.

Citizens of the WEN adopted the proposed constitution on November 19, 2013. It is a time for reflection, a time to tell our traditional stories and plan for the future. I began this book with creation and I want to end with re-creation. Anishinaabeg have many re-creation stories, and while the details vary among these versions, the same thing always happens.[1]

> And so the world was flooded. Nanaboozhoo and the animals were left clinging to a log. The land was somewhere deep beneath the water. Nanaboozhoo and the animals decided that some action must be taken; someone was going to have to dive down and get a piece of earth so that new land could be created.

Loon was the first to volunteer, diving down with great skill and determination. Loon floated back to the top and Nanaboozhoo looked in the loon's mouth but found no earth. Nanaboozhoo blew on Loon and she/he came back to life. Others including the otter, helldiver, and mink tried and failed. The group began to worry but did not give up hope. Finally, Zhaashkoonh (the lowly muskrat) offered to try. The animals did not think that Zhaashkoonh would be successful. Zhaashkoonh gathered all her/his strength and courage and dove down. When Zhaashkoonh floated to the top the animals thought that all hope was lost. Nanaboozhoo opened Zhaashkoonh's front paw and found a grain of earth. He found more in Zhaashkoonh's other paws and mouth. Nanaboozhoo then blew on Zhaashkoonh and life returned. Nanaboozhoo took the grains of earth in the palm of his hand and then threw it around onto the water. An island was created. They went onto the little island. Nanaboozhoo got more earth from the island and threw it all around. The island grew and grew. The animals danced in celebration. Nanaboozhoo kept throwing the earth around.[2]

In the end the earth is consistently re-created, but it always takes more than one try. This is a story of empowerment and transformation. Transformation plays a prominent role throughout Anishinaabe traditional stories and offers ample opportunities to be interpreted in a variety of ways that are useful for current circumstances. The earthdiver story is one of the finest examples of transformation and (re)creation, which are both connected to sovereignty. Gerald Vizenor's concept of transmotion is useful here. He writes that transmotion is a "sense of native motion and an active presence is sui generis sovereignty. Native transmotion is survivance, a reciprocal use of nature, not a monotheistic, territorial sovereignty. Native stories of survivance are the creases of transmotion and sovereignty."[3] He further asserts: "Sovereignty is in the visions of transformation."[4]

Sovereignty is inherently related to action: it must be exercised or it will diminish; it can continuously transform and adapt to changing circumstances. There are various ways in which Anishinaabeg have asserted identities that both challenge race and insist upon the importance of action and relationships. Anishinaabeg have consistently refused to be mere victims and, instead, acted in accordance with survivance and *mino-bimaadiziwin*. In the earthdiver story, a new world is created when the old one floods. If they had not taken action, Nanaboozhoo and the animals would have been the victims of the flood. Instead, they worked together to create a new place for themselves—they engaged in transmotion and rebuilt. This is an important story that offers many lessons.

The idea of creating a new world offers many possibilities for interpretation. In her work on the power of Odawa narratives, anthropologist Melissa Pflug has observed, "This earth diver theme, repeated frequently in various myths, illustrates the creative power of renewal. Working in ethical cooperation with other Great Persons of mythology, the earth diver is a transformer."[5] It is this power of transformation that is highly valued by the Anishinaabeg. So, here we get a sense of the remarkable and wonderful power of traditional Anishinaabe stories. We hold the power to create a new world. We also notice the importance of cooperation in the earthdiver story and carry that value into our lives. There is no savior here; the animals carried a responsibility to save themselves, and with the help of Nanaboozhoo they accomplished the unthinkable.

Anishinaabe scholar Basil Johnston has observed, "Because each Ojibway story may embody several themes and meanings, time and deliberation are required for adequate appreciation. There is no instantaneous understanding."[6] Johnston acknowledges that the flexible nature of Anishinaabe stories allows readers and listeners of different abilities to ascertain their own understandings of the significance of the story.[7] Additionally, the personal experiences and objectives of each reader or listener also influence their interpretations. It is this possibility of multiple interpretations and the flexibility of the stories to adapt to changing circumstances and needs of the community that provide the central power of these stories. There is no single, correct way to use and interpret these narratives; rather, these stories transform and adapt to new situations through interpretation. A single story can be used for multiple purposes depending on the way it is told, the audience, and the intent of the storyteller.[8]

What impact does this story have on the citizenship issue and the newly adopted constitution? Anishinaabe identity has surely transformed over time, and yet a consistent emphasis on family and relationships emerges. It was clear that the Anishinaabeg could not possibly survive if fictional measures of "blood" continued to be used to define who could become a tribal citizen. Our world was flooded; the blood-quantum requirement for citizenship drowned out many Anishinaabeg. On November 19, 2013, the power to change was placed in the hands of the citizens of the WEN. They were called upon to dive down and bring up the grains of earth necessary to create a new world. They fulfilled their responsibility. One of those grains of earth is the constitution. Scholar Lisa Brooks has astutely noted, "If we look to its roots in the English language, the word 'constitution' implies in its possible meanings the activity of creation."[9] The constitution is a grain of earth; it is a beginning point from which we will rebuild the nation. Nishnaabeg scholar Leanne Simpson has argued:

If we are to continue on a Nishnaabeg pathway, we must choose to live as Nishnaabeg, committing to mino bimaadziwin, and committing to building resurgence. We have a choice and that choice requires action, commitment, and responsibility. We are not simply born Nishnaabeg, even if we have "full-blood." We must commit to living the good life each day. We must act. We must live our knowledge.[10]

Simpson's message is empowering. The absence of victimry opens space for the presence of survivance and *mino-bimaadiziwin*. As Anishinaabeg we create our identities, families, and nations. We must take responsibility for our actions and choose to practice our core values.

Anishinaabe identity is complex, dynamic, and fluid. While Anishinaabe nations determine citizenship requirements, the U.S. government has strongly influenced these requirements. There have been dramatic changes in citizenship requirements as well as a consistent resistance to racialization and blood quantum. Citizens form the very foundation of a nation, and thus the question of citizenship defines the heart of the nation. Citizenship requirements answer the fundamental and profound question: Who are we? Each nation must find answers that fit their value systems and construct the kind of nation they desire. As Scott Lyons asserts: "*Require what you want to produce.*"[11]

Of course, this sounds easier than it is. No answer is perfect and some compromise is always necessary. Even if we can agree that we want to create a nation based the seven teachings (courage, humility, truth, respect, wisdom, honesty, and love) as well as on strong familial bonds to both honor our ancestors and plan for the seventh generation, the question of how to make that happen remains. We posit that a nation based on relationships will ensure a responsible, respectful, and reciprocal relationship between the nation and citizens. The hard truth is that there are no guarantees. Many of our families have elements of dysfunction and abuse. We have too many children growing up without a strong bond with their fathers. There is much work to be done to renew our families and work toward *mino-bimaadiziwin*. Citizenship is a beginning point, a journey of reflection and discovery, and, above all, it is a single grain of earth; we must make it grow.

The new citizenship requirement based on Anishinaabe values will not solve all social conflict in the nation. Undoubtedly, there will always be a diversity of viewpoints on Anishinaabe identity and the best ways to live out our values. There will always be family divisions, political factions, and differing strategies for how best to build a strong nation, but the new citizenship requirement is a powerful starting point that carries the power of transformation. How might our youth be changed now that they are accepted not on the basis of their blood, but on the basis of their relationships, which come with both rights and responsibilities? What will happen now that the WEN has rejected the externally imposed ideas of race and blood and, instead, rested its foundation on our families? I hope that a new political reality will emerge, that an influx of citizens committed to upholding their responsibilities will help us (re)build a strong Anishinaabe nation. I hope that together we will use the knowledge handed down to us by our ancestors' work towards decolonization.

Our ancestors were earthdivers. They lived through immense change and yet maintained their identities, families, communities, and nations. Each nation holds the power of creation; we have created and re-created ourselves many times. Our governance structures have undergone considerable changes, and yet we can find traces of core values and practices. Anishinaabeg have adapted while maintaining strong identities. Like our ancestors, we are earthdivers. This is our story, and Nanaboozhoo kept throwing the earth around.

Revised Constitution and Bylaws of the Minnesota Chippewa Tribe, Minnesota

PREAMBLE

WE, THE MINNESOTA CHIPPEWA TRIBE, CONSISTING OF THE CHIP-pewa Indians of the White Earth, Leech Lake, Fond du Lac, Bois Forte (Nett Lake), and Grand Portage Reservations and the Nonremoval Mille Lac Band of Chippewa Indians, in order to form a representative Chippewa tribal organization, maintain and establish justice for our Tribe, and to conserve and develop our tribal resources and common property; to promote the general welfare for ourselves and descendants, do establish and adopt this constitution for the Chippewa Indians of Minnesota in accordance with such privilege granted the Indians by the United States under existing law.

Article I—Organization and Purpose

Section 1. The Minnesota Chippewa Tribe is hereby organized under Section 16 of the Act of June 18, 1934 (48 Stat. 984), as amended.

Sec. 2. The name of this tribal organization shall be the "Minnesota Chippewa Tribe."

Sec. 3. The purpose and function of this organization shall be to conserve and develop tribal resources and to promote the conservation and development of individual Indian trust property; to promote the general welfare of the members of the Tribe; to preserve and maintain justice for its members and otherwise exercise all powers granted and provided the

Indians, and take advantage of the privileges afforded by the Act of June 18, 1934 (48 Stat. 984) and acts amendatory thereof or supplemental thereto, and all the purposes expressed in the preamble hereof.

Sec. 4. The Tribe shall cooperate with the United States in its program of economic and social development of the Tribe or in any matters tending to promote the welfare of the Minnesota Chippewa Tribe of Indians.

Article II—Membership

Section 1. The membership of the Minnesota Chippewa Tribe shall consist of the following:

(a) Basic Membership Roll. All persons of Minnesota Chippewa Indian blood whose names appear on the annuity roll of April 14, 1941, prepared pursuant to the Treaty with said Indians as enacted by Congress in the Act of January 14, 1889 (25 Stat. 642) and Acts amendatory thereof, and as corrected by the Tribal Executive Committee and ratified by the Tribal Delegates, which roll shall be known as the basic membership roll of the Tribe.

(b) All children of Minnesota Chippewa Indian blood born between April 14, 1941, the date of the annuity roll, and July 3, 1961, the date of approval of the membership ordinance by the Area Director, to a parent or parents, either or both of whose names appear on the basic membership roll, provided an application for enrollment was filed with the Secretary or the Tribal Delegates by July 4, 1962, one year after the date of approval of the ordinance by the Area Director.

(c) All children of at least one quarter (1/4) degree Minnesota Chippewa Indian blood born after July 3, 1961, to a member, provided that an application for enrollment was or is filed with the Secretary of the Tribal Delegates of the Tribal Executive Committee within one year after the date of birth of such children.

Sec. 2. No person born after July 3, 1961, shall be eligible for enrollment if enrolled as a member of another tribe, or if not an American citizen.

Sec. 3. Any person of Minnesota Chippewa Indian blood who meets the membership requirements of the Tribe, but who because of an error has not been enrolled, may be admitted to membership in the Minnesota Chippewa Tribe by adoption, if such adoption is approved by the Tribal Executive Committee, and shall have full membership privileges from the date the adoption is approved.

Sec. 4. Any person who has been rejected for enrollment as a member of the Minnesota Chippewa Tribe shall have the right of appeal within sixty days from the date of written notice of rejection to the Secretary of the Interior from the decision of the Tribal Executive Committee and the decision of the Secretary of Interior shall be final.

Sec. 5. Nothing contained in this article shall be construed to deprive any descendant of a Minnesota Chippewa Indian of the right to participate in any benefits derived from claims against the U.S. Government when awards are made for and on behalf and for the benefit of descendants of members of said tribe.

Article III—Governing Body

The governing bodies of the Minnesota Chippewa Tribe shall be the Tribal Executive Committee and the Reservation Business Committees of the White Earth, Leech Lake, Fond du Lac, Bois Forte (Nett Lake), and Grand Portage Reservations, and the Nonremoval Mille Lac Band of Chippewa Indians, hereinafter referred to as the six (6) Reservations.

Section 1. Tribal Executive Committee. The Tribal Executive Committee shall be composed of the Chairman and Secretary-Treasurer of each of the six (6) Reservation Business Committees elected in accordance with Article IV. The Tribal Executive Committee shall, at its first meeting, select from within the group a President, a Vice-President, a Secretary, and a Treasurer who shall continue in office for a period of two (2) years or until their successors are elected and seated.

Sec. 2. Reservation Business Committee. Each of the six (6) Reservations shall elect a Reservation Business Committee composed of not more than five (5) members nor less than three (3) members. The Reservation Business Committee shall be composed of a Chairman, Secretary-Treasurer, and one (1), two (2), or three (3) Committeemen. The candidates shall file for their respective offices and shall hold their office during the term for which they were elected or until their successors are elected and seated.

Article IV—Tribal Elections

Section 1. Right to Vote. All elections held on the six (6) Reservations shall be held in accordance with a uniform election ordinance to be adopted by the Tribal Executive Committee which shall provide that:

(a) All members of the tribe, eighteen (18) years of age or over, shall have the right to vote at all elections held within the reservation of their enrollment.[1]

(b) All elections shall provide for absentee ballots and secret ballot voting.

(c) Each Reservation Business Committee shall be the sole judge of the qualifications of its voters.

(d) The precincts, polling places, election boards, time for opening and closing the polls, canvassing the vote and all pertinent details shall be clearly described in the ordinance.

Sec. 2. Candidates. A candidate for Chairman, Secretary-Treasurer and Committeeman must be an enrolled member of the Tribe and reside on the reservation of his enrollment. No member of the Tribe shall be eligible to hold office, either as a Committeeman or Officer, until he or she shall have reached his or her twenty-first (21) birthday on or before the date of election.[2]

Sec. 3. Term of Office.

(a) The first election of the Reservation Business Committee for the six (6) Reservations shall be called and held within ninety (90) days after the date on which these amendments became effective in accordance with Section 1, of this Article.

(b) For the purpose of the first election, the Chairman and one (1) Committeeman shall be elected for a four-year term. The Secretary-Treasurer and any remaining Committeemen shall be elected for a two-year term. Thereafter, the term of office for Officers and Committeemen shall be four (4) years. For the purpose of the first election, the Committeeman receiving the greatest number of votes shall be elected for a four-year term.

Article V—Authorities of the Tribal Executive Committee

Section 1. The Tribal Executive Committee shall, in accordance with applicable laws or regulations of the Department of the Interior, have the following powers:

(a) To employ legal counsel for the protection and advancement of the rights of the Minnesota Chippewa Tribe; the choice of counsel and fixing of fees to be subject to the approval of the Secretary of the Interior, or his authorized representative.

(b) To prevent any sale, disposition, lease or encumbrance of tribal lands, interest in lands, or other assets including minerals, gas and oil.

(c) To advise with the Secretary of the Interior with regard to all appropriation estimates or Federal projects for the benefit of the Minnesota Chippewa Tribe, except where such appropriation estimates or projects are for the benefit of individual Reservations.

(d) To administer any funds within the control of the Tribe; to make expenditures from tribal funds for salaries, expenses of tribal officials, employment or other tribal purposes. The Tribal Executive Committee shall apportion all funds within its control to the various Reservations excepting funds necessary to support the authorized costs of the Tribal Executive Committee. All expenditures of tribal funds, under control of the Tribal Executive Committee, shall be in accordance with a budget, duly approved by resolution in legal session, and the amounts so expended shall be a matter of public record at all reasonable times. The Tribal Executive Committee shall prepare annual budgets, requesting advancements to the control of the Tribe of any money deposited to the credit of the Tribe in the United States Treasury, subject to the approval of the Secretary of the Interior or his authorized representative.

(e) To consult, negotiate, contract and conclude agreements on behalf of the Minnesota Chippewa Tribe with Federal, State and local governments or private persons or organizations on all matters within the powers of the Tribal Executive Committee, except as provided in the powers of the Reservation Business Committee.

(f) Except for those powers hereinafter granted to the Reservation Business Committees, the Tribal Executive Committee shall be authorized to manage, lease, permit, or otherwise deal with tribal lands, interests in lands or other tribal assets; to engage in any business that will further the economic well-being of members of the Tribe; to borrow money from the Federal Government or other sources and to direct the use of such funds for productive purposes, or to loan the money thus borrowed to Business Committees of the Reservations and to pledge or assign chattel or income, due or to become due, subject only to the approval of the Secretary of the Interior or his authorized representative, when required by Federal law or regulations.

(g) The Tribal Executive Committee may by ordinance, subject to the review of the Secretary of the Interior, levy licenses or fees on non-members or non-tribal organizations doing business on two or more Reservations.

(h) To recognize any community organizations, associations or committees open to members of the several Reservations and to approve such organizations, subject to the provision that no such organizations, associations or committees may assume any authority granted to the Tribal Executive Committee or to the Reservation Business Committees.

(i) To delegate to committees, officers, employees or cooperative associations any of the foregoing authorities, reserving the right to review any action taken by virtue of such delegated authorities.

Article VI—Authorities of the Reservation Business Committees

Section 1. Each of the Reservation Business Committees shall, in accordance with applicable laws or regulations of the Department of Interior, have the following powers:

(a) To advise with the Secretary of the Interior with regard to all appropriation estimates on Federal projects for the benefit of its Reservation.

(b) To administer any funds within the control of the Reservation; to make expenditures from Reservation funds for salaries, expenses of Reservation officials, employment or other Reservation purposes. All expenditures of Reservations funds under the control of the Reservation Business Committees shall be in accordance with a budget, duly approved by resolution in legal session, and the amounts so expended shall be a matter of public record at all reasonable times. The Business Committees shall prepare annual budgets requesting advancements to the control of the Reservation of tribal funds under the control of the Tribal Executive Committee.

(c) To consult, negotiate and contract and conclude agreements on behalf of its respective Reservation with Federal, State and local governments or private persons or organizations on all matters within the power of the Reservation Business Committee, provided that no such agreements or contracts shall directly affect any other Reservation or the Tribal Executive Committee without their consent. The Business Committee shall be authorized to manage, lease, permit or otherwise deal with tribal lands, interests in lands or other tribal assets, when authorized to do so by the Tribal Executive Committee but no such authorization shall be necessary in the case of lands or assets owned exclusively by the Reservation. To engage in any business that will further the economic well-being of members of the Reservation; to borrow money from the Federal Government or other sources and to direct the use of such funds for productive purposes or to loan the money thus borrowed to members of the Reservation and to pledge or assign Reservation chattel or income due or to become due, subject only to the approval of the Secretary of the Interior or his authorized representative when required by Federal law and regulations. The Reservation Business Committee may also, with the consent of the Tribal Executive Committee, pledge or assign tribal chattel or income.

(d) The Reservation Business Committee may by ordinance, subject to the review of the Secretary of the Interior, levy licenses or fees on non-members or non-tribal organizations doing business solely within their respective Reservations. A Reservation Business Committee may recognize any community organization, association or committee open to members of the Reservation or located within the Reservation and approve such organization, subject to the provision that no such organization, association or committee may assume any authority granted to the Reservation Business Committee or to the Tribal Executive Committee.

(e) To delegate to committees, officers, employees or cooperative associations any of the foregoing authorities, reserving the right to review any action taken by virtue of such delegated authorities.

(f) The powers heretofore granted to the bands by the charters issued by the Tribal Executive Committee are hereby superseded by this Article and said charters will no longer be recognized for any purposes.

Article VII—Duration of Tribal Constitution

Section 1. The period of duration of this tribal constitution shall be perpetual or until revoked by lawful means as provided in the Act of June 18, 1934 (48 Stat. 984), as amended.

Article VIII—Majority Vote

Section 1. At all elections held under this constitution, the majority of eligible voter cast shall rule, unless otherwise provided by an Act of Congress.

Article IX—Bonding of Tribal Officials

Section 1. The Tribal Executive Committee and the Reservation Business Committees, respectively, shall require all persons, charged by the Tribe or Reservation with responsibility for the custody of any of its funds or property, to give bond for the faithful performance of his official duties. Such bond shall be furnished by a responsible bonding company and shall be acceptable to the beneficiary thereof and the Secretary of the Interior or his authorized representative, and the cost thereof shall be paid by the beneficiary.

Article X—Vacancies and Removal

Section 1. Any vacancy in the Tribal Executive Committee shall be filled by the Indians from the Reservation on which the vacancy occurs by election under rules prescribed by the Tribal Executive Committee. During the interim, the Reservation Business Committee shall be empowered to select a temporary Tribal Executive Committee member to represent the Reservation until such time as the election herein provided for has been held and the successful candidate elected and seated.

Sec. 2. The Reservation Business Committee by a two-thirds (2/3) vote of its members shall remove any officer or member of the Committee for the following causes:

(a) Malfeasance in the handling of tribal affairs.
(b) Dereliction or neglect of duty.
(c) Unexcused failure to attend two regular meetings in succession.
(d) Conviction of a felony in any county, State or Federal court while serving on the Reservation Business Committee.
(e) Refusal to comply with any provisions of the Constitution and Bylaws of the Tribe.

The removal shall be in accordance with the procedures set forth in Section 3 of this Article.

Sec. 3. Any member of the Reservation from which the Reservation Business Committee member is elected may prefer charges by written notice supported by the signatures of no less than 20 percent of the resident eligible voters of said Reservation, stating any of the causes for removal set forth in Section 2 of this Article, against any member or members of the respective Reservation Business Committee. The notice must be submitted to the Business Committee. The Reservation Business Committee shall consider such notice and take the following action:

(a) The Reservation Business Committee within fifteen (15) days after receipt of the notice or charges shall in writing notify the accused of the charges brought against him and set a date for a hearing. If the Reservation Business Committee deems the accused has failed to answer charges to its satisfaction or fails to appear at the appointed time, the Reservation Business Committee may remove as provided in Section 2 or it may schedule a recall election which shall be held within thirty (30) days after the date set for the hearing. In either event, the action of the Reservation Business Committee or the outcome of the recall election shall be final.

(b) All such hearings of the Reservation Business Committee shall be held in accordance with the provisions of this Article and shall be open to the members of the Reservation. Notices of such hearings shall be duly posted at least five (5) days prior to the hearing.

(c) The accused shall be given opportunity to call witnesses and present evidence in his behalf.

Sec. 4. When the Tribal Executive Committee finds any of its members guilty of any of the causes for removal from office as listed in Section 2 of this Article, it shall in writing censor the Tribal Executive Committee member. The Tribal Executive Committee shall present its written censure to the Reservation Business Committee from which the Tribal Executive Committee member is elected. The Reservation Business Committee shall thereupon consider such censure in the manner prescribed in Section 3 of this Article.

Sec. 5. In the event the Reservation Business Committee fails to act as provided in Sections 3 and 4 of this Article, the Reservation membership may, by petition supported by the signatures of no less than 20 percent of the eligible resident voters, appeal to the Secretary of the Interior. If the Secretary deems the charges substantial, he shall call an election for the purpose of placing the matter before the Reservation electorate for their final decision.

Article XI—Ratification

Section 1. This constitution and the bylaws shall not become operative until ratified at a special election by a majority vote of the adult members of the Minnesota Chippewa Tribe, voting at a special election called by the Secretary of the Interior, provided that at least 30 percent of those entitled to vote shall vote, and until it has been approved by the Secretary of the Interior.

Article XII—Amendment

Section 1. This constitution may be revoked by Act of Congress or amended or revoked by a majority vote of the qualified voters of the Tribe voting at an election called for that purpose by the Secretary of the Interior if at least 30 percent of those entitled to vote shall vote. No amendment shall be effective until approved by the Secretary of the Interior. It shall be the duty of the Secretary to call an election when requested by two-thirds of the Tribal Executive Committee.

Article XIII—Rights of Members

All members of the Minnesota Chippewa Tribe shall be accorded by the governing body equal rights, equal protection, and equal opportunities to participate in the economic resources and activities of the Tribe, and no member shall be denied any of the constitutional rights or guarantees enjoyed by other citizens of the United States, including but not limited to freedom of religion and conscience, freedom of speech, the right to orderly association or assembly, the right to petition for action or the redress of grievances, and due process of law.

Article XIV—Referendum

Section 1. The Tribal Executive Committee, upon receipt of a petition signed by 20 percent of the resident voters of the Minnesota Chippewa Tribe, or by an affirmative vote of eight (8) members of the Tribal Executive Committee, shall submit any enacted or proposed resolution or ordinance of the Tribal Executive Committee to a referendum of the eligible voters of the Minnesota Chippewa Tribe. The majority of the votes cast in such referendum shall be conclusive and binding on the Tribal Executive Committee. The Tribal Executive Committee shall call such referendum and prescribe the manner of conducting the vote.

Sec. 2. The Reservation Business Committee, upon receipt of a petition signed by 20 percent of the resident voters of the Reservation, or by an affirmative vote of a majority of the members of the Reservation Business Committee, shall submit any enacted or proposed resolution or ordinance of the Reservation Business Committee to a referendum of the eligible voters of the Reservation. The majority of the votes cast in such referendum shall be conclusive and binding on the Reservation Business Committee. The Reservation Business Committee shall call such referendum and prescribe the manner of conducting the vote.

Article XV—Manner of Review

Section 1. Any resolution or ordinance enacted by the Tribal Executive Committee, which by the terms of this Constitution and Bylaws is subject to review by the Secretary of the Interior, or his authorized representative, shall be presented to the Superintendent or officer in charge of the Reservation who shall within ten (10) days after its receipt by him approve or disapprove the resolution or ordinance.

If the Superintendent or officer in charge shall approve any ordinance or resolution it shall thereupon become effective, but the Superintendent or officer in charge shall transmit a copy of the same, bearing his endorsement, to the Secretary of the Interior, who may within ninety (90) days from the date of approval, rescind the ordinance or resolution for any cause by notifying the Tribal Executive Committee.

If the Superintendent or officer in charge shall refuse to approve any resolution or ordinance subject to review within ten (10) days after its receipt by him he shall advise the Tribal Executive Committee of his reasons therefor in writing. If these reasons are deemed by the Tribal Executive Committee to be insufficient, it may, by a majority vote, refer the ordinance or resolution to the Secretary of the Interior, who may, within ninety (90) days from the date of its referral, approve or reject the same in writing, whereupon the said ordinance or resolution shall be in effect or rejected accordingly.

Sec. 2. Any resolution or ordinance enacted by the Reservation Business Committee, which by the terms of this Constitution and Bylaws is subject to review by the Secretary of the Interior or his authorized representative, shall be governed by the procedures set forth in Section 1 of this Article.

Sec. 3. Any resolution or ordinance enacted by the Reservation Business Committee, which by the terms of this Constitution and Bylaws is subject to approval by the Tribal Executive Committee, shall within ten (10) days of its enactment be presented to the Tribal Executive Committee. The Tribal Executive Committee shall at its next regular or special meeting, approve or disapprove such resolution or ordinance.

Upon approval or disapproval by the Tribal Executive Committee of any resolution or ordinance submitted by a Reservation Business Committee, it shall advise the Reservation Business Committee within ten (10) days, in writing, of the action taken. In the event of disapproval the Tribal Executive Committee shall advise the Reservation Business Committee, at that time, of its reasons therefor.

BYLAWS

Article I—Duties of the Officers of the Tribal Executive Committee

Section 1. The President of the Tribal Executive Committee shall:

(a) Preside at all regular and special meetings of the Tribal Executive Committee and at any meeting of the Minnesota Chippewa Tribe in general council.
(b) Assume responsibility for the implementation of all resolutions and ordinances of the Tribal Executive Committee.
(c) Sign, with the Secretary of the Tribal Executive Committee, on behalf of the Tribe all official papers when authorized to do so.
(d) Assume general supervision of all officers, employees and committees of the Tribal Executive Committee and, as delegated, take direct responsibility for the satisfactory performance of such officers, employees and committees.
(e) Prepare a report of negotiations, important communications and other activities of the Tribal Executive Committee and shall make this report at each regular meeting of the Tribal Executive Committee. He shall include in this report all matters of importance to the Tribe, and in no way shall he act for the Tribe unless specifically authorized to do so.
(f) Have general management of the business activities of the Tribal Executive Committee. He shall not act on matters binding the Tribe until the Tribal Executive Committee has deliberated and enacted appropriate resolution, or unless written delegation of authority has been granted.
(g) Not vote in meetings of the Tribal Executive Committee except in the case of a tie.

Sec. 2. In the absence or disability of the President, the Vice-President shall preside. When so presiding, he shall have all rights, privileges and duties as set forth under duties of the President, as well as the responsibility of the President.

Sec. 3. The Secretary of the Tribal Executive Committee shall:

(a) Keep a complete record of the meetings of the Tribal Executive Committee and shall maintain such records at the headquarters of the Tribe.
(b) Sign, with the President of the Tribal Executive Committee, all official papers as provided in Section 1 (c) of this Article.
(c) Be the custodian of all property of the Tribe.
(d) Keep a complete record of all business of the Tribal Executive Committee. Make and submit a complete and detailed report of the current year's business

and shall submit such other reports as shall be required by the Tribal Executive Committee.

(e) Serve all notices required for meetings and elections.

(f) Perform such other duties as may be required of him by the Tribal Executive Committee.

Sec. 4. The Treasurer of the Tribal Executive Committee shall:

(a) Receive all funds of the Tribe entrusted to it, deposit same in a depository selected by the Tribal Executive Committee, and disburse such tribal funds only on vouchers signed by the President and Secretary.

(b) Keep and maintain, open to inspection by members of the Tribe or representatives of the Secretary of the Interior, at all reasonable times, adequate and correct accounts of the properties and business transactions of the Tribe.

(c) Make a monthly report and account for all transactions involving the disbursement, collection or obligation of tribal funds. He shall present such financial reports to the Tribal Executive Committee at each of its regular meetings.

Sec. 5. Duties and functions of all appointive committees, officers, and employees of the Tribal Executive Committee shall be clearly defined by resolution of the Tribal Executive Committee.

Article II—Tribal Executive Committee Meetings

Section 1. Regular meetings of the Tribal Executive Committee shall be held once in every 3 months beginning on the second Monday in July of each year and on such other days of any month as may be designated for that purpose.

Sec. 2. Notice shall be given by the Secretary of the Tribal Executive Committee of the date and place of all meetings by mailing a notice thereof to the members of the Tribal Executive Committee not less than 15 days preceding the date of the meeting.

Sec. 3. The President shall call a special meeting of the Tribal Executive Committee upon a written request of at least one-third of the Tribal Executive Committee. The President shall also call a special meeting of the Tribal Executive Committee when matters of special importance pertaining to the Tribe arise for which he deems advisable the said Committee should meet.

Sec. 4. In case of special meetings designated for emergency matters pertaining to the Tribe, or those of special importance warranting immediate action of said Tribe, the President of the Tribal Executive Committee may waive the 15-day clause provided in Section 2 of this Article.

Sec. 5. Seven members of the Tribal Executive Committee shall constitute a quorum, and Robert's Rules shall govern its meetings. Except as provided in said Rules, no business shall be transacted unless a quorum is present.

Sec. 6. The order of business at any meeting so far as possible shall be:

(a) Call to order by the presiding officer.
(b) Invocation.
(c) Roll call.
(d) Reading and disposal of the minutes of the last meeting.
(e) Reports of committees and officers.
(f) Unfinished business.
(g) New business.
(h) Adjournment.

Article III—Installation of Tribal Executive Committee Members

Section 1. New members of the Tribal Executive Committee who have been duly elected by the respective Reservations shall be installed at the first regular meeting of the Tribal Executive Committee following election of the committee members, upon subscribing to the following oath:

"I, _____, do hereby solemnly swear (or affirm) that I shall preserve, support and protect the Constitution of the United States and the Constitution of the Minnesota Chippewa Tribe, and execute my duties as a member of the Tribal Executive Committee to the best of my ability, so help me God."

Article IV—Amendments

Section 1. These bylaws may be amended in the same manner as the Constitution.

Article V—Miscellaneous

Section 1. The fiscal year of the Minnesota Chippewa Tribe shall begin on July 1 of each year.

Section 2. The books and records of the Minnesota Chippewa Tribe shall be audited at least once each year by a competent auditor employed by the Tribal Executive Committee, and at such times as the Tribal Executive Committee or the Secretary of the Interior or his authorized representative may direct. Copies of audit reports shall be furnished the Bureau of Indian Affairs.

Article VI—Reservation Business Committee Bylaws

Section 1. The Reservation Business Committee shall by ordinance adopt bylaws to govern the duties of its officers and Committee members and its meetings.

Section 2. Duties and functions of all appointive committees, officers, and employees of the Reservation Business Committee shall be clearly defined by resolution of the Reservation Business Committee.

Certification of Adoption

Pursuant to an order approved September 12, 1963, by the Assistant Secretary of the Interior, the Revised Constitution and Bylaws of the Minnesota Chippewa Tribe was submitted for ratification to the qualified voters of the reservations, and was on November 23, 1963, duly adopted by a vote of 1,761 for and 1,295 against, in an election in which at least 30 percent of those entitled to vote cast their ballots in accordance with Section 16 of the Indian Reorganization Act of June 18, 1934 (48 Stat. 984), as amended by the Act of June 15, 1935 (49 Stat. 378).

(sgd) Allen Wilson, President
Tribal Executive Committee
(sgd) Peter DuFault, Secretary
Tribal Executive Committee
(sgd) H. P. Mittelholtz, Superintendent
Minnesota Agency

Approval

I, John A. Carver Jr., Assistant Secretary of the Interior of the United States of America, by virtue of the authority granted me by the Act of June 18, 1934 (48 Stat. 984), as amended, do hereby approve the attached Revised Constitution and Bylaws of the Minnesota Chippewa Tribe, Minnesota.

John A. Carver Jr.
Assistant Secretary of the Interior
Washington, D.C.
Date: March 3, 1964

The Constitution of the White Earth Nation

Gichi-manidoo-giizis midaasogonagizi ashi ningodwaaswi
Niizho-midaaswaak ashi zhaagaswi
Gaa-aanike-ozhibii'igaadeg Waa-apenimoyang Ogimaawiwin
Enaakonigaadeg Gaa-waababiganikaag
OGIMAAWIWIN ENAAKONIGAADEG GAA-WAABABIGANIKAAG
NAAGAANIBII'IGAADEG

GAA-WAABABIGANIKAAG DAZHI-ANISHINAABEG OBIMIWIIDOONAAWAA
gaa-izichigenid ogitiziimiwaan ishkweyaaang ji-giitaashkaagoosigwaa
bimaadiziwaad, odinawemaaganiwaan, odoodemiwaan. Geyaabi
odibaadododaanaawaa Anishinaabeg keyaa enendamowaad, zoongide'ewaad,
baapinendamowaad, zhaabwiiwaad, wiidookawaawaad wiijanisginaabemi-
waan, miinawaa go anishinaabe-ogimaawiwaad.

Niinawind sa anishinaabewiyaang Gaa-waababiganikaag
wii-kanawendamaang keyaa bimiwidooyaang indoogimaawiwininaan,
ji-biitaakoshkaagoosiwaang, ji-mino-doodaagooyaang, ji-bizaani-
bimaadiziyaang, ji-ganawendamaang indakiiminaan, miinawaa
ji-ganawendamaang keyaa ina'oonigooyaang ji-ogimaawiyaang, indinaa-
konigemin miinawaa indoozitoomin o'ow Ogimaawiwin Enaakonigaadeg
Gaa-waababiganikaag.

PREAMBLE

The Anishinaabeg of the White Earth Nation are the successors of a great tradition of continental liberty, a native constitution of families, totemic associations. The Anishinaabeg create stories of natural reason, of courage, loyalty, humor, spiritual inspiration, survivance, reciprocal altruism, and native cultural sovereignty.

We the Anishinaabeg of the White Earth Nation in order to secure an inherent and essential sovereignty, to promote traditions of liberty, justice, and peace, and reserve common resources, and to ensure the inalienable rights of native governance for our posterity, do constitute, ordain and establish this Constitution of the White Earth Nation.

CHAPTER 1: TERRITORY AND JURISDICTION

The White Earth Nation shall have jurisdiction over citizens, residents, visitors, altruistic relations, and the whole of the land, including transfers, conferrals, and acquisitions of land in futurity, water, wild rice, public and private property, right of way, airspace, minerals, natural resources, parks, and any other environmental estates or territories designated by and located within the boundaries of the White Earth Reservation, as established and described in the Treaty of March 19, 1867, and over the reserved rights within the ceded waterways and territories of the Treaty of 1855.

CHAPTER 2: CITIZENS OF THE WHITE EARTH NATION

Article 1

Citizens of the White Earth Nation shall be descendants of Anishinaabeg families and related by linear descent to enrolled members of the White Earth Reservation and Nation, according to genealogical documents, treaties and other agreements with the government of the United States.

Article 2

Services and entitlements provided by government agencies to citizens, otherwise designated members of the White Earth Nation, shall be defined according to treaties, trusts, and diplomatic agreements, state and federal laws, rules and regulations, and in policies and procedures established by the government of the White Earth Nation.

Article 3

The Anishinaabeg and their descendants shall have the right to appeal to the President and to the White Earth Court any decisions that deny citizenship in the White Earth Nation.

Article 4

No person or government has the privilege or power to diminish the sovereignty of the White Earth Nation.

CHAPTER 3: RIGHTS AND DUTIES

Article 1

The White Earth Nation shall make no laws that would establish a religion, or laws that would deny the free expression of religion, speech, or of the press and electronic communication.

Article 2

The White Earth Nation shall make no laws that deny the right of the people to peaceably gather or assemble for any reason, and shall make no laws that prohibit the right to petition the government for restitution, amendments, or redress of grievances, and no person shall be discriminated against for initiating or espousing an untimely or contrary petition about governance.

Article 3

The people shall not be denied the fundamental human rights of citizenship in the White Earth Nation.

Article 4

The people are equal under the law and no law, government policy, or agency practice shall discriminate in political, economic, social or cultural associations because of race, creed, sex, gender, disability, or social status.

Article 5

The freedom of thought and conscience, academic, artistic irony, and literary expression, shall not be denied, violated or controverted by the government.

Article 6

The secrecy of personal communication shall not be violated, and no censorship shall be practiced or maintained by the government.

Article 7

The right to own and transfer of private property is inviolable. The rights of property shall be protected, and private property expropriated for public use shall be according to due process of law and just compensation.

Article 8

No person shall be denied or deprived of life or liberty, except certain serious misdemeanors and felony convictions, and no criminal penalties shall be imposed without due process of law and judicial procedures.

Article 9

No person shall be apprehended by law enforcement officers without probable cause and due process of law or by warrant duly issued by a court.

Article 10

The people shall have the right to possess firearms except for convicted felons in accordance with state and federal laws.

Article 11

The people shall be secure in their homes, personal papers and documents, against entries, electronic and material searches, without a specific, descriptive warrant for adequate cause issued by a court. Each search and seizure shall require a separate, specific warrant issued by a court, except in cases of probable threats or potential emergencies.

Article 12

No person shall be obligated to testify or provide evidence in a court against himself or herself, and any confessions obtained under compulsion, torture, or threats, or after arrest and excessive detention, may not be admissible as evidence in court. No person shall be convicted or punished for a crime when the only evidence against him or her is a confession, except in cases of crimes that can be proven by other evidence.

Article 13

No person shall be subject to trial twice for the same criminal indictment or offence.

Article 14

No person shall be denied the right to be duly informed of the nature and cause of a warrant, indictment, or criminal proceeding, and shall not be denied the right to be represented by legal counsel.

Article 15

The people shall have the right to confront and challenge witnesses in a criminal court, and the legal option of a speedy court hearing or public jury trial shall not be refused or contradicted.

Article 16

Citizens shall never be banished from the White Earth Nation.

Article 17

The Constitution of the White Earth Nation is inspired by inherent and traditional sovereignty, and contains, embodies, and promotes the rights and provisions provided in the articles and amendments of the Indian Civil Rights Act of 1968, and the United States Constitution.

CHAPTER 4: SOVEREIGN IMMUNITY

The White Earth Nation declares sovereign territorial, political and cultural rights and powers as an independent government and immunity to civil law suits. The Legislative Council by certain formal policies and procedures shall have the right to waive the sovereign immunity of the government in the best interests of the White Earth Nation.

CHAPTER 5: BOARD OF ELECTIONS

Article 1

Citizens must be at least eighteen years old to vote in government referenda and elections.

Article 2

Election and voting procedures shall be established by an Election Code and managed by an independent Board of Elections appointed by the Legislative Council.

Article 3

The Board of Elections shall consist of five eligible citizen voters of the White Earth Nation. The Chief Judge of the Board of Elections shall administer and supervise election regulations and procedures according to provisions of the Election Code. The Chief Judge shall not vote as a member of the Board of Elections.

Article 4

Members of the Board of Elections shall ensure fair and impartial elections according to the Election Code and the Constitution of the White Earth Nation.

Article 5

The Legislative Council shall resolve any challenges or allegations of impropriety of election laws or procedures.

Article 6

Citizens who become candidates for elected positions in the government shall not be members of the Board of Elections. The Legislative Council shall appoint the Chief Judge and replacements to the Board of Elections.

CHAPTER 6: GOVERNANCE

Article 1

The White Earth Nation shall be governed by a representative and elected Legislative Council.

Article 2

The Legislative Council shall consist of a President, or White Earth Chief, the Secretary Treasurer, and elected Representatives of acknowledged communities of the White Earth Nation.

Article 3

The respective communities shall be entitled to one elected Representative to serve on the Legislative Council.

Article 4

Communities shall be established or changed by petition, by population, historic or totemic associations, and ratified by a simple majority of eligible citizen voters in a general referendum.

Article 5

The President and the Secretary Treasurer shall be elected at large by eligible citizen voters of the White Earth Nation.

Article 6

The President, Secretary Treasurer, and Representatives of the Legislative Council shall be elected for no more than two four year terms, and staggered elections shall be ordered every two years.

Article 7

Two citizens of the White Earth Nation shall be elected at large to serve constituencies outside the White Earth Reservation in the State of Minnesota.

Article 8

The Legislative Council shall have the authority to propose changes in the count of elected Representatives based on changes in population or the number of acknowledged communities. Proposals to change the count of Representatives shall be subject to a majority vote of citizens in a referendum.

Article 9

Candidates for elected government offices shall be citizens who reside within the treaty boundaries according to the Treaty of March 19, 1867, of the White Earth Nation, except two citizen members of the Legislative Council who shall be elected at large in the State of Minnesota.

Article 10

Citizens who have been convicted of a felony may vote in elections and referenda but shall not be eligible to hold elected offices in the White Earth Nation.

Article 11

Candidates for elected government office shall be at least twenty-five years of age at the time of the election.

Article 12

The Legislative Council shall appoint a new President in the event of the death, resignation, incapacity, or removal of the duly elected President. The appointed President shall serve the remainder of the elected term of the office.

Article 13

The Legislative Council has the power to initiate impeachment proceedings of elected representatives of the government for specific allegations of misconduct, criminal indictments, or felony convictions. To initiate impeachment procedures requires at least a two-thirds vote of the Legislative Council.

Article 14

There shall be two distinct procedures of impeachment. The first is admonition of misconduct but no other action or decree, and the second procedure is impeachment and removal from elected office.

Article 15

The White Earth Nation shall obligate candidates for elected offices not to disburse in campaign services, promotion and advertising more than three times the amount of the annual national family poverty guidelines, for one person in the Contiguous States, established and published in the Federal Register by the United States Department of Human Services.

Article 16

Candidates for elected office shall file a formal report no later than thirty days after the election with the Chief Judge of the Board of Elections. The report shall be an affirmation of total election contributions and disbursements of the candidate.

Article 17

The President and Legislative Council of the White Earth Nation shall maintain public records and documents for posterity. The President shall nominate an archive to secure the public records and documents.

CHAPTER 7: COMMUNITY COUNCILS

The Community Councils shall be initiated and established in geographically based communities by citizens of the White Earth Nation. The Community Councils shall provide communal information, guidance, and recommendations to both the Legislative Council and the President on matters of concern to the citizens. The Community Councils shall promote, advance and strengthen the philosophy of mino-bimaadiziwin, to live a good life, and in good health, through the creation and formation of associations, events and activities that demonstrate, teach and encourage respect, love, bravery, humility, wisdom, honesty and truth for citizens.

CHAPTER 8: COUNCIL OF ELDERS

The Council of Elders shall be nominated by citizens and designated by the Legislative Council. The Council of Elders shall provide ideas and thoughts on totemic associations, traditional knowledge, cultural and spiritual practices, native survivance, and considerations of resource management, and advice the Legislative Council. The Council of Elders shall consist of twenty citizens of the White Earth Nation who are at least fifty-five years of age at the time of appointment.

CHAPTER 9: YOUTH COUNCIL

The Youth Council shall be nominated by citizens and designated by the Legislative Council. The Youth Council shall provide information about matters that affect young people and advise the President and Legislative Council. The Youth Council shall consist of twenty citizens who are between the ages of twelve and eighteen, and who are residents of the White Earth Nation.

CHAPTER 10: SEPARATION OF POWERS

The White Earth Nation shall be divided into three separate branches of government. The Executive branch is the elected President, the Board of Elections, Council of Elders, Youth Council, and other executive designations. The Legislative branch includes the Representatives elected to the Legislative Council. The Judicial branch of government is the Judiciary and White Earth Courts. The three respective branches of government shall have no authority over any other branch, except for certain nominations and other provisions specified in the Constitution of the White Earth Nation.

CHAPTER 11: THE PRESIDENT

Article 1

The President, or White Earth Chief, shall be the official national and international elected representative of the White Earth Nation.

Article 2

The President shall have the authority to secure and accept grants, negotiate agreements with associations, foundations, organizations, institutions, corporations, municipal, state, federal, and local governments, and other states and nations in the world with the ratification of the Legislative Council.

Article 3

The President shall be responsible for the administration and management of the government, and shall implement and execute the laws, ordinances, resolutions, and other enactments of the Legislative Council.

Article 4

The President shall approve by signature the laws, ordinances, measures, resolutions and appropriations of the Legislative Council.

Article 5

The President shall have the power to veto proposed laws, ordinances, measures, and resolutions initiated by the Legislative Council.

Article 6

The President shall return within five days vetoed or rejected proposed laws, ordinances and measures with a required statement of objection.

Article 7

The Legislative Council may overcome any veto of proposed laws, ordinances and resolutions by a two-thirds vote of the elected Representatives.

Article 8

The President shall have the authority to appoint executive branch administrators and other officials to serve the White Earth Nation.

Article 9

The President shall have the power to schedule and preside over sessions of the Legislative Council.

Article 10

The President shall not vote except in the case of a tie vote of the Legislative Council.

Article 11

The President shall deliver an annual address dedicated to the State of the White Earth Nation.

Article 12

The President shall be bonded as an elected official.

Article 13

The President may serve no more than two four year elected terms.

Article 14

The President shall promote, protect, and defend cultural and political sovereignty and the Constitution of the White Earth Nation.

Article 15

The President shall have the authority to nominate honorary ambassadors, consuls, citizens, and to initiate and establish embassies of the White Earth Nation to serve the national and international concerns of native survivance and moral equity.

CHAPTER 12: THE LEGISLATIVE COUNCIL

Article 1

Representatives of the Legislative Council shall propose and enact laws, codes, ordinances, resolutions, and statutes of the White Earth Nation.

Article 2

The Legislative Council shall have the authority to raise general revenue, levy and collect taxes for government services and operations, establish license and service fees, and initiate other specific levies and taxes for the welfare of the citizens of the White Earth Nation.

Article 3

The Legislative Council shall have the authority to borrow money, issue public bonds, appropriate funds for the operation of the government, and to initiate other monetary policies in the interests of the White Earth Nation.

Article 4

The Legislative Council shall promote and protect the health, public welfare, safety, education, and the cultural and political sovereignty of the citizens of the White Earth Nation.

Article 5

The Legislative Council shall establish subordinate and secondary boards, appoint delegates, and reserves the right to review the initiatives and actions of the delegates and boards.

Article 6

The Legislative Council shall be responsible for the proper management of government programs, land, waterways, resources, commerce, public housing, transportation, casino operations, business enterprises, and other assets of the White Earth Nation.

Article 7

The Legislative Council shall have the authority to control the distribution and sale of alcoholic beverages within the treaty boundaries of the White Earth Nation.

Article 8

The Legislative Council shall not establish, support, or embody any covert political, military, or intelligence operations, without due process of law and legal warrants, against peaceable citizens of the White Earth Nation.

Article 9

The Legislative Council shall have residual powers, and the powers of governance provided, specified and entrusted in the Constitution shall not be construed as the limitation of legislative power or authority. The powers of the government not specifically expressed or entrusted to the Legislative Council shall be reserved to the citizens of the White Earth Nation.

CHAPTER 13: THE SECRETARY TREASURER

Article 1

The Secretary Treasurer shall be bonded and responsible for monetary and financial matters, resources, documents and records of the Legislative Council. Government records shall be available for public inspection and review.

Article 2

The Secretary Treasurer shall schedule an annual audit of funds, monetary transactions and records, deposits and expenditures by a duly certified independent auditor.

Article 3

The Secretary Treasurer shall carry through official duties and responsibilities of the President and the Representatives of the Legislative Council.

Article 4

The Secretary Treasurer shall be a voting member of the Legislative Council.

Article 5

The Secretary Treasure shall provide and publish an annual fiscal report and accounting of the White Earth Nation.

CHAPTER 14: THE JUDICIARY

Article 1

The Judiciary shall consist of the White Earth Court, Court of Appeals, and other courts established by the Legislative Council.

Article 2

The White Earth Court shall have the power of judicial review and jurisdiction over any legal matters, disputes, civil procedures and criminal laws, ordinances, regulations, codes and customs of family relations, protection, and dissolution, adoption, domestic violence, juvenile justice, and probate, housing and property, conservation, taxation, governance, the corporate code, election disputes, and constitutional issues of the White Earth Nation.

Article 3

The Court of Appeals shall have original and appellate jurisdiction. The Court of Appeals shall hear case appeals and issues initiated by the Legislative Council. Decisions of the Court of Appeals are conclusive.

CHAPTER 15: POWERS OF THE WHITE EARTH COURTS

Article 1

The Courts shall have the authority to interpret and construe the laws, ordinances, and regulations of the Legislative Council and the Constitution of the White Earth Nation.

Article 2

The Courts shall issue legal decisions, injunctions, reviews, writs of mandamus, extradition, certiorari, writs of habeas corpus, and other legal orders, instruments and documents.

Article 3

The Courts shall establish procedures, rules, legal forms, and review by formal requests of citizens the specific and comprehensive constitutional validity of laws, ordinances and codes initiated and passed by the Legislative Council.

Article 4

The Courts shall ensure and practice restorative justice in civil actions, minor criminal offences, juvenile and family matters, whenever appropriate to resolve complaints and disputes of the White Earth Nation.

Article 5

The Courts shall establish and publish a code of judicial ethics.

CHAPTER 16: THE WHITE EARTH JUDGES

Article 1

The White Earth Court shall consist of a Chief Judge and Associate Judges. The Chief Judge shall be elected by a majority plus one of the eligible votes in a duly called election.

Article 2

The Chief Judge shall appoint the necessary number of Associate Judges for five-year terms with the consent of the Legislative Council.

Article 3

The Court of Appeals shall consist of three judges and shall be appointed by the Legislative Council in consultation with the Chief Judge.

Article 4

The Chief Judge shall not be a member of the Court of Appeals.

Article 5

Judges of the Court of Appeals shall serve for five-years, and may otherwise practice law or be associated with a law firm.

Article 6

The judges of the courts shall be at least twenty-five years of age, of proven moral character, and who have not been convicted of a felony.

Article 7

The judges shall be graduates of a law school accredited by the American Bar Association.

Article 8

The judges shall be admitted to the bar to practice law in native communities, state, or federal courts.

Article 9

The judges shall be experienced lawyers, magistrates, or judges.

Article 10

The judges shall have knowledge of Anishinaabe culture, traditions, and general history.

Article 11

The judges shall recuse themselves, an assertion of judicial disqualification, as unsuitable to perform legal duties where there are possible conflicts of interest, or the appearance of personal interests, or potential challenges of partiality.

Article 12

The judges shall be impeached by the Legislative Council and removed from judicial practice for abuses of impartiality, bribery, political impropriety, or felony conviction.

CHAPTER 17: LEGISLATIVE COUNCIL MEETINGS

Article 1

The Legislative Council shall meet at least once each month to conduct government business. The time and place of each session shall be posted in advance.

Article 2

Citizens of the White Earth Nation have the right to attend sessions of the Legislative Council.

Article 3

The President has the authority to schedule special and emergency sessions of the Legislative Council.

Article 4

The Legislative Council by a majority vote and written request shall have the authority to schedule a special session.

Article 5

The President shall be obligated to schedule a special session of the Legislative Council by an official petition of thirty percent of eligible citizen voters of the White Earth Nation.

Article 6

The President may schedule an emergency session of the Legislative Council without written notice to consider urgent matters, services, protection of the health, welfare and safety of the citizens and communities of the White Earth Nation.

Article 7

The Legislative Council shall conduct no other business than the specific stated purpose of an emergency session.

Article 8

The Legislative Council shall have the authority to meet in closed executive sessions with the President to discuss matters of litigation, proposed and discreet negotiations, and other concerns of confidentiality.

Article 9

The Legislative Council shall not decide actions on matters of litigation or confidentiality in closed executive sessions except when the outcome of the session has been fully reported in subsequent public sessions of the Legislative Council. The results of executive sessions shall be decided by vote at a public meeting.

Article 10

Legislative Council motions, votes, resolutions and decisions shall be noted and preserved in the official minutes of the sessions.

Article 11

Legislative Council actions, decisions, and enactments of record shall be available for inspection by citizens during normal business hours of the government.

Article 12

The Legislative Council shall date and number each and every resolution, ordinance, law and statute, and cite the appropriate authority of the Constitution of the White Earth Nation.

Article 13

The Legislative Council shall prepare a certificate for each resolution, ordinance, and statute that confirms the presence of a quorum and indicates the number of members voting for or against each enactment.

Article 14

The Legislative Council shall constitute a quorum by a simple majority of fifty-one percent of the elected members at a duly schedule session.

CHAPTER 18: ETHICS AND IMPEACHMENT

Article 1

Elected members of the government may be impeached or removed from office by a recorded two-thirds vote of the entire Legislative Council.

Article 2

The Legislative Council may impeach or remove from office an elected member of government for a felony conviction in a court of competent jurisdiction.

Article 3

The Legislative Council may impeach or remove from office an elected member of the government for two misdemeanor convictions, including driving while intoxicated, but not including ordinary traffic violations.

Article 4

Elected officials of the government may not be suspended or removed from office without due process of law.

Article 5

The Legislative Council may impeach for cause an elected member of the government. The impeachment may be a form of admonition, a warning or legal statement of charges, or the impeachment may be based on an indictment or conviction for a felony, and the forcible removal of an official of the government.

Article 6

The White Earth Nation shall provide for a recall election of an elected official of the government. Citizens have the right to initiate a petition to recall an elected official. The petition shall secure at least two-thirds of the eligible voters for a recall election. The petition may be political and may include allegations, grievances, complaints and assertions of misconduct, nonfeasance, or mismanagement by an elected official of the government.

CHAPTER 19: PETITIONS AND REFERENDA

Article 1

The Legislative Council may initiate a referendum by a vote of two-thirds of the elected Representatives.

Article 2

Citizens of the White Earth Nation may initiate a referendum by evidence of a vote of thirty percent of the eligible citizen voters.

Article 3

The Legislative Council and eligible citizens may present proposed laws, ordinances, and initiatives to a referendum vote of the electorate, according to certified evidence of the constitutional process.

Article 4

The referendum vote shall be held within one hundred and eighty days from the official receipt of the petition, unless the scheduled date of the referendum is within six months of a general election, in that event the referendum would be presented to the eligible voters in the general election.

Article 5

Scheduled referenda shall be conducted according to the rules and regulations of the Board of Elections and the Election Code.

CHAPTER 20: AMENDMENTS TO THE CONSTITUTION

The Constitution of the White Earth Nation may be amended by two-thirds of the recorded eligible votes in a duly called election or referendum to amend the Constitution. Eligible voters must be formally informed by written and published notices of the proposed amendment to the Constitution of the White Earth Nation.

RATIFICATION OF THE CONSTITUTION

The sworn delegates to the White Earth Constitutional Convention hereby duly ratify for a citizen referendum the Constitution of the White Earth Nation. The Constitution of the White Earth Nation was duly ratified on April 4, 2009, at the Shooting Star Casino Hotel, Mahnomen, Minnesota. The ratification was by secret ballots of twenty-four delegates present. Sixteen delegates voted for ratification, and eight delegates votes against ratification.

Gerald Vizenor, Distinguished Professor of American Studies at the University of New Mexico, was a delegate to the Constitutional Convention and the Principal Writer of the proposed Constitution of the White Earth Nation.

The Constitution Proposal Team included Erma Vizenor, President of the White Earth Nation, Jill May Doerfler, Assistant Professor, Department of Indian Studies, University of Minnesota, Duluth, Jo Anne E. Stately, Vice President of Development for the Indian Land Tenure Foundation, and Anita Fineday, Chief Tribal Court Judge, White Earth Nation.

David E. Wilkins, Professor of American Indian Studies, University of Minnesota, was a Special Consultant to the Constitutional Convention and the Proposal Team.

Anton Treuer, Professor, American Indian Resource Center, Languages and Ethnic Studies, Bemidji State University, was the translator of the Preamble to the Constitution.

Notes

PREFACE

1. LeAnne Howe, "Blind Bread and the Business of Theory Making," in *Reasoning Together: The Native Critics Collective*, ed. Craig S. Womack, Daniel Heath Justice, and Christopher B. Teuton (Norman: University of Oklahoma Press, 2008), 338.
2. Anishinaabeg is the plural form of Anishinaabe. I discuss my decision to use this term and its history in the introduction.
3. I explore the types of Anishinaabe stories more fully with my fellow coeditors Niigaanwewidam James Sinclair and Heidi Stark in "Bagijige: An Offering," in *Centering Anishinaabeg Studies: Understanding the World through Stories* (East Lansing: Michigan State University Press, 2013), xv–xxviii.
4. Gerald Vizenor, *The Everlasting Sky: Voices of the Anishinabe People* (Minneapolis: Minnesota Historical Society Press, 2000), 69.
5. Kimberly Blaeser, "The New 'Frontier' of Native American Literature: Dis-Arming History with Tribal Humor," in *Native American Perspectives on Literature and History*, ed. Alan R. Velie (Norman: University of Oklahoma Press, 1994), 49.
6. Maureen Konkle, *Writing Indian Nations: Native Intellectuals and the Politics of Historiography, 1827–1863* (Chapel Hill: University of North Carolina Press, 2004), 162. Konkle also notes that many nineteenth-century American Indian authors "maintained that EuroAmericans' knowledge about Indians' racial difference was politically motivated" (5). Some early Anishinaabe authors include Bame-wa-wa-ge-zhik-a-quay/Jane Johnson Schoolcraft, Kah-ge-ga-gah-bowh/George Copway, Keh-ke-wa-guo-na-ba/Peter Jones, Maung-wudaus/George Henry, and William Warren.
7. In *Red on Red*, Craig Womack argues: "Traditional stories teach the origins not only of the material culture but worldview, values, and religious beliefs of the nation." Craig Womack, *Red on Red: Native American Literary Separatism* (Minneapolis: University of Minnesota Press, 1999), 53.
8. John Borrows, *Recovering Canada: The Resurgence of Indigenous Law* (Toronto: University of Toronto Press, 2002), 13–14.

9. Minnesota Chippewa Tribe, *White Earth: A History* (Minnesota Chippewa Tribe, 1989), 1.

10. The Minnesota Chippewa Tribe organized under the Indian Reorganization Act. It is an umbrella government with six member nations, including White Earth. The structure of the MCT will be discussed at length in chapter 2.

11. It is currently estimated that by 2040 it is unlikely that any children being born will have one quarter or more MCT blood and, thus, there will be no new MCT citizens. Furthermore, by 2090 no living person will have one-quarter MCT blood and the nation will cease to exist. Jill Doerfler, "Population Projections: 75% of WE Members Are Over the Age of 40," *Anishinaabeg Today: A Monthly Chronicle of the White Earth Nation*, September 5, 2012, 15.

12. As Elizabeth Cook-Lynn has observed, "The 'blood quantum debate,' the '*ethnic* identity' issue, has finally obscured or dismissed one of the important sovereign rights of Indian nations, and neither Congress nor the Supreme Court had to act in its usual dubious ways." Quoted in Gerald Vizenor, *Manifest Manners: Narratives on Postindian Survivance* (Lincoln: University of Nebraska Press, 1999), 88.

13. Robert Desjarlait, "Blood Quantum v. Lineal Descent: How Much Indian Are You?," *The Circle: Native American News and Arts* 22, no. 11 (November 2001): 13.

14. Ibid., 13.

15. For example, Anishinaabe scholar Anton Treuer has written about his own family, noting that he is not a citizen of any Native nation but his mother is a White Earth citizen. He has a blended family with nine children, three of whom are citizens of the Leech Lake Nation. Treuer describes a poignant event that gets at the heart of citizenship and belonging. He brought his children to a holiday celebration at Leech Lake. They all lined up to receive a gift from "Santa," but tribal employees only gave the enrolled children gifts and told the others they would not be given a gift. Treuer confesses: "Enrolled or not, all of my children know who they are, but I cannot protect them all from the very tangible pain of exclusion by their own tribe—exclusion from a petty Christmas ritual, yes, and from the deep sense of belonging that accompanies tribal citizenship." Anton Treuer, "How Has Tribal Enrollment Affected You Personally?," in *Everything You Wanted to Know about Indians but Were Afraid to Ask* (St. Paul: Borealis Books, Minnesota Historical Society, 2012), 115–16.

16. Carol Goldberg, "Members Only: Designing Citizenship Requirements for Tribal Nations," in *American Indian Constitutional Reform and the Rebuilding of Native Nations*, ed. Eric D. Lemont (Austin: University of Texas Press, 2006), 108.

17. Gerald Vizenor and Jill Doerfler, *The White Earth Nation: Ratification of a Native Democratic Constitution* (Lincoln: University of Nebraska Press, 2012).

INTRODUCTION

1. Ransom Judd Powell Papers, undated, 1843, and 1896–1938, R.5: p. 69–70/ frame 71–72, Minnesota Historical Society, St. Paul.
2. Jill Doerfler, "Population Projections: 75% of WE Members Are over the Age of 40," *Anishinaabeg Today: A Monthly Chronicle of the White Earth Nation*, September 5, 2012, 15. The MCT followed up with a more comprehensive study, and the final report was issued in May 2014. Wilder Research, "Minnesota Chippewa Tribe: Population Projections," May 2014, http://www .whiteearth.com/news/?news_id=102.
3. Doerfler, "Population Projections," 15.
4. Anishinaabe historian William Warren gave several possibilities for the origin and meaning of "Ojibwa," including the suggestion that the word denotes a specific aspect of popular moccasins, which were named Ojibwa moccasins. However, Warren believes the word more likely means "to roast and pucker up," a meaning he estimates refers to the way that enemy captives were roasted or tortured using fire. Warren notes that this name is relatively new, and that "as a race or distinct people they denominate themselves A-wish-in-aub-ay," commonly spelled as "Anishinaabe" today. William Warren, *History of the Ojibway People* (St. Paul: Minnesota Historical Society Press, 1984), 35–37.

   For more on names, see Gerald Vizenor, *The Everlasting Sky: Voices of the Anishinabe People*, especially chapter 1, "The Sacred Names Were Changed" (Minneapolis: Minnesota Historical Society Press, 2000), 1–13.
5. Kathy Davis Graves and Elizabeth Ebbott, *Indians in Minnesota*, 5th ed. (Minneapolis: University of Minnesota Press, 2006), 26.
6. For more information on the word "Ojibwe," see Anton Treuer, "What's in a Name: The Meaning of Ojibwe," *Oshkaabewis Native Journal* 2, no. 1 (Fall 1995): 39–41.
7. Dennis Jones, "The Etymology of Anishinaabe," *Oshkaabewis Native Journal* 2, no. 1 (Fall 1995): 43.
8. In using Anishinaabe(g), I also work to support what Gerald Vizenor terms "postindian identity." He asserts that *indian*, which he insists be used only in lowercase letters and in italics, is a misnomer that enacts manifest destiny. On the other hand, postindian names work to "transpose the *indian* simulations" and allow Anishinaabeg to endure humanity. He writes: "Consider the burden of the name *indian*, and other names that modify the situation, such as *chippewa indian*. The natives who must bear these names are known, in their own language, as *anishinaabe*." Gerald Vizenor and A. Robert Lee, *Postindian Conversations* (Lincoln: University of Nebraska Press, 1999), 156.

9. The term "band" often refers to the divisions within the Anishinaabe collective. Stark has observed, "Bands were originally constituted by a number of families that lived together in the same village. Today, the Anishinaabe continue to divide along band lines yet maintain a shared identity through common ancestry as Anishinaabe people." Heidi Kiiwetinepinesiik Stark, "Marked by Fire: Anishinaabe Articulations of Nationhood in Treaty Making with the United States and Canada," *American Indian Quarterly* 36, no. 2 (Spring 2012): 146 n. 26. Like Stark, I primarily employ the term "nation" in place of band because it more accurately reflects the political autonomy of these entities.

10. Vizenor and Lee, *Postindian Conversations*, 21.

11. Vine Deloria Jr., *Custer Died for Your Sins: An Indian Manifesto* (Norman: University of Oklahoma Press, 1988), 81–82.

12. Natives are not immune to the *indian*. Comanche author and curator Paul Chaat Smith reveals that some Natives find the romantic stereotypes of Native identity compelling: "For our part, we dimly accept the role of spiritual masters and first environmentalists as we switch cable channels and videotape our weddings and ceremonies. We take pride in westerns that make us look gorgeous (which we are!) and have good production values. We secretly wish we were more like the Indians in the movies." Paul Chaat Smith, *Everything You Know about Indians Is Wrong* (Minneapolis: University of Minnesota Press, 2009), 6.

13. Vizenor and Lee, *Postindian Conversations*, 84–85.

14. Ibid., 157.

15. Ibid., 85.

16. Vizenor, *The Everlasting Sky*, 19–20.

17. Scott Lyons, "Actually Existing Indian Nations: Modernity, Diversity, and the Future of Native American Studies," *American Indian Quarterly* 35, no. 3 (Summer 2011): 302–3.

18. Paul Spruhan, "A Legal History of Blood Quantum in Federal Indian Law to 1935," *South Dakota Law Review* 51, no. 1 (2006): 23–36.

19. For a detailed analysis of Galton's theory of fractional inheritance, see Daniel J. Kevles, *In the Name of Eugenics: Genetics and the Uses of Human Heredity* (Cambridge, MA: Harvard University Press, 1995).

20. American definitions of whiteness have changed over time; see David R. Roediger, *Working toward Whiteness: How America's Immigrants Became White: The Strange Journey from Ellis Island to the Suburbs* (New York: Basic Books, 2006).

21. Joanne Barker, *Native Acts: Law, Recognition, and Cultural Authenticity* (Durham, NC: Duke University Press, 2011), 94.

22. Patrick Wolfe, "Land, Labour, and Difference: Elementary Structures of Race," *American Historical Review* 106, no. 3 (June 2001): 887. For a comparison of the racialization of American Indians and African Americans, see Bethany Berger, "Red: Racism and the American Indian," *UCLA Law Review* 56 (2009): 591–656.

23. Historian Patricia Limerick deduced that the United States "set the blood quantum at one quarter, hold to it as a rigid definition of Indians, let intermarriage proceed as it had for centuries, and eventually Indians will be defined out of existence. When that happens, the federal government will be freed of its persistent 'Indian problem.'" Limerick, *The Legacy of Conquest: The Unbroken Past of the American West* (New York: W.W. Norton, 1987), 338.

24. Angela Gonzales, Judy Kertész, and Gabrielle Tayac, "Eugenics as Indian Removal: Sociohistorical Processes and the De(con)struction of American Indians in the Southeast," *Public Historian* 39, no. 3 (Summer 2007): 53–67.

25. J. Kēhaulani Kauanui, *Hawaiian Blood: Colonialism and the Politics of Sovereignty and Indigeneity* (Durham, NC: Duke University Press, 2008), 9.

26. Chadwick Allen, *Blood Narrative: Indigenous Identity in American Indian and Maori Literary and Activist Texts* (Durham, NC: Duke University Press, 2002), 176.

27. For detailed cases of how Native land titles declined in New England and how Natives disappeared in the minds of Europeans, see Jean M. O'Brien, *Dispossession by Degrees: Indian Land and Identity in Natick, Massachusetts, 1650–1790* (Cambridge: Cambridge University Press, 1997).

28. Eva Marie Garroutte, *Real Indians: Identity and the Survival of Native America* (Berkeley: University of California Press, 2003), 42.

29. In the *History of the Ojibway People* (St. Paul: Minnesota Historical Society Press, 2009), Anishinaabe historian William Warren described the extensive intermarriage that occurred between the Anishinaabeg and the Dakota prior to the twentieth century. Warren told how after a period of warfare, the Anishinaabeg and Dakota "intermingled freely" on the St. Croix, where they camped together and intermarriages took place. In addition to creating relatives through intermarriage, the Anishinaabeg and Dakota adopted tribal members. Often during a period of peace, a Dakota and Anishinaabe would exchange presents and adopt each other. Those who had lost relations during the previous fighting sought to fill the void left by those who passed on, and members most often entered into this adoptive relationship. Adoptive ties were strong and meaningful. Warren noted many instances in which during periods of warfare adoptive relatives saved the lives of one another. This classic work gives some insight into Anishinaabe understandings of the ways in

which "others" could be accepted and incorporated. Intermarriage and adoption were processes of merger and incorporation and served to create large kinship networks and alliances. These fluid and flexible boundaries served Anishinaabeg well and were important survival strategies during periods of high death rates due to warfare, disease, and decreased resources. During this time period, separation and exclusion would have not served Anishinaabe interests or contributed to their survivance (164–65).

See also Patricia Albers and Jeanne Kay, "Sharing the Land: A Study in American Indian Territoriality," in *A Cultural Geography of North American Indians*, ed. Thomas Ross and Tyrel Moore (Boulder, CO: Westview Press, 1987) for a discussion of intermarriage and identity among the Anishinaabe during the 1800s.

In addition, nearly every story about Anishinaabe life in the late nineteenth and early twentieth centuries in *Rainy River Lives* contains a story of adoption. Maggie Wilson, *Rainy River Lives: Stories by Maggie Wilson*, ed. Sally Cole (Lincoln: University of Nebraska Press, 2009).

30. Scott L. Gould, "Mixing Bodies and Beliefs: The Predicament of Tribes," *Columbia Law Review* 101, no. 4 (May 2001): 748, 757.

31. Russell Thornton, *American Indian Holocaust and Survival: A Population History since 1492* (Norman: University of Oklahoma Press, 1987), 236–37.

32. Kevin Leecy, quoted in "Tribal/State Pact Keeps Kids with Indian Families," *Anishinaabeg Today: A Chronicle of the White Earth Band*, March 7, 2007.

33. Pamela D. Palmater, *Beyond Blood: Rethinking Indigenous Identity* (Saskatoon, Saskatchewan: Purich Publishing, 2011), 178.

34. David E. Wilkins and Heidi Kiiwetinepinesiik Stark, *American Indian Politics and the American Political System*, 3rd ed. (Lanham, MD: Rowman & Littlefield Publishers, 2011), 312–13.

35. Joanne Barker, "For Whom Sovereignty Matters," in *Sovereignty Matters: Locations of Contestation and Possibility in Indigenous Struggles for Self-Determination*, ed. Joanne Barker (Lincoln: University of Nebraska Press, 2005), 26.

36. For an in-depth analysis of these cases, see David E. Wilkins, *American Indian Sovereignty and the U.S. Supreme Court: The Masking of Justice* (Austin: University of Texas Press, 1997); Robert A. Williams Jr., *Like a Loaded Weapon: The Rehnquist Court, Indian Rights, and the Legal History of Racism in America* (Minneapolis: University of Minnesota Press, 2005).

37. Cherokee Nation v. Georgia, 30 U.S. (5 Pet.) 1, 20 (1831).

38. Worcester v. Georgia, 31 U.S. (6 Pet.) 515, 559 (1832).

39. Ibid., 560–61.

40. A good collection of essays exploring sovereignty is Joanne Barker's *Sovereignty Matters*. See also Amanda Cobb, "Understanding Tribal Sovereignty:

Definitions, Conceptualizations, and Interpretations," joint publication of the *Journal of Indigenous Studies* 1 (Fall 2005/Spring 2006) and *American Studies* 46 (Fall/Winter 2005): 115–32; Wallace Coffey and Rebecca Tsosie, "Rethinking the Tribal Sovereignty Doctrine: Cultural Sovereignty and the Collective Future of Indian Nations," *Stanford Law and Policy Review* 12, no. 2 (Spring 2001): 191–210; Vine Deloria Jr., "Self-Determination and the Concept of Sovereignty," in *Economic Development in American Indian Reservations*, ed. Roxanne Dunbar Ortiz (Albuquerque: University of New Mexico, Native American Studies, 1979), 22–28.

41. Taiaiake Alfred, *Peace, Power, and Righteousness* (Oxford: Oxford University Press Canada, 1999), 55–56.

42. Ibid., 59.

43. Gerald Vizenor, *The Heirs of Columbus* (Hanover, NH: University Press of New England, 1991), 7.

44. Gerald Vizenor, *Fugitive Poses* (Lincoln: University of Nebraska Press, 2000), 182.

45. For a longer discussion of transmotion and sovereignty, see Niigonwedom James Sinclair, "A Sovereignty of Transmotion: Imagination and the 'Real,' Gerald Vizenor, and Native Literary Nationalism," in *Stories through Theories/Theories through Stories: North American Indian Writing, Storytelling, and Critique*, ed. Gordon D. Henry Jr., Nieves Pascual Soler, and Silvia Martinez-Falquina (East Lansing: Michigan State University Press, 2009), 123–58.

46. Vizenor, *Fugitive Poses*, 184.

47. Following the practice set forth by Gerald Vizenor, I use italics and a lower case "i" here to draw attention to the fictional image, which has too often taken the place of actual Natives. He has noted that the "misrecognition of natives as *indians* is both oppressive and a prison of false identities"; Vizenor, *Fugitive Poses*, 22.

48. Simon J. Ortiz, "Towards a National Indian Literature: Cultural Authenticity in Nationalism," *MELUS* 8, no. 2 (1981): 10.

49. Jace Weaver, Craig S. Womack, and Robert Warrior, *American Indian Literary Nationalism* (Albuquerque: University of New Mexico Press, 2005), 111.

50. Federal acknowledgement or recognition is the establishment of the government-to-government relationship that American Indian nations have with the United States. For a variety of reasons, some nations are not recognized as such by the United States and can gain that status through the Federal Acknowledgment Process. For an excellent study of federal recognition, see Brian Klopotek, *Indigeneity, Race, and Federal Tribal Recognition Policy in Three Louisiana Indian Communities* (Durham, NC: Duke University Press, 2011); Amy E. Den Ouden and Jean M. O'Brien, eds., *Recognition,*

Sovereignty Struggles, and Indigenous Rights in the United States (Chapel Hill: University of North Carolina Press, 2013).

51. Renee Ann Cramer, *Cash, Color, and Colonialism: The Politics of Tribal Acknowledgment* (Norman: University of Oklahoma Press, 2005), 107.

52. Indeed, some have challenged the racial and cultural identity of the Pequots. In *Without Reservation*, Jeff Benedict asserts that Congress was tricked into granting federal recognition to the Mashantucket Pequots and raises serious questions about their identity as American Indians, going so far as to suggest they are opportunistic frauds simply "cashing in" on casinos. Jeff Benedict, *Without Reservation: The Making of America's Most Powerful Indian Tribe and Foxwoods, the World's Largest Casino* (New York: HarperCollins, 2000). In her article "Identity at Mashantucket," Mary Lawlor observes that there is a diversity of opinions on the identity of the Pequots, noting, "While non-Native as well as Native supporters of the Pequots found historical justice in their federal acknowledgment, others have been indignant from the start at what they claim are the tribe's dubious origins." Lawlor, "Identity in Mashantucket," *American Quarterly* 57, no. 1 (2005): 156.

    The story of the Mashantucket Pequots has garnered much attention, and several books have recently been published that address their story as well as broader themes of identity, gaming, and tribal sovereignty. See Kim Isaac Eisler, *Revenge of the Pequots: How a Small Native American Tribe Created the World's Most Profitable Casino* (Lincoln: University of Nebraska Press, 2002); Brett Duval Fromson, *Hitting the Jackpot: The Inside Story of the Richest Indian Tribe in History* (New York: Grove Press, 2004); Eve Darian-Smith, *New Capitalists: Law, Politics, and Identity surrounding Casino Gaming on Native American Land* (Belmont, CA: Wadsworth Publishing, 2003); Steve Andrew Light and Kathryn R. L. Rand, *Indian Gaming and Tribal Sovereignty: The Casino Compromise* (Lawrence: University of Kansas Press, 2005).

53. Cramer, *Cash, Color, and Colonialism*, 59.

54. A classic work on the construction of Indians is Robert F. Berkhofer, *The White Man's Indian: Images of the American Indian from Columbus to the Present* (New York: Vintage, 1979).

55. In *The Nations Within: The Past and Future of American Indian Sovereignty*, Deloria and Lytle argue that self-government "implies a recognition by the superior political power that some measure of local decision making is necessary but that this process must be monitored very carefully so that its products are compatible with the goals and policies of the larger political power." While Deloria and Lytle contend that sovereignty is not an American Indian conception, they also concede that self-government has been a useful concept to use when dealing with Western nation-states because it opens space to negotiate.

Self-government is not the final answer, and now that space has been opened, it is time to push for American Indian conceptions of power. Vine Deloria Jr. and Clifford M. Lytle, *The Nations Within: The Past and Future of American Indian Sovereignty* (Austin: University of Texas Press, 1998), 14.

56. Alfred, *Peace, Power, and Righteousness*, 62–65.

57. For a discussion of the term and its history, see Gerald Vizenor, ed., *Survivance: Narratives of Native Presence* (Lincoln: University of Nebraska Press, 2008).

58. Gerald Vizenor, *Manifest Manners* (Lincoln: University of Nebraska Press, 1999), vii.

59. Vizenor and Lee, *Postindian Conversations*, 93.

60. John D. Nichols and Earl Nyholm, *A Concise Dictionary of Minnesota Ojibwe* (Minneapolis: University of Minnesota Press, 1995), 85.

61. Melissa A. Pflug, *Ritual and Myth in Odawa Revitalization: Reclaiming a Sovereign Place* (Norman: University of Oklahoma Press, 1998), 6, 25.

62. Vizenor and Lee, *Postindian Conversations*, 93.

63. For example, in "The Baron of Patronia," Vizenor's mixed-blood character Luster Brown "over-turned an instance in racial hocus-pocus" through his ability to raise and nurture children at White Earth. This ability of those who have been defined by the federal government as mixed-blood to survive and create new generations is a reversal of blood quantum. This story rejects the idea that those who are mixed-blood cannot create new generations of Indian people. Much of Vizenor's work deals with mixed-bloods—or "cross-bloods," as he would say. I think Vizenor is using these characters to make the point that blood quantum is not an appropriate means to define a person's identity. Gerald Vizenor, "The Baron of Patronia," in *Talking Leaves: Contemporary Native American Short Stories*, ed. Craig Lesley (New York: Dell Publishing, 1991), 284–93.

64. See "Indigenous Peoples Are Nations, Not Minorities," chapter 2 in David E. Wilkins and Heidi Kiiwetinepinesiik Stark's *American Indian Politics and the American Political System*, 3rd ed. (Lanham, MD: Rowman & Littlefield, 2011), for a more detailed explanation of this complex issue.

65. Scott Lyons, *X-Marks: Native Signatures of Assent* (Minneapolis: University of Minnesota Press, 2010), 126.

66. Felix S. Cohen, *Handbook of Federal Indian Law* (1942; New York: AMS Press, 1982), 19. A notable departure from this is *United States v. Rogers*, in which for the first time the Supreme Court established a biologically defined racial constraint on the federal definition of "Indian." For a full analysis of how race has functioned in Indian law, with specific attention to *United States v. Rogers*, see Bethany R. Berger, "Power over This Unfortunate Race: Race, Politics, and Indian Law in United States v. Rogers," *William & Mary Law Review* 45, no. 5 (2004): 1957–2052.

67. In fact, the American Anthropological Association has created a traveling museum exhibit, an interactive website, and educational materials entitled "RACE: Are We So Different?" to educate Americans about the history of the construction of race. See http://www.aaanet.org/resources/A-Public -Education-Program.cfm and http://www.understandingrace.org.

68. American Anthropological Association Statement on "Race," adopted on May 17, 1998, http://www.understandingrace.org/about/statement.html.

69. See Paul Spruhan, "A Legal History of Blood Quantum in Federal Indian Law to 1935," *South Dakota Law Review* 51, no. 1 (2006): 1–50.

70. There has been much legal debate about the degree of political sovereignty held by American Indian nations. This work does not examine the degree of sovereignty held by American Indian nations nor the precise details of their complex relationships with the United States. In addition, the term "nationhood" and its various possible definitions have become popular scholarly debate.

 For more information on nationhood, see Benedict Anderson, *Imagined Communities: Reflections on the Origin and Spread of Nationalism*, rev. ed. (New York: Verso, 2006); Ernest Gellner, *Nations and Nationalism*, 2nd ed. (Ithaca, NY: Cornell University Press, 2009); Rogers Brubaker, *Citizenship and Nationhood in France and Germany* (Cambridge, MA: Harvard University Press, 1998). The academic journal *Nations and Nationalism* is devoted to "the growing research interest in nationalism that has been simulated by the increasing proliferation of nationalist movements throughout the world." On American Indian conceptions of nationhood, see Audra Simpson, *Mohawk Interruptus: Political Life across the Borders of Settler States* (Durham, NC: Duke University Press, 2014); Jean Dennison, *Colonial Entanglement: Constituting a Twenty-first Century Osage Nation* (Chapel Hill: University of North Carolina Press, 2012); Weaver et al., *American Indian Literary Nationalism*; Cheryl Walker, *Indian Nation: Native American Literature and Nineteenth-Century Nationalisms* (Durham, NC: Duke University Press, 1997); David A. Chang, "'An Equal Interest in the Soil': Creek Small-Scale Farming and the Work of Nationhood, 1866– 1889," *American Indian Quarterly* 33, no. 1 (Winter 2009): 98–130; Pauline Turner Strong and Barrik van Winkle, "Tribe and Nation: American Indians and American Nationalism," *Social Analysis* 33 (September 1993): 9–26.

71. Raymond Williams, *Keywords*, rev. ed. (New York: Oxford University Press, 1983), 213.

72. Alfred, *Peace, Power, and Righteousness*, 65. Emphasis original.

73. Wilkins and Stark, *American Indian Politics and the American Political System*, 310–11.

74. Stark, "Marked by Fire," 123.

75. Ibid., 124.

76. Brubaker, *Citizenship and Nationhood in France and Germany*, 3.

77. Ibid.

78. Brubaker asserts: "Modern national citizenship was an invention of the French Revolution. The formal delimitation of the citizenry; the establishment of civil equality, entailing shared rights and shared obligations; the institutionalization of political rights; the legal rationalization and ideological accentuation of the distinction between citizens and foreigners; the articulation of the doctrine of national sovereignty and of the link between citizenship and nationhood; the substitution of immediate, direct relations characteristic of the ancient regime—the Revolution brought all these developments together on a national level for the first time." Ibid., 35.

79. Ibid., 10–17.

80. Felix S. Cohen, *Handbook of Federal Indian Law* (1942; New York: AMS Press, 1982), 20.

81. *Waldron v. the United States et al.*, 1 July 1905, No. 43, Circuit Court, D. South Dakota, 143 F. 413, U.S. App. (1905).

82. *Santa Clara Pueblo et al., v. Julia Martinez et al.*, 15 May 1978, 36 U.S. 49, Supreme Court (1978). Despite this recognition, there are a few exceptional cases in which tribes are federally required to have specific criteria defining tribal citizenship. Eva Marie Garroutte, "The Racial Formation of American Indians: Negotiating Legitimate Identities within Tribal and Federal Law," *American Indian Quarterly* 25, no. 2 (Spring 2001): 224.

    In addition, federal legislation that defines Indians as anyone other than tribal citizens has also eroded the authority of Native nations to determine citizenship criteria. For a discussion of the ways in which federal legislation, including the General Allotment Act, Indian Reorganization Act, Indian Civil Rights Act, and Indian Gaming Regulatory Act, has infringed upon tribal authority, see Nicole J. Laughlin, "Identity Crisis: An Examination of Federal Infringement on Tribal Authority to Determine Membership," *Hamline Law Review* 30, no. 1 (Winter 2007): 97–123.

83. Santa Clara Pueblo v. Martinez, 436 U.S. 49, 72 n. 32 (1978) cited in Ibid, 98.

84. Matthew L. M. Fletcher, "Santa Clara Pueblo v. Martinez," *Encyclopedia of American Civil Liberties* (New York: Routledge, 2006). For more information on this case, see Catharine A. MacKinnon, "Whose Culture? A Case Note on Martinez v. Santa Clara Pueblo," in *Feminism Unmodified: Discourses on Life and Law* (Cambridge, MA: Harvard University Press, 1987), 63–69; Rina Swentzell, "Testimony of a Santa Clara Woman," *Kansas Journal of Law & Public Policy* 14, no. 1 (2004): 97–102; Gloria Valencia-Weber, "Santa Clara Pueblo v. Martinez: Twenty-five Years of Disparate Cultural Visions," *Kansas Journal of Law & Public Policy* 14, no. 1 (2004): 49–66.

85. *The New American Webster Handy College Dictionary*, 3rd ed., edited by Albert and Loy Morehead (New York: Penguin Books, 1995), 130.

86. About two-thirds of American Indians had already become U.S. citizens via the General Allotment Act of 1887 and other means.

87. While some American Indians desired citizenship, there was and continues to be resistance to U.S. citizenship. For example, after the passage of the act, the Grand Council of the Iroquois Confederacy wrote to Congress expressing their rejection of U.S. citizenship. See Chief Oren Lyons and John Mohawk, eds., *Exiled in the Land of the Free: Democracy, Indian Nations, and the U.S. Constitution* (Santa Fe, NM: Clear Light Publishers, 1992).

88. Lilias C. Jones Jarding, "Citizenship: United States and State," in *Encyclopedia of United States Indian Policy and Law*, ed. Paul Finkelman and Tim Alan Garrison (Washington, DC: CQ Press, 2009), 178–81. See also Wilkins and Stark, *American Indian Politics and the American Political System*, 174–79.

89. However, it is important to note that about sixty tribes adopted constitutions prior to the passage of the IRA. Felix S. Cohen, *On the Drafting of Tribal Constitutions*, ed. David E. Wilkins (Norman: University of Oklahoma Press, 2006), xxi.

90. Vine Deloria Jr. and Clifford M. Lytle, *The Nations Within* (Austin: University of Texas Press, 1984), 18–19.

91. For example, in chapter 2, I will closely examine the interventions of the U.S. secretary of the Interior and other officials in the establishment of citizenship criteria for the Minnesota Chippewa Tribe.

92. Kirsty Gover, *Tribal Constitutionalism: States, Tribes, and the Governance of Membership* (Oxford: Oxford University Press, 2010), 6.

93. Ibid., 132.

94. Ibid., 133.

95. Garroutte, "Racial Formation," 225–26. See also Melissa L. Meyer, "American Indian Blood Quantum Requirements: Blood Is Thicker Than Family," in *Over the Edge: Remapping the American West*, ed. Valerie J. Matsumoto and Blake Allmendinger (Berkeley: University of California Press, 1999), 231–44.

96. Carol Goldberg, "Members Only: Designing Citizenship Requirements for Tribal Nations," in *American Indian Constitutional Reform and the Rebuilding of Native Nations*, ed. Eric D. Lemont (Austin: University of Texas Press, 2006), 132.

97. Some examples include Elizabeth Larson, "Indian Disenrollments a Statewide, Nationwide Issue," *Lake Country News*, December 6, 2008; Jodi Rave, "Tribal Enrollment a Contentious Issue for Native People," *Missoulian*, October 31, 2008; Ray Henry, "Members Removed from Indian Tribes Complain of Unfairness," *South Coast Today*, October 26, 2007; Mary Pierpoint,

"Seminole Nation Changes Tribal Enrollment," *Indian Country Today*, July 19, 2000.

98. David Wilkins, "Self-Determination or Self-Decimation? Banishment and Disenrollment in Indian Country," *Indian Country Today*, August 25, 2006.

99. David Wilkins, "Depopulation in Indian Country: 21st Century Style," paper delivered at University of Minnesota-Duluth, April 9, 2009.

CHAPTER 1. NO, NO THERE WAS NO MIXED-BLOODS: MAPPING ANISHINAABE CONCEPTIONS OF IDENTITY

1. Janet A. McDonnell, *The Dispossession of the American Indian, 1887–1934* (Bloomington: Indiana University Press, 1991), 2. Political rhetoric surrounding the policy was that individual European-style landownership would teach Indians individualism and selfishness, which were seen as necessary characteristics for the assimilation of Native people into dominant society. Sharon O'Brien, *American Indian Tribal Governments* (Norman: University of Oklahoma Press, 1989), 78.

   While many scholars argue that the trust relationship was established in treaties, some scholars argue that it was established through a variety of other means. See David E. Wilkins and K. Tsianina Lomawaima, "'With the Greatest Trust and Fidelity': The Trust Doctrine," in *Uneven Ground: American Indian Sovereignty and Federal Indian Law* (Norman: University of Oklahoma Press, 2002).

2. Quoted in John P. LaVelle, "The General Allotment Act 'Eligibility' Hoax: Distortions of Law, Policy, and History in Derogation of Indian Tribes," *Wicazo Sa Review* 14, no. 1 (Spring 1999): 257.

3. Ibid.

4. Melissa L. Meyer, "American Indian Blood Quantum Requirements: Blood Is Thicker Than Family," in *Over the Edge: Remapping the American West*, ed. Valerie J. Matsumoto and Blake Allmendinger (Berkeley: University of California Press, 1999), 232–33.

5. Carol Goldberg, "Members Only: Designing Citizenship Requirements for Tribal Nations," in *American Indian Constitutional Reform and the Rebuilding of Native Nations*, ed. Eric D. Lemont (Austin: University of Texas Press, 2006), 122.

6. Katherine Ellinghaus, "The Benefits of Being Indian: Blood Quanta, Intermarriage, and Allotment Policy on the White Earth Reservation, 1889–1920," *Frontiers: A Journal of Women Studies*, nos. 2 & 3 (2008): 89–90.

7. Chairman to Commission of Indian Affairs, 8 March 1893, E1298 Letters Sent by the Chairman, 1893–1900, Chippewa Commission Records, RG 75, NARA-Great Lakes Region, quoted in Ellinghaus, "The Benefits of Being Indian," 91.

8. Ibid., 90–91.

9. The vague terms used in this legislation caused confusion, and in 1895 the assistant attorney general ruled that in order for an individual to qualify as "Chippewa Indian" under the Nelson Act, they must have Chippewa Indian blood, have a recognized connection with one of the bands in Minnesota, have been a Minnesota resident when the act was passed, and move to a reservation with the intention of living there permanently. This ruling did not necessarily provide much clarification. In addition, it excluded children of Anishinaabe women who had married non-Indians, but extended qualification to those who had received "half-breed script" under the 1854 and 1855 treaties. Melissa L. Meyer, *The White Earth Tragedy: Ethnicity and Dispossession at a Minnesota Anishinaabe Reservation, 1889–1920* (Lincoln: University of Nebraska Press, 1994), 59–60.

10. See pp. 50–67 in Meyer's *White Earth Tragedy* for a detailed discussion of both the commission and the migration to White Earth. See also Minnesota Chippewa Tribe, *White Earth A History* (Minnesota Chippewa Tribe, 1989), 30–34; Kathy Davis Graves and Elizabeth Ebbott, *Indians in Minnesota*, 5th ed. (Minneapolis: University of Minnesota Press, 2006), 45–46.

11. Edward Michael Peterson Jr., "That So-Called Warranty Deed: Clouded Land Titles on the White Earth Indian Reservation in Minnesota," *North Dakota Law Review* 59, no. 2 (1983): 162.

12. This counts additional allotments that were made after 1904 when the President was authorized to allot pine lands, which had been previously exempted. Ibid., 162–65.

13. C. F. Larrabee to Mrs. Stella Tourville, 20 September 1907, National Archives and Records Administration Facility at Washington, DC, Record Group 75, Records of the Bureau of Indian Affairs, Central Classified Files [hereafter NARA-DC, RG 75, CCF], White Earth File 72487, 1907, 053.

14. More information on the reasons for Tourville's denial would be helpful because it could reveal a great deal about how and why individuals were accepted and rejected from White Earth. Alexandra Harmon has done excellent work on the complexities of enrollment in "Tribal Enrollment Councils: Lessons on Law and Indian Identity," in which she details the complexities of blood/race, kinship, culture, politics, and economics that the enrollment council on the Colville Indian Reservation balanced and negotiated during the early twentieth century. Alexandra Harmon, "Tribal Enrollment Councils: Lessons on Law and Indian Identity," *Western Historical Quarterly* 32 (Summer 2001): 175–200.

15. Meyer, *The White Earth Tragedy*, 5.
16. Ibid., 5.
17. Ibid., 118–20, 180–83.
18. While competency was not linked to blood quantum in this legislation, it would be federal policy that all allottees with one-half or less Indian blood be issued fee patents from 1917 to 1920. Commissioner of Indian Affairs Cato Sells introduced this policy with no legislative authority, and it was abandoned in 1920 when John Barton Payne became secretary of the Interior, when applications for fee patents were again decided on a case-by-case basis using competency as the litmus test. McDonnell, *The Dispossession of the American Indian*, 107–12.
19. Peterson, "That So-Called Warranty Deed," 165.
20. This legislation only applied to the White Earth Reservation; however, in 1917 Commissioner of Indian Affairs Cato Sells created a policy to unilaterally release all allotted lands held by American Indians of less than one-half Indian blood. While he knew the rationale was not foolproof, he felt "it is almost an axiom that an Indian who has a larger portion of white blood than Indian partakes more of the latter." Only a few years after the implementation of the policy, Sells abandoned it. Sells quoted in Paul Spruhan, "A Legal History of Blood Quantum in Federal Indian Law to 1935," *South Dakota Law Review* 51, no. 1 (2006): 45, emphasis added.
21. Meyer, *The White Earth Tragedy*, 142–43, 152–53.
22. "White blood" was the terminology used by the court. It was assumed that "blood" from European countries was "white blood," but the court did not specifically name the countries that would be included under this designation.
23. Meyer, *The White Earth Tragedy*, 166–67.
24. Stephen Jay Gould, *The Mismeasure of Man* (New York: W.W. Norton and Co., 1996), 88–101. Gould gives a detailed history of the development of racial theory in America during the nineteenth century.
25. Meyer, *The White Earth Tragedy*, 153–55.
26. Ibid., 159–60.
27. John R. Howard to Commissioner of Indian Affairs, 22 August 1908, NARA-DC, RG 75, CCF, White Earth File 57849, 1908, 040.
28. Ibid.
29. Ibid.
30. Meyer, *The White Earth Tragedy*, 159–61.
31. Ibid., 162.
32. Ibid., 163.
33. Special Agent John H. Hinton created the Hinton Roll. He attended the September 1910 annuity payment at White Earth and, in consultation with

Anishinaabe leaders, established the blood quantum of each individual to the sixteenth fraction. Ibid., 162.

34. Peterson, "That So-Called Warranty Deed," 169.

35. Index to Ransom Judd Powell Papers, undated, 1843, 1896–1938, M455, Minnesota Historical Society, St. Paul. Powell was well known as an attorney for Minnesota lumber companies and had represented their interests on many occasions. He continued to advise his clients on their cases while he worked on the blood roll. In *The White Earth Tragedy*, Meyer details the devious and illegal activities Powell engaged in (163–71; quote on 164).

36. Meyer, *The White Earth Tragedy*, 166–67.

37. There is a vast literature on the symbolism of blood in a wide variety of cultures. Yet no such study exists for Anishinaabeg, making unclear what role blood played in society during the nineteenth century.

38. Melissa L. Meyer, *Thicker Than Water: The Origins of Blood as Symbol and Ritual* (New York: Routledge, 2005), 5.

39. Brackette Williams, "The Impact of the Precepts of Nationalism on the Concept of Culture: Making Grasshoppers out of Naked Apes," *Cultural Critique* 24, no. 2 (1993): 162. See also Brackette Williams, "A Class Act: Anthropology and the Race to Nation across Ethnic Terrain," *Annual Review of Anthropology* 18 (1989): 401–44.

40. Meyer, "American Indian Blood," 238–39.

41. Yet it remains unclear why "blood" became so central in United States policy. In 1999, Melissa Meyer asserted, "No one has explored in a serious scholarly fashion how the enrollment process evolved or how 'blood quantum' or degree of Indian 'blood' came to be one of the most important criteria used first by federal policy makers." Ibid., 231.

Additionally, the courts were not consistent in their rulings. For example, Michael A. Elliott has noted, "In 1880 . . . a federal district court in Oregon ruled that a person with equal parts of white and Indian ancestry is 'strictly speaking' neither Indian nor white." Michael A. Elliott, "Telling the Difference: Nineteenth-Century Legal Narratives of Racial Taxonomy," *Law & Social Inquiry* 24, no. 3 (Summer 1999): 626, n. 23.

42. Charles J. Kappler, ed. and comp., *Indian Affairs: Laws and Treaties*, vol. 2 (Washington, DC: Government Printing Office, 1904), 543.

43. Quoted in Theresa M. Schenck, *William W. Warren: The Life, Letters, and Times of an Ojibwe Leader* (Lincoln: University of Nebraska Press, 2007), 22.

44. Ibid., 23–24.

45. Ibid., 35–40.

46. Kappler, *Indian Affairs*, 568.

47. Ibid., 975.

48. John D. Nichols, ed., *"A Statement Made by the Indians": A Bilingual Petition of the Chippewas of Lake Superior, 1864* (London, Ontario: Center for Research and Teaching of Canadian Native Languages, 1988), 16–17.

49. David Beaulieu, "Curly Hair and Big Feet: Physical Anthropology and Implementation of Land Allotment on the White Earth Chippewa Reservation," *American Indian Quarterly* (Fall 1984): 288.

50. R. R. Bishop Baraga, *A Dictionary of the Otchipwe Language* (1878; repr., Minneapolis: Ross & Hanes, Inc., 1973), 124.

51. Beaulieu, "Curly Hair and Big Feet," 286–87.

52. Following the practice of Gerald Vizenor, I use a lowercase "i" and italics because it is a "simulation and a loan word of dominance; the *indian* is an ironic crease." Gerald Vizenor, *Fugitive Poses* (Lincoln: University of Nebraska Press, 2000), 14. Vizenor asserts, "The *indian* is a simulation, the absence of natives; the *indian* transposes the real, and the simulation of the real has no referent, memories, or native stories" (15).

53. Ibid., 145.

54. Robert F. Berkhofer, *The White Man's Indian: Images of the American Indian from Columbus to the Present* (New York: Vintage, 1979).

55. In *The White Earth Tragedy*, Meyer makes a brief reference to the testimonies collected by this investigation (169), but focuses her efforts on political factionalisms after the land fraud cases and relies on other sources, including letters, newspaper accounts, and government reports for her analysis.

56. John D. Nichols to Jill Doerfler, 12 June 2007, personal communication. "Blood" and "red" in John D. Nichols and Earl Nyholm, *A Concise Dictionary of Minnesota Ojibwe* (Minneapolis: University of Minnesota Press, 1995), 147, 234.

57. Scott Lyons, *X-Marks: Native Signatures of Assent* (Minneapolis: University of Minnesota Press, 2010), 52–53.

58. Ibid., 56. In addition, he notes that for Anishinaabeg "an Indian was someone who lived with and like Indians: it was about the proximity, practice, and principles that people lived by" (56).

59. Meyer, *The White Earth Tragedy*, 118–22.

60. See Vizenor's discussion of the testimony of Anishinaabe Charles Aubid and Native mappers in *Fugitive Poses*, 167–70.

61. Ransom Judd Powell Papers, undated, 1843, and 1896–1938, Minnesota Historical Society, St. Paul [hereafter Ransom Judd Powell Papers], R.4: 409.

62. Ibid., R.4: 414.

63. Ibid., R.4: 416.

64. Ibid., R.5: 968.

65. This is not the famous artist of the same name.

66. Ransom Judd Powell Papers, R.6: 51. I have to thank Kim Tallbear for pointing out that I conflated blood with genes in an earlier version of this analysis. I have revised my assertions and conclusions to reflect the fact that scientists did not articulate the DNA double helix until 1953. She asserts, "I have learned that we need to keep clear the difference between genetic properties and blood quantum as a semiotic and bureaucratic object constituted through other forms of science, namely, the *social* and *policy* sciences" (emphasis original). Kim Tallbear, *Native American DNA: Tribal Belonging and the False Promise of Genetic Science* (Minneapolis: University of Minnesota Press, 2013), 54–55.

67. Ransom Judd Powell Papers, R.6: 51.

68. Ibid., R.6: 100. McIntosh was fifty-seven years old at the time of the interview. She was born at Crow Wing. Ibid., R.6: 95.

69. Ibid., R.6: 142–43.

70. Ibid., R.4: 451.

71. Ibid., R.4: 552.

72. Ibid., R.4: 451–52.

73. See Ellinghaus, "The Benefits of Being Indian," 81–105 for an excellent discussion of intermarriage and some examples of individuals who claimed to be "mixed-blood" as a strategy to control their resources.

74. Vizenor, *Fugitive Poses*, 173.

75. Gerald Vizenor and A. Robert Lee, *Postindian Conversations* (Lincoln: University of Nebraska Press, 1999), 21.

76. Shon-ne-yah-quay, quoted in Meyer, *The White Earth Tragedy*, 166.

77. Ibid., 166.

78. Me-zhug-e-ge-shig is more commonly spelled May-zhuck-ke-ge-shig; however, as with all the names, I have retained the spelling in the testimony records. Historian Bruce White has noted that Me-zhug-e-ge-shig was "a long time leader at White Earth in the late nineteenth century. He had been a war leader and a compatriot of Hole-in-the-Day before the Mississippi Ojibwe moved to White Earth." Bruce White, *We Are at Home: Pictures of the Ojibwe People* (St. Paul: Minnesota Historical Society Press, 2007), 48.

79. Ransom Judd Powell Papers, R.5: 678.

80. John R. Howard to Commissioner of Indian Affairs, 23 June 1914, NARA-DC, RG 75, CCF, White Earth Agency File 20600, 1914, 056.

81. Ibid.

82. Ibid.

83. Ransom Judd Powell Papers, R.4: 494.

84. Ibid.

85. Ibid.

86. Ibid., R.4: 613–14.

87. Ibid.
88. Ibid., R:5: 1038.
89. Ibid., R.4: 681.
90. Ibid., R.5: 422.
91. Vizenor, *Fugitive Poses*, 89.
92. Ransom Judd Powell Papers, R.4: 494; R.6: 50–51.
93. Ibid., R.5: 596.
94. Ibid., R.5: 480.
95. Ibid., R.5: 474.
96. Beaulieu writes: "The terms mixed-blood and half-breed in the Ojibwa language were the same word regardless of percentage of blood. The Chippewa classified a person Indian if he lived with them and adopted their habits and mode of life and classified him a half-breed if he adopted the white man's life." Beaulieu, "Curly Hair and Big Feet," 288.
97. Ransom Judd Powell Papers, R.5: 247.
98. "Swallowing bones" is part of traditional medicinal ceremonies.
99. Ransom Judd Powell Papers, R.5: 459.
100. Vizenor, *Fugitive Poses*, 182.
101. Ransom Judd Powell Papers, R.5: 459; R.6: 83–84.
102. Ibid., R.6: 83–84.
103. Indeed, Gerald Vizenor has argued that "Motion is a natural human right that is not bound by borders." Vizenor, *Fugitive Poses*, 189.
104. The Midewiwin, also spelled Midewin, is known as the Grand Medicine Society. It was and is a powerful and prominent religion among the Anishinaabe as well as the Ottawa and Potawatomi. Members of the Midewiwin are both spiritual leaders and healers. The teachings of the society are recorded on birch-bark scrolls. For more information on this topic, see Michael Angel, *Preserving the Sacred: Historical Perspectives on the Ojibwa Midewiwin* (Winnipeg: University of Manitoba Press, 2002); Frances Densmore, *Chippewa Customs*, reprint (St. Paul: Minnesota Historical Society Press, 1929); Basil Johnston, *Ojibway Ceremonies*, reprint (Lincoln: University of Nebraska Press, 1990); Ruth Landes, *Ojibwa Religion and the Midewiwin* (Madison: University of Wisconsin Press, 1968).
105. Ransom Judd Powell Papers, R.5: 557.
106. Ibid., R.5: 591.
107. Ibid., R.5: 202.
108. Meyer, *The White Earth Tragedy*, 5.
109. Ransom Judd Powell Papers, R.5: 458.
110. Ibid., R.5: 1044.
111. Ibid., R.5: 466.

112. Ibid., R.5: 1025.
113. Gerald Vizenor argues that the invented *indian* is the absence of natives. In this case the absence of the racialized images of the *indian* is the presence of Anishinaabeg. He has observed that "The cultural and political histories of the anishinabe were written in the language of those who invented the *indian* . . . divided ancestry by geometric degrees—the federal government identifies the anishinabe by degrees of *indian* blood. . . . The inventions of the dominant society have nothing to do with the heart of the people." Vizenor, *The Everlasting Sky*, 13.
114. For detailed information on the findings of the physical examinations, see Aleš Hrdlička, "Anthropology of the Chippewa," *Holmes Anniversary Volume of Anthropological Essays* (1916), found at the Newberry Library, Chicago; and Albert Ernest Jenks, "Indian-White Amalgamation: An Anthropometic Study," *Studies in the Social Sciences*, no. 6 (Minneapolis: Bulletin of the University of Minnesota, 1916).
115. In his dissertation, "Weeds in Linnaeus's Garden: Science and Segregation, Eugenics, and the Rhetoric of Racism at the University of Minnesota and the Big Ten, 1900–45," Mark Soderstrom uses Jenks's life and career to "examine the evolution of anthropology as a discipline within its national context." Due in part to his work at White Earth, Jenks was one of a hundred people appointed by the secretary of the Interior to assist the United States in creating Indian policy in 1923. Mark Soderstrom, "Weeds in Linnaeus's Garden: Science and Segregation, Eugenics, and the Rhetoric of Racism at the University of Minnesota and the Big Ten, 1900–45" (PhD diss., University of Minnesota, 2004), 49, 70. For a short summary of Jenks's career, see Tim Brady, "Primitive Thinking," *Minnesota: The Magazine of the University of Minnesota Alumni Association* (March–April 2008), 26–31.
116. Soderstrom, "Weeds in Linaeus's Garden," 73. In addition to his work at the Smithsonian, Hrdlička was the founder and editor of the *American Journal of Physical Anthropology*, and cofounder of the American Association of Physical Anthropologists.
117. Beaulieu, "Curly Hair and Big Feet," 282, 293–98.
118. Ibid., 282, 288; Richard H. Weil, "Destroying a Homeland: White Earth, Minnesota," *American Indian Culture and Research Journal* 13, no. 2 (1989): 71–73; Meyer, *The White Earth Tragedy*, 118–28.
119. Meyer, "American Indian Blood," 240.
120. Vizenor, *Fugitive Poses*, 154.
121. There were 5,173 allottees listed on the roll, of which, 408 were classified as "full-bloods." Meyer, *The White Earth Tragedy*, 170; Peterson, "That So-Called Warranty Deed," 169–70; Minnesota Chippewa Tribe, *White Earth*, 37.

122. Beaulieu, "Curly Hair and Big Feet," 286–96; Soderstrom, "Weeds in Linaeus's Garden," 71–72; Holly Youngbear-Tibbetts, "Without Due Process: The Alienation of Individual Trust Allotments of the White Earth Anishinaabeg," *American Indian Culture and Research Journal* 15, no. 2 (1991): 106–8.
123. Beaulieu, "Curly Hair and Big Feet," 282.
124. Furthermore, one year after the cases had been decided, Jenks tested the hair of himself and several of his colleagues and found that his hair and that of Dr. Hrdlička was of the most typical negro type. He concluded: "Either the old classification of human races by hair texture is not of scientific value or Dr. Hrdlička and I are related to the negro." Ibid., 305.

Numerous investigations have taken up the issue of the legality of the land sales. In her article "Without Due Process: The Alienation of Individual Trust Allotments of the White Earth Anishinaabeg," Holly Youngbear-Tibbetts "focuses on the equity suits filed by the United States on behalf of the Anishinaabeg who had been wrongfully dispossessed," and details the community's response to the White Earth Land Settlement Act of 1987, which might be the last word in the cases. Youngbear-Tibbetts, "Without Due Process," 96–97.
125. John R. Howard to Delia A. Gubbon, 17 May 1913, NARA-DC, RG 75, CCF, White Earth File 75401, 1914, 056.
126. Willis and Cahill on behalf of Antoine Lafond to Ransom J. Powell and Gordon Cain, March 1914, NARA-DC, RG 75, CCF, White Earth, File 75401, 1914, 056.
127. Affidavit of Antoine Lafond, n.d., NARA-DC, RG 75, CCF, White Earth File 75401, 1914, 056.
128. Ibid.
129. Ibid.
130. Vizenor, *Fugitive Poses*, 182.
131. Lyons, *X-Marks*, 57.

CHAPTER 2. CONSIDER THE RELATIONSHIP: CITIZENSHIP REGULATIONS OF THE MINNESOTA CHIPPEWA TRIBE

1. *Constitution and By-Laws of the Minnesota Chippewa Tribe, Minnesota Chippewa Tribe*, official website, http://www.mnchippewatribe.org.
2. Deloria and Lytle argue that Congress approved the Indian Reorganization Act (IRA) because of concerns that due to divisions, many American Indian nations did not have officials with whom the United States could deal, not because they were concerned with the rights of Native nations to govern

themselves. Additionally, they critique the model constitutions provided to tribes and the power of oversight given to the secretary of the Interior within those models. Vine Deloria Jr. and Clifford M. Lytle, *The Nations Within: The Past and Future of American Indian Sovereignty* (Austin: University of Texas Press, 1998). See also Sharon O'Brien, *American Indian Tribal Governments* (Norman: University of Oklahoma Press, 1989).

3. *To Grant to Indians Living under Federal Tutelage the Freedom to Organize for Purposes of Local Self-Government and Economic Enterprise: Hearing before the Committee on Indian Affairs United States Senate*, 73rd Congress 263–64 (1934), Statement of Senator Wheeler, quoted in Paul Spruhan, "A Legal History of Blood Quantum in Federal Indian Law to 1935," *South Dakota Law Review* 51, no. 1 (2006): 46, emphasis added.

4. Spruhan, "A Legal History," 46. Clearly, Wheeler's conception of American Indian identity was tied closely to race and low mental abilities.

5. Ibid., 46–48. For an in-depth look at how the BIA determined blood quantum in accordance with the one-half provision of the IRA, see Paul Spruhan, "Indian as Race/Indian as Political Status: Implementation of the Half-Blood Requirement under the Indian Reorganization Act, 1934–1945," *Rutgers Race and Law Review* 8 (August 2006).

6. Spruhan, "A Legal History," 49–50.

7. While the IRA authorized 10 million dollars for the loan program, only $5,245,000 was actually appropriated during the Collier administration. In addition, the cost of administering the program was very high. By 1942, administrative costs each year were consuming more than 20 percent of the monies available for loans. Lawrence C. Kelly, "The Indian Reorganization Act: The Dream and the Reality," in *Major Problems in American Indian History: Documents and Essays*, ed. Albert L. Hurtado and Peter Iverson (Lexington, MA: D.C. Heath Co., 1994), 473.

8. By 1952, the MCT had acquired 91,000 acres of land, which were placed in trust status, under this program. Kathy Davis Graves and Elizabeth Ebbott, *Indians in Minnesota*, 5th ed. (Minneapolis: University of Minnesota Press, 2006), 30.

9. This was due to a variety of circumstances. For example, seventeen Pueblo tribes did not want written constitutions because they were too inflexible and would lead to factionalism. Kelly, "The Indian Reorganization Act," 469.

10. Graves and Ebbott, *Indians in Minnesota*, 17.

11. Scott L. Gould, "Mixing Bodies and Beliefs: The Predicament of Tribes," *Columbia Law Review* 101, no. 4 (May 2001): 720–21.

12. White Earth Reservation Curriculum Committee (Marshall Brown, Chairman; Jerry Rawley, Georgia Wiemer, Everett Goodwin; and Kathy Roy

Goodwin) served as an advisory group to the preparation of the publication, *White Earth: A History* (Minnesota Chippewa Tribe, 1989), 40.

13. *Constitution and By-Laws of the Minnesota Chippewa Tribe, Minnesota Chippewa Tribe*, official website, http://www.mnchippewatribe.org.

14. In *History of the Minnesota Chippewa Tribe*, Schaaf and Robertson report that there was some resistance and "considerable confusion" over the subcharters. For example, at a meeting held in the community of Nay-tah-waush on the White Earth Reservation in 1938, Frank Broker stated that "The charters will be just a little different on each reservation to meet their modes of living . . . so I believe that there will be no two charters alike." Joe Morrison, tribal delegate, stated: "You (Mr. Frank Broker) know as well as I do that the constitutions and by-laws have tied the Indians hand and foot in such a way that we can hardly wiggle, of course, naturally since the Indian office make this charter we are kind of afraid that it will give the government employees more authority than it should. We did not have our attorney explain these things to us, but we can construct the words to suit the government office and if this is the case, we do not want the charter." Quoted in William Schaaf and Charles Robertson, in conjunction with the Minnesota Chippewa Tribe Curriculum Development Committee, *History of the Minnesota Chippewa Tribe* (N.p.: n.p., n.d), 86–87.

15. White Earth Reservation Curriculum Committee, *White Earth: A History* (Minnesota Chippewa Tribe, 1989), 40. Timothy G. Roufs, *The Anishinabe of the Minnesota Chippewa Tribe* (Indian Tribal Series: Phoenix, 1975), 79–82. In 1963, they were renamed Reservation Business Committees, reflecting new powers granted to them by the MCT. In 1985, the White Earth band changed the name to the White Earth Reservation Tribal Council because they felt that the title "Business Committee" did not accurately reflect their duties. They have several powers granted to them by the MCT, including advising the secretary of the Interior about funding federal projects for the reservation; administering reservation lands; making agreements on behalf of the reservation with federal, state, and local governments; managing, leasing, or otherwise dealing with tribal lands as authorized by the tribe; engaging in business to further the economic well-being of the reservation; borrowing money from the federal government; drafting ordinances with the approval of the secretary of the Interior; levying license fees on nonmembers or nontribal organizations; and delegating these powers to officers, committees, employees, or associations, reserving the right to review. Minnesota Chippewa Tribe, *White Earth*, 44–46.

16. *Constitution and By-Laws of the Minnesota Chippewa Tribe*, Article II, Section 3, 24 July 1936, Minnesota Chippewa Tribe Archives, Cass Lake, Minnesota.

17. *Constitution and By-Laws of the Minnesota Chippewa Tribe*, Article II, Section 2, 24 July 1936, Minnesota Chippewa Tribe Archives, Cass Lake, Minnesota. This issue was further clarified in Article I of the By-Laws, which states: "In the determination of membership under Article II, Section 2, of the constitution, the Government annuity rolls, as such rolls may be corrected under this Constitution, shall be used to determine the enrollment status in the Tribe and the same shall be conclusive, the said rolls being the Government official register of the recognized members of the Tribe." *Minnesota Chippewa Tribe By-Laws*, Article I, "Determination of Membership," n.d., Minnesota Chippewa Tribe Archives, Cass Lake, Minnesota.

18. I have not found a resolution requiring residence for tribal citizenship within the MCT, but the Department of the Interior might have required it. At a TEC meeting in July 1941, Mr. Rogers noted, "The present policy of the Department is to enroll only those who were born or are born in the Indian country." Quoted in Memorandum to Mr. Flanery Chief (signature illegible), 31 March 1942, NARA-DC, RG 75, CCF, Consolidated Chippewa, File 32610–1941, 053.

19. The Minnesota Chippewa Tribe further clarifies the election process and role of the TEC, noting: "These twelve persons are elected by enrolled members of their reservations to serve four year terms. The terms of the Chairman and Secretary/Treasurers are staggered so that elections are held every two years. The Bylaws of the Minnesota Chippewa Tribe specifically delegate various administrative duties to the four officers of the Tribe who are the President, Vice-President, Secretary, and Treasurer. Officers are elected from within the Tribal Executive Committee, by its twelve members, every two years following general elections." "Tribal Executive Committee and Sub-committees," *Minnesota Chippewa Tribe*, http://www.mnchippewatribe.org.

20. Proposed Amendments to the Constitution and Bylaws of the Minnesota Chippewa Tribe, n.d., NARA, CCF, Consolidated Chippewa, File 7314–1948, 053.

21. While the Mille Lacs Reservation was established in the 1855 treaty, and some treaties and acts of Congress recognized the reservation, some individuals interpreted these documents to mean that Mille Lacs was not a reservation and all Anishinaabeg should be removed. Many Anishinaabeg did move, but some stayed, and in the 1920s they were finally given allotments on the reservation. Graves and Ebbott, *Indians in Minnesota*, 37.

Only individuals who were citizens of the MCT could be chosen as tribal delegates. Instructions for Holding Election for Tribal Delegates, 3 October 1936, Minnesota Chippewa Tribe Archives, Cass Lake, Minnesota.

22. *Constitution and By-Laws of the Minnesota Chippewa Tribe*, Article IV, Section 2, 24 July 1936, Minnesota Chippewa Tribe Archives, Cass Lake, Minnesota.

23. At this time, the TEC wanted to have Tribal Delegates elected to three-year terms rather than annually. Resolution No. 71, 1950, NARA-DC, RG 75, CCF, Consolidated Chippewa, File 7314–1948, 053.

24. Tribal Executive Committee, As elected, 9 October 1936, Minnesota Chippewa Tribe Archives, Cass Lake, Minnesota.

25. Resolution No. 1, Minnesota Chippewa Tribe, Minutes of Special Meeting of Tribal Executive Committee, 3 April 1937, Minnesota Chippewa Tribe Archives, Cass Lake, Minnesota, 145–46.

26. Minnesota Chippewa Tribe, Minutes of Special Meeting of Tribal Executive Committee, 19 July 1940, Minnesota Chippewa Tribe Archives, Cass Lake, Minnesota, 165.

27. For example, in 1912 Congress restricted funding for American Indian education to individuals with one-quarter or more Indian blood, and in 1928 Congress extended restrictions on allotments to 1956 for citizens of the Five Civilized Tribes who were one-half or more Indian blood. Spruhan, "A Legal History," 45.

28. Ibid., 10. In addition, many BIA policies did or do not have explicit written guidelines. For example, in recent years the BIA has worked to create a written policy for Certificate of Degree of Indian Blood cards, which it issued for several decades with no established uniform guidelines. Gould, "Mixing Bodies and Beliefs," 761, n. 370.

29. Minnesota Chippewa Tribe, Minutes of a Special Meeting of Tribal Executive Committee, 19 July 1940, Minnesota Chippewa Tribe Archives, Cass Lake, Minnesota, 166.

30. Minnesota Chippewa Tribe, Minutes of Special Meeting of Tribal Executive Committee, 17–20 May 1940, Minnesota Chippewa Tribe Archives, Cass Lake, Minnesota, 284.

31. Ibid., 284.

32. Ibid., 31.

33. Ibid., 22.

34. Ibid., 22.

35. Ibid., 22.

36. Ibid., 23.

37. Savage is likely referencing treaties such as those in 1847 and 1867, which specifically included "mixed-bloods." See ibid., 51–52.

38. Ibid., 28–29.

39. Ibid., 29.

40. Ibid., 18. Despite Sanders's comment about a policy requiring residence for enrollment, I have been unable to find it. This may be a rule that was inconsistently enforced and/or introduced by the BIA and not by the MCT.
41. The signature on the letter is illegible; I am unsure exactly who wrote it.
42. Quoted in Assistant Commissioner (signature illegible) to Mr. Flanery, memorandum, 31 March 1942, NARA-DC, RG 75, CCF, Consolidated Chippewa, File 32610–1941, 053.
43. Ibid.
44. Ibid. Here we see further evidence that the residence requirement was instituted by the BIA.
45. Ibid.
46. When he spoke at other meetings, he did not speak in Anishinaabe (or it wasn't noted that he did), so this, combined with the time period, makes it likely that he could speak English if he wanted to.
47. Quoted in Assistant Commissioner (signature illegible) to Mr. Flanery, memorandum, 31 March 1942, NARA-DC, RG 75, CCF, Consolidated Chippewa, File 32610–1941, 053.
48. Ibid.
49. Ibid.
50. As discussed in the previous chapter, the Anishinaabeg had already experienced devastating land losses as a consequence of racialized identities insisted upon by the U.S. governments.
51. Quoted in Assistant Commissioner (signature illegible) to Mr. Flanery, memorandum, 31 March 1942, NARA-DC, RG 75, CCF, Consolidated Chippewa, File 32610–1941, 053.
52. Ibid.
53. Resolution No. 4, Rules Governing the Qualifications for Enrollment in the Minnesota Chippewa Tribe, 26 July 1941, NARA-DC, RG 75, CCF, Consolidated Chippewa, File 32610–1941, 053.
54. Ibid.
55. Ibid.
56. In the 1920s the Indian population in Minneapolis and St. Paul was less than 1,000, but by the end of World War II an estimated 6,000 lived there. Many were attracted by jobs. White Earth Anishinaabeg had long played an important role in the urban Indian community in Minneapolis. For example, Frederick W. Peake was active in the urban Indian community as early as 1915, and during the 1920s he had offices for the Twin Cities Chippewa Council, the Minnesota Wigwam Indian Welfare Society, and the Twin Cities Indian Republican Club in his home. In addition, William Mason founded the Ojibway Research Society with his friends

from White Earth in 1942. Indeed, White Earth emigrants dominated the membership of several urban Indian organizations. For more detail, see Nancy Shoemaker, "Urban Indians and Ethnic Choices: American Indian Organizations in Minneapolis, 1920–1950," *Western Historical Quarterly* (November 1988): 431–47.

57. Minnesota Chippewa Tribe, *White Earth*, 40–41.

58. F. J. Scott to Commissioner of Indian Affairs, 5 August 1941, NARA-DC, RG 75, CCF, Consolidated Chippewa, File 32610–1941, 053.

59. W. H. Flanery to Commissioner of Indian Affairs, memorandum, 14 January 1942, NARA-DC, RG 75, CCF, Consolidated Chippewa, File 32610–1941, 053.

60. Ibid.

61. Holst. abbreviates his name, and I have been unable to find it unabbreviated.

62. John H. Holst. to the Indian Office, memorandum, 25 February 1942, NARA-DC, RG 75, CCF, Consolidated Chippewa, File 32610–1941, 053.

63. Ibid.

64. Ibid.

65. George E. Fox to Mr. McCaskill, memorandum, 28 February 1942, NARA-DC, RG 75, CCF, Consolidated Chippewa, File 32610–1941, 053.

66. Oscar L. Chapman to Ed. M. Wilson, 23 December 1942, NARA-DC, RG 75, CCF, Consolidated Chippewa, File 32610–1941, 053.

67. Ibid.

68. Chapman went on to note: "This Department is charged with the responsibility of protecting the Indian tribes in their identity and their property, and of securing to them the benefits of the system of orderly tribal self-government established by the Indian Reorganization Act. This responsibility has been implemented by giving this Department the right to approve or disapprove certain tribal resolutions, and especially those dealing with admission to membership. I believe that Resolution No. 4 would have undesirable consequences which were not made manifest in the consideration given to that resolution by the Council, and that in disapproving that resolution the Department will protect the tribe and its future generations from the damage to their property and to their tribal organization which that resolution might cause." Ibid.

69. Francis J. Scott to William Zimmerman, 9 June 1943, NARA-DC, RG 75, CCF, Consolidated Chippewa, File 32610–1941, 053.

70. William Zimmerman to Francis J. Scott, 7 April 1944, NARA-DC, RG 75, CCF, Consolidated Chippewa, File 32610–1941, 053.

71. Ibid.

72. Ibid.

73. Ibid.
74. John Herrick to Mr. Youngdahl, 31 May 1940, NARA-DC, RG 75, CCF, Consolidated Chippewa, File 35275, 1940, 053.
75. Ibid.
76. Ibid.
77. Resolution No. 5, 19 July 1940, Minnesota Chippewa Tribe Archives, Cass Lake, Minnesota.
78. F. J. Scott to Commissioner of Indian Affairs, 30 July 1940, NARA-DC, RG 75, CCF, Consolidated Chippewa, File 52897, 1940, 053.
79. Ibid.
80. Fred H. Daiker to F. J. Scott, 16 August 1940, NARA-DC, RG 75, CCF, Consolidated Chippewa, File 52897, 1940, 053.
81. Ibid.
82. F. J. Scott to Commissioner of Indian Affairs, 14 December 1940, NARA-DC, RG 75, CCF, Consolidated Chippewa, File 81544, 1940, 053.
83. Robert Pearson to F. J. Scott, 1 September 1944, NARA-DC, RG 75, CCF, Consolidated Chippewa, File 26968, 1941, 053.
84. Ibid.
85. Walter V. Woshlhe to Francis J. Scott, 31 October 1944, NARA-DC, RG 75, CCF, Consolidated Chippewa, File 26968, 1941, 053.
86. Resolution No. 31, Minnesota Chippewa Tribe, 22 May 1945, NARA-DC, RG 75, CCF, Consolidated Chippewa, File 32610–1941, 053.
87. Resolution No. 6, Minnesota Chippewa Tribe, 8 June 1948, NARA-DC, RG 75, CCF, Consolidated Chippewa, File 7314–1948, 053.
88. Charles Wilkinson, *Blood Struggle: The Rise of Modern Indian Nations* (New York: W.W. Norton & Co., 2005), 64–66.
89. Minutes, Meeting of the Tribal Executive Committee, Minnesota Chippewa Tribe, Duluth, Minnesota, 9–11 December 1948, NARA-DC, RG 75, CCF, Consolidated Chippewa, File 7314–1948, 056.
90. Ibid., Resolution No. 14.
91. Ibid., Resolution No. 6.
92. Resolution No. 14, Minnesota Chippewa Tribe, 21 May 1949, NARA-DC, RG 75, CCF, Consolidated Chippewa, File 32610–1941, 053.
93. Lyzeme Savage to John R. Nichols, 25 August 1949, NARA-DC, RG 75, CCF, Consolidated Chippewa, File 32610–1941, 053.
94. William Warne to Lyzeme Savage, 9 December 1949, NARA-DC, RG 75, CCF, Consolidated Chippewa, File 32610–1941, 053.
95. Resolution No. 2, Minnesota Chippewa Tribe, passed 9–10 June 1950, NARA-DC, RG 75, CCF, Consolidated Chippewa, File 32610–1941, 053. This resolution by the tribal delegates reaffirmed TEC Resolution No. 3,

Minnesota Chippewa Tribe, passed 9 June 1949, NARA-DC, RG 75, CCF, Consolidated Chippewa, File 32610–1941, 053.

96. Lyzeme Savage to Commissioner of Indian Affairs, 20 June 1950, NARA-DC, RG 75, CCF, Consolidated Chippewa, File 32610–1941, 053. The letter explicitly lists: "1. Our men and women in the armed forces who married and bore children off reservation but returned to their reservation on their release from the Services. 2. Enrollees who are employed in government service. 3. Seasonal workers who go off reservation but, upon release from employment because of a reduction and other economic reasons, returned to the reservation."

97. Ibid.

98. Lyzeme Savage to D. S. Meyer, 19 July 1950, NARA-DC, RG 75, CCF, Consolidated Chippewa, File 32610–1941, 053.

99. D. S. Meyer to Lyzeme Savage, 2 August 1950, NARA-DC, RG 75, CCF, Consolidated Chippewa, File 32610–1941, 053.

100. Resolution No. 14, Minnesota Chippewa Tribe, passed 8–10 June 1950, NARA-DC, RG 75, CCF, Consolidated Chippewa, File 32610–1941, 053.

101. D. S. Meyer to Don C. Foster, 19 September 1951, NARA-DC, RG 75, CCF, Consolidated Chippewa, File 32610–1941, 053.

102. Ibid.

103. Watkins quoted in Wilkinson, *Blood Struggle*, 69, emphasis original.

104. Wilkinson, *Blood Struggle*, 67–71.

105. Resolution No. 32, Minnesota Chippewa Tribe, 1–2 December 1956, Minnesota Chippewa Tribe Archives, Cass Lake, Minnesota.

106. Minutes, Tribal Executive Committee Meeting at Grand Portage, Minnesota, August 8–10, 1957, Minnesota Chippewa Tribe Archives, Cass Lake, Minnesota.

107. Ibid.

108. Indeed, the TEC unanimously passed a resolution that noted Buckanaga left the meeting "with all current minutes and resolutions, leaving the Executive Committee no alternative but to adjourn the meeting without fully completing its duties." Ibid., Resolution No. 34.

109. Resolution No. 77, Minnesota Chippewa Tribe, Tribal Executive Committee, March 23, 1959, Minnesota Chippewa Tribe Archives, Cass Lake, Minnesota.

110. Ibid.

111. James E. Officer, "The Bureau of Indian Affairs since 1945: An Assessment," *Annals of the American Academy of Political and Social Science* 436, no. 1 (1978): 64.

112. An Ordinance Relating to Enrollment and Membership in the Minnesota Chippewa Tribe, May 12, 1961, Minnesota Chippewa Tribe Archives, Cass Lake, Minnesota.

113. Ibid.
114. Minnesota Chippewa Tribe, Delegates Meeting, May 13–14, 1961, Minnesota Chippewa Tribe Archives, Cass Lake, Minnesota.
115. Ibid.
116. Ibid.
117. "Revised Constitution and Bylaws of the Minnesota Chippewa Tribe, Minnesota," Certification of Adoption.
118. "Revised Constitution and Bylaws of the Minnesota Chippewa Tribe, Minnesota," Article 2.
119. Minnesota Chippewa Tribe, Tribal Executive Committee Meeting, October 1, 1965, NARA-DC, RG 75, CCF, Consolidated Chippewa, File 32610–1941, 053.
120. Minnesota Chippewa Tribe, Tribal Executive Committee, January 13–14, 1967, Minnesota Chippewa Tribe Archives, Cass Lake, Minnesota.
121. Alvin M. Josephy Jr., *Now That the Buffalo's Gone* (Norman: University of Oklahoma Press, 1989), 225.
122. For more information on both the ISDEAA and this era in federal Indian policy, see George Pierre Castile, *Taking Charge: Native American Self-Determination and Federal Indian Policy, 1975–1993* (Tucson: University of Arizona Press, 2006).
123. Schaaf and Robertson, *History of the Minnesota Chippewa Tribe*, 139.
124. Ibid.
125. Ibid.
126. Ibid.
127. Resolution 40–72, Minnesota Chippewa Tribe, Tribal Executive Committee Meeting, February 5, 1972, Minnesota Chippewa Tribe Archives, Cass Lake, Minnesota.
128. Minnesota Chippewa Tribe, Tribal Executive Committee Meeting, March 15–16, 1971, Minnesota Chippewa Tribe Archives, Cass Lake, Minnesota.
129. Ibid.
130. Wilder Research Center, "Minnesota Chippewa Tribe: Population Projections," May 2014, 2. Http://www.whiteearth.com/programs/?page_id=539&program_id=24.
131. For details of the charges, see *United States v. Darrell Chip Wadena*, United States, 8th Circuit Court of Appeals, 152 F3d 831.
132. "The End of an Era: White Earth Chairman of 20 Years Sentenced to 51 Months Prison; Clark, Rawley to Do 46, 33 Months," *Native American Press/Ojibwe News* (Bemidji, MN), November 22, 1996.
133. Ibid.
134. "No More Business as Usual in the Minnesota Chippewa Tribe," *Ojibwe News* (Bemidji, MN), October 27, 1995.

135. "White Earth's Poverty Wadena's Wealth," *The Circle: Native American News and Arts* (Minneapolis), January 31, 1996.

136. Dr. Leah J. Carpenter, Associate Professor and 3M Chair of Accounting, Department of Accounting, Bemidji State University, http://www.bemidjistate.edu/academics/departments/accounting/faculty/lcarpenter.

137. Leah J. Carpenter, "Shawanima or Divide and Conquer? Constitutional Reform at a Crossroads," *Ojibwe News* (St. Paul, MN), March 28, 1997.

138. Ibid.

139. Ibid.

140. McArthur quoted in "White Earth Open Meeting a Welcome Change, but Questions Left Unanswered," *Ojibwe News* (St. Paul, MN), July 18, 1997.

141. *The Constitution of the White Earth Ojibwe Nation of Anishinaabeg* (draft), February 21, 1998, White Earth Constitutional Drafting Committee, personal collection of the author.

142. Ibid.

143. Ibid.

144. Suggestions for Revision of the Minnesota Chippewa Tribe's Constitution, Constitutional Reform Committee Meeting, May 12, 2001, Shooting Star Casino, Mahnomen, Minnesota, personal collection of the author.

145. Author's notes on White Earth Tribal Council Meeting, July 7, 2001, Shooting Star Casino, Mahnomen, Minnesota, personal collection of the author.

CHAPTER 3. IT IS TIME TO TAKE OUR OWN LEADERSHIP: THE CONSTITUTION OF THE WHITE EARTH NATION

1. Erma J. Vizenor, "White Earth 2007 State of the Nation Address," *Anishinaabeg Today*, March 7, 2007, 10–14.

2. Ibid., 14.

3. Jill Doerfler, *Fictions and Fractions: Reconciling Citizenship Regulations with Cultural Values among the White Earth Anishinaabeg* (PhD diss., University of Minnesota, 2007), 94–122.

4. LaGarde already knew about some of the great sources I had found because I had discussed them on several occasions on the NDN News radio program he cohosted with Paul Schultz. Our conversations often continued over brunch after the program ended.

5. "Sovereignty and the Minnesota Chippewa Tribe," *Anishinaabeg Today*, April 18, 2007, 2; "A Short History of Chippewa Blood Quantum," *Anishinaabeg Today*, May 9, 2007, 2, 17; "Anishinaabe Understandings of Identity

in the 1910s," *Anishinaabeg Today*, May 30, 2007, 2, 23; "More 1910s Anishinaabe Conceptions of Identity," *Anishinaabeg Today*, June 20, 2007, 2, 17.
See also "Responsibilities and Importance of Tribal Citizenship," *Anishinaabeg Today*, July 11, 2007, 2, 18; "The Minnesota Chippewa Tribe Addresses
the Citizenship Question in the 1940s," *Anishinaabeg Today*, August 1, 2007;
"The MCT Holds Strong against the Use of Blood Quantum," *Anishinaabeg Today*, August 22, 2007, 2, 16; and "Blood Quantum Becomes the Sole
Requirement for Tribal Citizenship," *Anishinaabeg Today*, September 12,
2007, 2, 22.

6. Carol Goldberg, "Members Only: Designing Citizenship Requirements for
   Tribal Nations," in *American Indian Constitutional Reform and the Rebuilding of Native Nations*, ed. Eric D. Lemont (Austin: University of Texas Press,
   2006), 107.

7. Scott Lyons, *X-Marks: Native Signatures of Assent* (Minneapolis: University of
   Minnesota Press, 2010), 181.

8. The delegates were a very diverse group. Although the vast majority were
   over the age of forty, there was a relatively broad age range represented. They
   came from a variety of educational and professional backgrounds and family
   situations.

9. Eric D. Lemont, "Introduction," in *American Indian Constitutional Reform
   and the Rebuilding of Native Nations*, ed. Eric D. Lemont (Austin: University
   of Texas Press, 2006), 5.

10. Revised Constitution and Bylaws of the Minnesota Chippewa Tribe, Minne-
    sota, Article 5, "Authorities of the Tribal Executive Committee," and Article
    6, "Authorities of the Reservation Business Committees," November 23,
    1963, available at http://thorpe.ou.edu/constitution/chippewa.

11. Official website for the Harvard Project on American Indian Economic
    Development, Harvard University, http://hpaied.org/about-hpaied/overview.

12. Official website for the Native Nations Institute for leadership, management,
    and policy, University of Arizona, http://nni.arizona.edu/whatwedo/index
    .php.

13. Miriam Jorgensen, ed. *Rebuilding Native Nations: Strategies for Governance
    and Development* (Tucson: University of Arizona Press, 2007).

14. David E. Wilkins, "Seasons of Change: Of Reforms, Melees, and Revolu-
    tions in Indian Country," in *American Indian Constitutional Reform and the
    Rebuilding of Native Nations*, ed. Eric D. Lemont (Austin: University of Texas
    Press, 2006), 39.

15. Ibid.

16. Unless otherwise noted, all material for this chapter is based on my notes and
    other personal materials from the Constitutional Conventions.

17. The delegates were Pam Aspinwall, Michael Bellanger, Gabriel Brisbois, Phyllis Bunker, Bev Carlson, Celeste Cloud, Julie Doerfler, Sharon Enjady-Mitchell, Donna Fairbanks, Marlin Farley, Ralph Goodman, Kathy Goodwin, Janice Goodwin, Marcy Hart, Jerry Helgren, Joe Holstien, Alice M. Johnson, Louie Johannson, Darla Kier, Shirley LaDuke, Teresa LaDuke, Charlotte Lee, Pam Lehmann, George LeQuier, Jane Leuer, Peggy Lewis, Cindy Lindsay, Tara Mason, Leo Murray, Ken Perrault, Gerald Roberts, Paul Schultz, Lucile Silk, Sandra Smith, Karen Solberg, JoAnne Stately, Leonard Thompson, Donald Vizenor, Gerald Vizenor, and Roberta Wind.

18. I have decided to keep the comments of the delegates and nondelegates at the conventions anonymous. I will indicate if the person was a delegate or not. I find the use of "he or she" draws unnecessary attention and will instead use "s/he" as a substitute.

19. Martha Berry, "Firsthand Accounts: Membership and Citizenship," in *American Indian Constitutional Reform and the Rebuilding of Native Nations*, ed. Eric D. Lemont (Austin: University of Texas Press), 2006, 183.

20. Kirsty Gover, "Genealogy as Continuity: Explaining the Growing Tribal Preference for Descent Rules in Membership Governance in the United States," *American Indian Law Review* 33, no. 1 (2009): 295.

21. Ibid., 248.

22. In her interdisciplinary study of American Indian identity, *Real Indians*, sociologist Eva Garroutte notes: "The original, stated intention of blood quantum distinctions was to determine the point at which the various responsibilities of the dominant society to Indian people ended. The ultimate and explicit federal intention was to use the blood quantum standard as a means to liquidate tribal lands and to eliminate government trust responsibility to tribes, along with entitlement programs, treaty rights, and reservations." Eva Marie Garroutte, *Real Indians: Identity and the Survival of Native America* (Berkeley: University of California Press, 2003), 42.

23. Doerfler, *Fictions and Fractions*, 94–122.

24. Gover, "Genealogy as Continuity," 248.

25. Quoted in Mr. Flanery Chief (signature illegible), memorandum, March 31, 1942, NARA-DC, RG 75, CCF, Consolidated Chippewa, File 32610–1941, 053.

26. Dennis Jones, "The Etymology of Anishinaabe," *Oshkaabewis Native Journal* 2, no. 1 (Fall 1995): 43.

27. Ibid., 45.

28. *White Earth Reservation*, official website, http://www.whiteearth.com.

29. Kim Tallbear's *Native American DNA: Tribal Belonging and the False Promise of Genetic Science* (Minneapolis: University of Minnesota Press, 2013) is the

foremost resource on this issue, but it was not out at the time of the convention. I did write a couple of newspaper articles addressing this misconception: "Hamline Symposium Discusses If Race, Genetics Play a Role in Defining American Indian Identity," *Anishinaabeg Today: A Chronicle of the White Earth Band of Ojibwe*, April 30, 2008, 2, 15; and "Scholars Ask, 'Does "Indian Blood" Still Matter?,'" *Anishinaabeg Today: A Monthly Chronicle of the White Earth Nation*, October 5, 2011, 2, 16.

30. For more on the timber settlement, see Emily Kaiser, "Plans Duel for Chippewa Cash," *(Minneapolis) Star Tribune*, June 25, 2008; Tom Robertson, "Chippewa Bands Can't Agree How to Split Multi-Million Dollar Settlement," *Minnesota Public Radio*, July 22, 2008, http://minnesota.publicradio.org.

31. For a detailed explanation of the Seven Grandfather Teachings (also sometimes called the Seven Teachings or Seven Grandmother Teachings), see Leanne Simpson, *Dancing on Our Turtle's Back: Stories of Nishinaabeg Re-Creation, Resurgence and a New Emergence* (Winnipeg, Manitoba: Arbeiter Ring Publishing, 2010), 124–27.

32. When he spoke at other meetings, he did not speak in Anishinaabe (or it wasn't noted that he did), so this, combined with the time period, makes it likely that he could speak English if he wanted to.

33. Quoted in Mr. Flanery Chief (signature illegible), memorandum, March 31, 1942, NARA-DC, RG 75, CCF, Consolidated Chippewa, File 32610–1941, 053.

34. W. H. Flanery to Commissioner of Indian Affairs, memorandum, January 14, 1942, NARA-DC, RG 75, CCF, Consolidated Chippewa, File 32610–1941, 053.

35. Minnesota Chippewa Tribe, Delegates meeting, Bemidji, Minnesota, May 13–14, 1961, Minnesota Chippewa Tribe Archive, Cass Lake, Minnesota.

36. Gover, "Genealogy as Continuity," 295. Gover attributes the marked increase in blood-quantum requirements to higher numbers of individuals living away from the reservation and increased rates of out-marriage; however, MCT records do not reflect concern about this trend.

37. Joseph Thomas Flies-Away, Carrie Garrow, and Miriam Jorgensen, "Native Nation Courts: Key Players in Nation Rebuilding," in *Rebuilding Native Nations: Strategies for Governance and Development*, ed. Miriam Jorgensen (Tucson: University of Arizona Press, 2007), 115–16, 121–22.

38. Ibid., 123–26.

39. *The Constitution of the White Earth Ojibwe Nation of Anishinaabeg* (draft), 21 February 1998, White Earth Constitutional Drafting Committee, personal collection of the author.

40. Lemont, "Introduction," 1.
41. Duane Champagne, "Remaking Tribal Constitutions: Meeting the Challenges of Tradition, Colonialism, and Globalization," in *American Indian Constitutional Reform and the Rebuilding of Native Nations*, ed. Eric D. Lemont (Austin: University of Texas Press, 2006), 25.
42. John Borrows, *Drawing Out Law: A Spirit's Guide* (Toronto: University of Toronto Press), 2010.
43. Philip P. Mason, ed., "Introduction," in *Schoolcraft: The Literary Voyager or Muzzeniegun* (East Lansing: Michigan State University Press, 1962), xxiii–xxvi. See also *Schoolcraft's Indian Legends from Algic Researches, The Myth of Hiawatha, Oneota, The Red Race in America, and Historical and Statistical Information Respecting . . . the Indian Tribes of the United States*, ed. Mentor L. Williams (East Lansing: Michigan State University Press, 1956), xxi. These stories were first published in 1839 under the title *Algic Researches*, but the two-volume set received little public attention. After Longfellow's great success with *Hiawatha* in 1855, Schoolcraft attempted again to gain attention to American Indian traditional stories with *The Myth of Hiawatha* in 1856, with omissions and additions from *Algic Researches*, but once again it was not as popular as Schoolcraft had hoped.
44. Henry R. Schoolcraft, "Shingebiss," from *The Indian in His Wigwam, or Characteristics of the Red Race of America, from Original Notes and Manuscripts* (New York: Dewitt & Davenport, 1848), 85–86.
45. Anishinaabe scholar Basil Johnston has observed: "Because each Ojibway story may embody several themes and meanings, time and deliberation are required for adequate appreciation. There is no instantaneous understanding." Johnson, *Ojibway Heritage: The Ceremonies, Rituals, Songs, Dances, Prayers and Legends of the Ojibway* (Toronto: McClelland and Stewart, 1967), 8. Johnston acknowledges that the flexible nature of Anishinaabe stories allows readers and listeners of different abilities to ascertain their own understandings of the significance of the story. Additionally, the personal experiences and objectives of each reader or listener also influence their interpretations. It is this possibility of multiple interpretations, and the flexibility of the stories to adapt to changing circumstances and needs of the community that provide the central power of these stories. There is no single, correct way to use and interpret these narratives; rather, these stories transform and adapt to new situations through interpretation. A single story can be used for multiple purposes depending on the way it is told, the audience, and the intent of the storyteller.
46. I was inspired to take this approach by the works of several scholars, including Julie Cruikshank, who asserts that the "oral tradition may tell us about the past, but its meanings are not exhausted with reference to the past. Good

stories from the past continue to provide legitimate insights about contemporary events." Cruikshank, *The Social Life of Stories: Narrative and Knowledge in the Yukon Territory* (Lincoln: University of Nebraska Press, 2000), 43–44.

47. Melissa A. Pflug, *Ritual and Myth in Odawa Revitalization: Reclaiming a Sovereign Place* (Norman: University of Oklahoma Press, 1998), 96.

48. Later I published a newspaper article on this same topic: "A Model for Action: Shingebiss Is an Important Story of Strength and Resiliency," *Anishinaabeg Today: A Chronicle of the White Earth Band of Ojibwe*, December 2, 2009, 7, 19.

49. Felix S. Cohen, *Handbook of Federal Indian Law* (1942; reprint, New York: AMS Press, 1982), 20.

50. Goldberg, "Members Only," 108.

51. Ibid, 132.

52. *The Constitution of the White Earth Ojibwe Nation of Anishinaabeg* (draft), 21 February 1998, White Earth Constitutional Drafting Committee, personal collection of the author.

53. As a means to help the delegates understand this option, I used an invented example of an individual who had some Minnesota Chippewa Tribe–White Earth Band blood, some Bad River Band of Lake Superior Tribe of Chippewa Indians blood, and some Saginaw Chippewa Tribe of Michigan blood. I explained that this person would be eligible for tribal citizenship as long as the total blood equaled at least ¼. Non-Anishinaabe blood would not count, and it is unclear if blood from Anishinaabe tribes that are not officially recognized by the U.S. government would count or not. I further noted that it was also unclear if Anishinaabe blood from Canadian Nations would be eligible or not.

54. The vote was made by a simple show of hands by the delegates. The motion was not adopted unanimously, but there was a clear majority in favor.

55. While lineal descent is far more inclusive than the previous requirement of one-quarter MCT blood, it is not a perfect answer to the citizenship question. Biological relationship is privileged here—someone who has an Anishinaabe father but never met him would still be eligible for citizenship. It would be up to that person to decide if they wanted to become a White Earth citizen or not. There is also a requirement to provide genealogical documentation, which may be a barrier for some. Lineal descent excludes adopted family members as well as those related by marriage. Yet, despite these shortcomings, delegates decided that it was the best option they had. I think it is a better determiner than blood quantum and brings us closer to uniting our families and gives individuals a much stronger role in choosing whether or not they want to become a citizen of the WEN. Personal autonomy is a key component of Anishinaabe life, and because lineal descent is more inclusive than blood quantum, it gives parents and individuals increased decision-making authority.

56. Gerald Vizenor and Erma Vizenor are related by marriage. Erma's late husband was Gerald's father's cousin. Gerald Vizenor and James MacKay, "Constitutional Narratives: A Conversation with Gerald Vizenor," in *Centering Anishinaabeg Studies: Understanding the World through Stories*, ed. Jill Doerfler, Heidi Kiiwetinepinesiik Stark, Niigaanwewidam James Sinclair (East Lansing: Michigan State University Press, 2013), 138.

57. I have provided a more detailed summary and analysis in *The Constitution of the White Earth Nation*, coauthored with Gerald Vizenor (Lincoln: University of Nebraska Press, 2012).

58. Constitution of the White Earth Nation, Preamble, available at http://www.d .umn.edu/~umdais/images/WECONSTITUTION.pdf.

59. Also see James MacKay's analysis of the Preamble in Vizenor and MacKay, "Constitutional Narratives," 135–36.

60. Lyons, *X-Marks*, 59.

61. Constitution of the White Earth Nation, Chapter 2, Article 1.

62. Constitution of the White Earth Nation, Chapter 2, Article 2.

63. Jill Doerfler, "Weaving Cultural Requirements into Services," *Anishinaabeg Today: A Monthly Chronicle of the White Earth Nation*, February 6, 2013, 2, 28.

64. For example, under the White Earth Constitution the president can veto legislation passed by the Legislative Council; however, the Legislative Council can override a veto with a two-thirds majority. In this system, the power of both the president and the Legislative Council are balanced in a reasonable manner so that neither has supreme authority. In the case of a tie vote, the president also has the authority to vote on legislation.

65. Chapter 17, "Legislative Council Meetings," describes procedural issues relating to meetings of the Legislative Council. The level of detail provides assurances to citizens that with the noted emergency exceptions, meetings will be both publicly announced and open. Additionally, Legislative Council motions, votes, resolutions, and decisions must be recorded in the official minutes of the sessions. The decisions made by the Legislative Council must be available for examination by citizens. These provisions ensure transparency and permit citizens to be informed on all actions taken by the government. This important information empowers citizens and will impact (re)elections.

66. The petition requires at least two-thirds of the eligible voters for a recall election. There are a variety of reasons for a petition, including allegations of misconduct or mismanagement by an elected official.

67. Nondelegates who arrived late accused me of skipping the chapter on the powers of the president but had simply missed that portion. In addition, they argued that the constitution gave the president too much power. It is likely

that they had not read the chapter and were, therefore, unaware of the system of checks and balances and the provisions for impeachment of the president. In addition, Article 13 of Chapter 11 establishes a term limit of no more than two four-year elected terms.

68. There was a motion to allow for representation for citizens who live anywhere in the United States, but delegates rejected the motion by a narrow margin.

69. There were concerns about nondelegates attempting to vote, so the method of having delegates sign for their ballot was employed to ensure that only official delegates voted.

70. Jason Adkins, "Some Shout Rejection of Tribal Process," *DL-Online*, April 8, 2009.

71. Delegates who were present at the final convention and voted include: Pam Aspinwall, Michael Bellanger, Gabriel Brisbois, Bev Carlson, Celeste Cloud, Julie Doerfler, Sharon Enjady-Mitchell, Ralph Goodman, Marcy Hart, Jerry Helgren, Joe Holstien, Alice M. Johnson, Louie Johannson, Charlotte Lee, Peggy Lewis, Ken Perrault, Gerald Roberts, Lucile Silk, Karen Solberg, JoAnne Stately, Leonard Thompson, Donald Vizenor, Gerald Vizenor, and Roberta Wind.

72. "Rebuilding and Renewing Tribal Sovereignty," *Anishinaabeg Today: A Chronicle of the White Earth Band of Ojibwe* (White Earth: MN), August 4, 2010, 9, 17; "The Inaccuracy of Blood Quantum," *Anishinaabeg Today*, July 7, 2010, 5; "The Fight against Blood Quantum in the 1940s," *Anishinaabeg Today*, June 2, 2010, 7, 25; "The White Earth Blood Quantum Scam," *Anishinaabeg Today*, May 5, 2010, 6; "The Tenuous History of Blood Quantum," *Anishinaabeg Today*, April 7, 2010, 5, 11; "Colonial Legacies, Opportunities for Change," *Anishinaabeg Today*, March 3, 2010, 5, 19; "New Constitution Would Strengthen Sovereignty," *Anishinaabeg Today*, February 3, 2010, 5; "A Model for Action: Shingebiss Is an Important Story of Strength and Resiliency," *Anishinaabeg Today*, December 2, 2009, 7, 19; "Anishinaabe Society One Hundred Years from Now," *Anishinaabeg Today*, October 7, 2009, 4, 22; "'A Philosophy for Living': Ignatia Broker and Constitutional Reform," *Anishinaabeg Today*, September 2, 2009, 2, 26; "Families First: Tribal Citizenship and the Future of the White Earth Nation," *Anishinaabeg Today*, August 5, 2009, 2, 23; "Reviewing the Constitution," *Anishinaabeg Today*, July 1, 2009, 2, 25.

73. The Bush Foundation funding was critical to the process moving ahead. The foundation also provided important resources and networks. The Bush Foundation "support(s) the self-determination of the 23 sovereign Native nations that share the same geographic area as Minnesota, North Dakota, and South Dakota. Our goal is that, by 2020, all 23 Native nations are exercising

self-determination to actively rebuild the infrastructure of nationhood." Http://www.bushfoundation.org/native-nations-building/overview.

74. While this is only about 20 percent of eligible voters, it is more than double the number of votes cast in an average election at White Earth.

75. "White Earth Voters Approve New Constitution," *Anishinaabeg Today*, December 4, 2013, 1.

76. Flies-Away et al., "Native Nation Courts," 136.

77. Vizenor and MacKay, "Constitutional Narratives," 146.

CONCLUSION

1. This story continues to represent core Anishinaabe values and traditions; yet the different versions change over time, sometimes adding new elements to reflect the growing diversity of religions among the Anishinaabeg. This ability to adjust yet remain fundamentally the same shows the ways in which individual storytellers were able to apply the story to new circumstances while retaining the core elements and lessons. The Earthdiver story is not stagnant and fixed, but fluid and able to adapt to new situations.

2. Many different versions of this story exist, including Edward Benton-Banai, *The Mishomis Book* (Hayward, WI: Indian Country Communications, 1998), 30–36; Basil Johnston, *Ojibway Heritage: The Ceremonies, Rituals, Songs, Dances, Prayers and Legends of the Ojibway* (Toronto: McClelland and Stewart, 1967), 13–16; Truman Michelson, ed., and William Jones, comp., *Ojibwa Texts*, vol. 7, pt. 1, Publications of the American Ethnological Society, ed. Franz Boas (New York: E. J. Brill, Ltd., 1917), 150–53; Thomas Peacock and Marlene Wisuri, *The Good Path: Ojibwe Learning and Activity Book for Kids* (Afton, MN: Afton Historical Society Press, 2002), 19–22; Leanne Simpson, *Dancing on Our Turtle's Back: Stories of Nishinaabeg Re-Creation, Resurgence and a New Emergence* (Winnipeg, Manitoba: Arbeiter Ring Publishing, 2010), 68–70; Gerald Vizenor, *Earthdivers: Tribal Narratives on Mixed Descent* (Minneapolis: University of Minnesota Press, 1981), ix–xix.

3. Gerald Vizenor, *Fugitive Poses* (Lincoln: University of Nebraska Press, 2000), 15–16.

4. Ibid., 184.

5. Melissa A. Pflug, *Ritual and Myth in Odawa Revitalization: Reclaiming a Sovereign Place* (Norman: University of Oklahoma Press, 1998), 90.

6. Johnston, *Ojibway Heritage*, 8.

7. Ibid., 8.

8. Similarly, in *The Social Life of Stories*, Cruikshank demonstrates how one story can be employed to communicate different meanings to different audiences and how the underlying message contained within a story can be used by a community to address contemporary issues. Julie Cruikshank, "Pete's Song," chapter 2 in *The Social Life of Stories: Narrative and Knowledge in the Yukon Territory* (Lincoln: University of Nebraska Press, 1998), 25–44.

9. Lisa Brooks, "The Constitution of the White Earth Nation: A New Innovation in a Longstanding Indigenous Literary Tradition," *Studies in American Indian Literature* 23, no. 4 (Winter 2011): 61.

10. Leanne Simpson, "Our Elder Brothers: The Lifeblood of Resurgence," in *Lighting the Eighth Fire: The Liberation, Resurgence, and Protection of Indigenous Nations*, ed. Leanne Simpson (Winnipeg, Manitoba: Arbeiter Ring Publishing, 2008), 74.

11. Scott Lyons, *X-Marks: Native Signatures of Assent* (Minneapolis: University of Minnesota Press, 2010), 171. Italics original.

APPENDIX 1. REVISED CONSTITUTION AND BYLAWS OF THE MINNESOTA CHIPPEWA TRIBE, MINNESOTA

1. As amended per Amendment I, approved by Secretary of Interior 11/6/72.
2. As amended per Amendment II, approved by Secretary of Interior 11/6/72.

Bibliography

Adkins, Jason. "Some Shout Rejection of Tribal Process." *DL-Online*, April 8, 2009. Http://www.dl-online/event/article/id/43228.

Albers, Patricia, and Jeanne Kay. "Sharing the Land: A Study in American Indian Territoriality." In *A Cultural Geography of North American Indians*, ed. Thomas Ross and Tyrel Moore. Boulder, CO: Westview Press, 1987, 47–91.

Alfred, Taiaiake. *Peace, Power and Righteousness*. Oxford: Oxford University Press Canada, 1999.

Allen, Chadwick. *Blood Narrative: Indigenous Identity in American Indian and Maori Literary and Activist Texts*. Durham, NC: Duke University Press, 2002.

Anderson, Benedict. *Imagined Communities: Reflections on the Origin and Spread of Nationalism*. Rev. ed. New York: Verso, 2006.

Angel, Michael. *Preserving the Sacred: Historical Perspectives on the Ojibwa Midewiwin*. Winnipeg: University of Manitoba Press, 2002.

Archuleta, Elizabeth. "Refiguring Indian Blood through Poetry, Photography, and Performance Art." *Studies in American Indian Literature* (Winter 2005), 1–26.

Baraga, R. R. Bishop. *A Dictionary of the Otchipwe Language*. 1878; reprint, Minneapolis: Ross & Hanes, Inc., 1973.

Barker, Joanne. "For Whom Sovereignty Matters." In *Sovereignty Matters: Locations of Contestation and Possibility in Indigenous Struggles for Self-Determination*, ed. Joanne Barker. Lincoln: University of Nebraska Press, 2005, 1–31.

———. *Native Acts: Law, Recognition, and Cultural Authenticity*. Durham, NC: Duke University Press, 2011.

Beaulieu, David. "Curly Hair and Big Feet: Physical Anthropology and Implementation of Land Allotment on the White Earth Chippewa Reservation." *American Indian Quarterly* (Fall 1984), 181–314.

Benedict, Jeff. *Without Reservation: The Making of America's Most Powerful Indian Tribe and Foxwoods, the World's Largest Casino*. Darby, PA: Diane Publishing Company, 2000.

Benton-Banai, Edward. *The Mishomis Book*. Hayward, WI: Indian Country Communications, 1998.

Berger, Bethany R. "Power over This Unfortunate Race: Race, Politics, and Indian Law in United States v. Rogers." *William & Mary Law Review* 45 (2004) 1957–2052.

———. "Red: Racism and the American Indian." *UCLA Law Review* 56 (2009), 591–656.

Berry, Martha. "Firsthand Accounts: Membership and Citizenship." In *American Indian Constitutional Reform and the Rebuilding of Native Nations*, ed. Eric D. Lemont. Austin: University of Texas Press, 2006, 183.

Bieder, Robert E. "Henry Rowe Schoolcraft and the Ethologist as Historian and Moralist." *Science Encounters the Indian, 1820–1880: The Early Years of American Ethology*. Norman: University of Oklahoma Press, 1986.

Blaeser, Kimberly M. *Gerald Vizenor: Writing in the Oral Tradition*. Norman: University of Oklahoma Press, 1996.

———. "The New Frontier of Native American Literature: Dis-arming History with Tribal Humor." In *Native American Perspectives on Literature and History*, ed. Alan R. Velie. Norman: University of Oklahoma, 1994, 37–50.

Borrows, John. *Drawing Out Law: A Spirit's Guide*. Toronto: University of Toronto Press, 2010.

———. *Recovering Canada: The Resurgence of Indigenous Law*. Toronto: University of Toronto Press, 2002.

Brady, Tim. "Primitive Thinking." *Minnesota: The Magazine of the University of Minnesota Alumni Association*, March–April 2008, 26–31.

Broker, Ignatia. *Night Flying Woman: An Ojibway Narrative*. St. Paul: Minnesota Historical Society Press, 1983.

Brooks, Lisa. "The Constitution of the White Earth Nation: A New Innovation in a Longstanding Indigenous Literary Tradition." *Studies in American Indian Literature* 23, no. 4 (Winter 2011), 48–76.

Brubaker, Rogers. *Citizenship and Nationhood in France and Germany*. Cambridge, MA: Harvard University Press, 1998.

Carpenter, Leah J. "Shawanima or Divide and Conquer? Constitutional Reform at a Crossroads," *Ojibwe News* (St. Paul, MN), March 28, 1997.

Champagne, Duane. "Remaking Tribal Constitutions: Meeting the Challenges of Tradition, Colonialism, and Globalization." In *American Indian Constitutional Reform and the Rebuilding of Native Nations*, ed. Eric D. Lemont. Austin: University of Texas Press, 2006, 11–34.

Chang, David A. "'An Equal Interest in the Soil': Creek Small-Scale Farming and the Work of Nationhood, 1866–1889." *American Indian Quarterly* 33, no. 1 (Winter 2009): 98–130.

Cobb, Amanda. "Understanding Tribal Sovereignty: Definitions, Conceptualizations, and Interpretations." Joint publication of the *Journal of Indigenous*

Studies 1 (Fall 2005/Spring 2006) and *American Studies* 46 (Fall/Winter 2005): 115–32.

Coffey, Wallace, and Rebecca Tsosie. "Rethinking the Tribal Sovereignty Doctrine: Cultural Sovereignty and the Collective Future of Indian Nations." *Stanford Law and Policy Review* 12, no. 2 (Spring 2001): 191–210.

Cohen, Felix S. *Handbook of Federal Indian Law.* 1942; reprint, New York: AMS Press, 1982.

———. *On the Drafting of Tribal Constitutions.* Edited by David E. Wilkins. Norman: University of Oklahoma Press, 2006.

Copway, George (Kahgegagahbowh). *Traditional History and Characteristic Sketches.* Edited by Donald B. Smith and A. Lavonne Brown Ruoff. Norman: University of Nebraska Press, 1997.

Cramer, Renee Ann. *Cash, Color, and Colonialism: The Politics of Tribal Acknowledgment.* Norman: University of Oklahoma Press, 2005.

Cruikshank, Julie. "Discovery of Gold on the Klondike: Perspectives from Oral Tradition." In *Reading beyond Words: Contexts for Native Histories,* ed. Jennifer S. H. Brown and Elizabeth Vibert. Peterborough, Ontario: Broadview Press, 2001, 433–59.

———. *The Social Life of Stories: Narrative and Knowledge in the Yukon Territory.* Lincoln: University of Nebraska Press, 1998.

Danzinger, Edmond Jefferson, Jr. *The Chippewas of Lake Superior.* Norman: University of Oklahoma Press, 1979.

Darian-Smith, Eve. *New Capitalists: Law, Politics, and Identity surrounding Casino Gaming on Native American Land.* Belmont, CA: Wadsworth Publishing, 2004.

Deloria, Vine, Jr., and Clifford M. Lytle. *The Nations Within.* Austin: University of Texas Press, 1984.

———. "Self-determination and the Concept of Sovereignty." In *Economic Development in American Indian Reservations,* ed. Roxanne Dunbar Ortiz, 22–28. Albuquerque: University of New Mexico, Native American Studies, 1979.

Dennison, Jean. *Colonial Entanglement: Constituting a Twenty-first Century Osage Nation.* Chapel Hill: University of North Carolina Press, 2012.

Den Ouden, Amy E., and Jean M. O'Brien, eds. *Recognition, Sovereignty Struggles, and Indigenous Rights in the United States.* Chapel Hill: University of North Carolina Press, 2013.

Densmore, Frances. *Chippewa Customs.* 1929; reprint, St. Paul: Minnesota Historical Society Press, 1979.

Desjarlait, Robert. "Blood Quantum v. Lineal Descent: How Much Indian Are You?" *The Circle: Native American News and Arts* (Minneapolis, MN) 22, no. 11 (November 2001).

Doerfler, Jill. "Anishinaabe Society One Hundred Years from Now." *Anishinaabeg Today: A Chronicle of the White Earth Band of Ojibwe* (White Earth, MN) 14, no. 11 (October 7, 2009): 4, 22.

———. "Anishinaabe Understandings of Identity in the 1910s." *Anishinaabeg Today: A Chronicle of the White Earth Band of Ojibwe* (White Earth, MN) 12, no. 8 (May 30, 2007): 2, 23.

———. "Blood Quantum Becomes the Sole Determiner for Tribal Citizenship." *Anishinaabeg Today: A Chronicle of the White Earth Band of Ojibwe* (White Earth, MN) 2, no. 12 (September 12, 2007): 2, 22.

———. "Colonial Legacies, Opportunities for Change." *Anishinaabeg Today: A Chronicle of the White Earth Band of Ojibwe* (White Earth, MN) 15, no. 3 (March 3, 2010): 5, 19.

———. "Families First: Tribal Citizenship and the Future of the White Earth Nation." *Anishinaabeg Today: A Chronicle of the White Earth Band of Ojibwe* (White Earth, MN) 14, no. 9 (August 5, 2009): 2, 23.

———. "Fictions and Fractions: Reconciling Citizenship Regulations with Cultural Values among the White Earth Anishinaabeg." PhD diss., University of Minnesota, 2007.

———. "The Fight against Blood Quantum in the 1940s." *Anishinaabeg Today: A Chronicle of the White Earth Band of Ojibwe* (White Earth, MN) 15, no. 6 (June 2, 2010): 7, 25.

———. "Hamline Symposium Discusses If Race, Genetics Play a Role in Defining American Indian Identity." *Anishinaabeg Today: A Chronicle of the White Earth Band of Ojibwe* (White Earth, MN) 13, no. 6 (April 30, 2008): 2, 15.

———. "The Inaccuracy of Blood Quantum." *Anishinaabeg Today: A Chronicle of the White Earth Band of Ojibwe* (White Earth, MN) 15, no. 7 (July 7, 2010): 5.

———. "MCT Holds Strong against the Use of Blood Quantum." *Anishinaabeg Today: A Chronicle of the White Earth Band of Ojibwe* (White Earth, MN) 12, no. 11 (August 22, 2007): 2, 17.

———. "The Minnesota Chippewa Tribe Addresses the Citizenship Question in the 1940s." *Anishinaabeg Today: A Chronicle of the White Earth Band of Ojibwe* (White Earth, MN) 12, no. 11 (August 1, 2007): 2, 16.

———. "A Model for Action: Shingebiss Is an Important Story of Strength and Resiliency." *Anishinaabeg Today: A Chronicle of the White Earth Band of Ojibwe* (White Earth, MN) 14, no. 10 (December 2, 2009): 7, 19.

———. "More 1910s Anishinaabe Conceptions of Identity." *Anishinaabeg Today: A Chronicle of the White Earth Band of Ojibwe* (White Earth, MN) 12, no. 9 (June 20, 2007): 2, 17.

———. "New Constitution Would Strengthen Sovereignty." *Anishinaabeg Today:*

A Chronicle of the White Earth Band of Ojibwe (White Earth, MN) 15, no. 2 (February 3, 2010): 5.

———. "'A Philosophy for Living': Ignatia Broker and Constitutional Reform." *Anishinaabeg Today: A Chronicle of the White Earth Band of Ojibwe* (White Earth, MN) 14, no. 10 (September 2, 2009): 2, 26.

———. "Rebuilding and Renewing Tribal Sovereignty." *Anishinaabeg Today: A Chronicle of the White Earth Band of Ojibwe* (White Earth, MN) 15, no. 8 (August 4, 2010): 9, 17.

———. "Responsibilities and Importance of Tribal Citizenship." *Anishinaabeg Today: A Chronicle of the White Earth Band of Ojibwe* (White Earth, MN) 12, no. 10 (July 11, 2007): 2, 18.

———. "Reviewing the Constitution." *Anishinaabeg Today: A Chronicle of the White Earth Band of Ojibwe* (White Earth, MN) 14, no. 8 (July 1, 2009): 2, 25.

———. "Scholars Ask, 'Does "Indian Blood" Still Matter?'" *Anishinaabeg Today: A Monthly Chronicle of the White Earth Nation* (White Earth, MN) 16, no. 11 (October 5, 2011): 2, 16.

———. "A Short History of Chippewa Blood Quantum." *Anishinaabeg Today: A Chronicle of the White Earth Band of Ojibwe* (White Earth, MN) 12, no. 7 (May 9, 2007): 2, 17.

———. "Sovereignty and the Minnesota Chippewa Tribe." *Anishinaabeg Today: A Chronicle of the White Earth Band of Ojibwe* (White Earth, MN) 12, no. 6 (April 18, 2007): 2.

———. "The Tenuous History of Blood Quantum." *Anishinaabeg Today: A Chronicle of the White Earth Band of Ojibwe* (White Earth, MN) 15, no. 4 (April 7, 2010): 5, 11.

———. "Weaving Cultural Requirements into Services." *Anishinaabeg Today: A Monthly Chronicle of the White Earth Nation* (White Earth, MN) 18, no. 2 (February 6, 2013): 2, 28.

———. "The White Earth Blood Quantum Scam." *Anishinaabeg Today: A Chronicle of the White Earth Band of Ojibwe* (White Earth, MN) 15, no. 5 (May 5, 2010): 6.

Doerfler, Jill, Niigaanwewidam James Sinclair, and Heidi Stark. "Bagijige: An Offering." In *Centering Anishinaabeg Studies: Understanding the World through Stories*, xv–xxviii. East Lansing: Michigan State University Press, 2013.

Eisler, Kim Isaac. *Revenge of the Pequots: How a Small Native American Tribe Created the World's Most Profitable Casino*. Lincoln: University of Nebraska Press, 2002.

Ellinghaus, Katherine. "The Benefits of Being Indian: Blood Quanta, Intermarriage, and Allotment Policy on the White Earth Reservation, 1889–1920." *Frontiers: A Journal of Women Studies*, nos. 2 & 3 (2008), 81–105.

Elliott, Michael A. "Telling the Difference: Nineteenth-Century Legal Narratives of Racial Taxonomy." *Law & Social Inquiry* 24, no. 3 (Summer 1999): 611–36.

"The End of an Era: White Earth Chairman of 20 Years Sentenced to 51 Months Prison; Clark, Rawley To Do 46, 33 Months." *Native American Press/Ojibwe News* (Bemidji, MN), November 22, 1996.

Fletcher, Matthew L. M. "Looking to the East: The Stories of Modern Indian People and the Development of Tribal Law." Http://digitalcommons.law.msu.edu/cgi/viewcontent.cgi?article=1160&context=facpubs.

———. "Santa Clara Pueblo v. Martinez." In *Encyclopedia of American Civil Liberties*, ed. Paul Finkelman. New York: Routledge, 2006.

Flies-Away, Joseph Thomas, Carrie Garrow, and Miriam Jorgensen. "Native Nation Courts: Key Players in Nation Rebuilding." In *Rebuilding Native Nations: Strategies for Governance and Development*, ed. Miriam Jorgensen. Tucson: University of Arizona Press, 2007.

Fogelson, Raymond. "Ethnohistory of Events and Nonevents." *Ethnohistory* 36, no. 2 (Spring 1989), 133–47.

Fromson, Brett Duval. *Hitting the Jackpot: The Inside Story of the Richest Indian Tribe in History*. Reprint. New York: Grove Press, 2004.

Garroutte, Eva Marie. "The Racial Formation of American Indians: Negotiating Legitimate Identities within Tribal and Federal Law." *American Indian Quarterly* 25, no. 2 (Spring 2001), 224–39.

———. *Real Indians: Identity and Survival in Native America*. Berkeley: University of California Press, 2003.

Gellner, Ernest. *Nations and Nationalism*. 2nd ed. Ithaca, NY: Cornell University Press, 2009.

Ghezzi, Ridie Wilson. "Nanabush Stories from the Ojibwe." In *Coming to Light: Contemporary Translations of the Native Literatures of North America*, ed. Brian Swann. New York: Vintage, 1996.

Goldberg, Carol. "Members Only: Designing Citizenship Requirements for Tribal Nations." In *American Indian Constitutional Reform and the Rebuilding of Native Nations*, ed. Eric D. Lemont. Austin: University of Texas Press, 2006, 107–43.

Gonzales, Angela, Judy Kertész, and Gabrielle Tayac. "Eugenics as Indian Removal: Sociohistorical Processes and the De(con)struction of American Indians in the Southeast." *Public Historian* 39, no. 3 (Summer 2007), 53–67.

Gould, Scott L. "Mixing Bodies and Beliefs: The Predicament of Tribes." *Columbia Law Review* 101, no. 4 (May 2001), 702–72.

Gould, Stephen Jay. *The Mismeasure of Man*. New York: W.W. Norton and Co., 1996.

Gover, Kirsty. "Genealogy as Continuity: Explaining the Growing Tribal Preference for Descent Rules in Membership Governance in the United States." *American Indian Law Review* 33, no. 1 (2009), 243–309.

———. *Tribal Constitutionalism: States, Tribes, and the Governance of Membership*. Oxford: Oxford University Press, 2010.

Graves, Kathy Davis, and Elizabeth Ebbott. *Indians in Minnesota.* 5th ed. Minneapolis: University of Minnesota Press, 2006.

Gross, Lawrence W. "Cultural Sovereignty and Native American Hermeneutics in the Interpretation of the Sacred Stories of the Anishinaabe." *Wicazo Sa Review* (Fall 2003), 127–43.

Harmon, Alexandra. "Tribal Enrollment Councils: Lessons on Law and Indian Identity." *Western Historical Quarterly* 32 (Summer 2001), 175–200.

Henry, Ray. "Members Removed from Indian Tribes Complain of Unfairness." *South Coast Today,* October 26, 2007. Http://www.southcoasttoday.com/apps /pbcs.dll/article?AID=/20071026/NEWS/710260340.

Hickerson, Harold. *The Chippewa and Their Neighbors: A Study in Ethnohistory.* New York: Holt, Rinehart and Winston, Inc., 1970.

———. "The Chippewa of the Upper Great Lakes: A Study in Sociopolitical Change." In *North American Indians in Historical Perspective,* ed. Eleanor Burke Leacock and Nancy Oestreich Lurie. New York: Random House, 1971.

Horwich, Jeff. "How Indian Are You?" *Minnesota Public Radio,* April 2001. Http:// news.minnesota.publicradio.org/projects/2001/04/brokentrust/horwichj _quantum-m/index.shtml.

Howe, LeAnne. "Blind Bread and the Business of Theory Making." In *Reasoning Together: The Native Critics Collective,* ed. Craig S. Womack, Daniel Heath Justice, and Christopher B. Teuton. Norman: University of Oklahoma Press, 2008, 325–39.

———. "The Story of America: A Tribalography." In *Clearing a Path: Theorizing the Past in Native American Studies,* ed. Nancy Shoemaker (New York: Routledge, 2002), 29–50.

Hoxie, Frederick E. *A Final Promise: The Campaign to Assimilate the Indians, 1880– 1920.* New edition. Lincoln: University of Nebraska Press, 2001.

Hrdlička, Aleš. "Anthropology of the Chippewa." In *Holmes Anniversary Volume of Anthropological Essays.* Washington, DC: Privately printed, 1916. Https:// archive.org/stream/holmesanniversar00hodg#page/n7/mode/2up.

Jenks, Albert Ernest. "Indian-White Amalgamation: An Anthropometric Study." *Studies in the Social Sciences,* no. 6. Minneapolis: Bulletin of the University of Minnesota, 1916.

Johnston, Basil. *Ojibway Ceremonies.* Reprint. Lincoln: University of Nebraska Press, 1990.

———. *Ojibway Heritage: The Ceremonies, Rituals, Songs, Dances, Prayers and Legends of the Ojibway.* Toronto: McClelland and Stewart, 1967.

Jones, Dennis. "The Etymology of Anishinaabe." *Oshkaabewis Native Journal* 2, no. 1 (Fall 1995), 43–48.

Jones Jarding, Lilias C. "Citizenship: United States and State." In *Encyclopedia of*

United States Indian Policy and Law, ed. Paul Finkelman and Tim Alan Garrison, 178–81. Washington, DC: CQ Press, 2009.

Jorgensen, Miriam, ed. *Rebuilding Native Nations: Strategies for Governance and Development*. Tucson: University of Arizona Press, 2007.

Josephy, Alvin M., Jr. *Now That the Buffalo's Gone*. Norman: University of Oklahoma Press, 1989.

Kaiser, Emily. "Plans Duel for Chippewa Cash." *Star Tribune*, June 25, 2008. Http://www.startribune.com/politics/state/21606029.html?location_refer =Entertainment.

Kappler, Charles J., ed. and comp. *Indian Affairs: Laws and Treaties*. Vol. 2. Washington, DC: Government Printing Office, 1904.

———. *Indian Treaties, 1778–1883*. Reprint. New York: Interland Publishing Inc., 1972.

Kauanui, J. Kēhaulani. *Hawaiian Blood: Colonialism and the Politics of Sovereignty and Indigeneity*. Durham, NC: Duke University Press, 2008.

Kegg, Maude, and John Nichols. *Portage Lake: Memories of an Ojibwe Childhood*. Minneapolis: University of Minnesota Press, 1993.

Kehow, Alice Beck. *The Ghost Dance: Ethnohistory and Revitalization*. New York: Thompson Publishing, 1989.

Kelly, Lawrence C. "The Indian Reorganization Act: The Dream and the Reality." In *Major Problems in American Indian History: Documents and Essays*, ed. Albert L. Hurtado and Peter Iverson. Lexington, MA: D.C. Heath and Co., 1994, 463–73.

Kevles, Daniel J. *In the Name of Eugenics: Genetics and the Uses of Human Heredity*. Cambridge, MA: Harvard University Press, 1995.

King, Thomas. *The Truth about Stories: A Native Narrative*. Minneapolis: University of Minnesota Press, 2005.

Klopotek, Brian. *Indigeneity, Race, and Federal Tribal Recognition Policy in Three Louisiana Indian Communities*. Durham, NC: Duke University Press, 2011.

Konkle, Maureen. *Writing Indian Nations: Native Intellectuals and the Politics of Historiography, 1827–1863*. Chapel Hill: University of North Carolina Press, 2004.

Kugel, Rebecca. *To Be the Main Leaders of Our People: A History of Minnesota Ojibwe Politics, 1825–1898*. East Lansing: Michigan State University Press, 1998.

Landes, Ruth. *Ojibwa Religion and the Midewiwin*. Madison: University of Wisconsin Press, 1968.

———. *Ojibwa Sociology*. Columbia University Contributions to Anthropology, vol. 29. New York: Columbia University Press, 1940.

Larson, Elizabeth. "Indian Disenrollments a Statewide, Nationwide Issue." *Lake Country News*, December 6, 2008. Http://lakeconews.com/content/view /6567/764/.

LaVelle, John P. "The General Allotment Act 'Eligibility' Hoax: Distortions of Law, Policy, and History in Derogation of Indian Tribes." *Wicazo Sa Review* 14, no. 1 (Spring 1999), 251–302.

Lawlor, Mary. "Identity in Mashantucket." *American Quarterly* 57, no. 1 (2005), 153–77.

Lemont, Eric D., ed. *American Indian Constitutional Reform and the Rebuilding of Native Nations.* Austin: University of Texas Press, 2006.

Light, Steve Andrew, and Kathryn R. L. Rand. *Indian Gaming and Tribal Sovereignty: The Casino Compromise.* Lawrence: University of Kansas Press, 2005.

Lyons, Chief Oren, and John Mohawk, eds. *Exiled in the Land of the Free: Democracy, Indian Nations, and the U.S. Constitution.* Santa Fe, NM: Clear Light Publishers, 1992.

Lyons, Scott, "Actually Existing Indian Nations: Modernity, Diversity, and the Future of Native American Studies." *American Indian Quarterly* 35, no. 3 (Summer 2011), 294–312.

———. *X-Marks: Native Signatures of Assent.* Minneapolis: University of Minnesota Press, 2010.

MacKinnon, Catharine A. "Whose Culture? A Case Note on Martinez v. Santa Clara Pueblo." In *Feminism Unmodified: Discourses on Life and Law.* Cambridge, MA: Harvard University Press, 1987, 63–68.

Mason, Philip P., ed. *Schoolcraft: The Literary Voyager or Muzzeniegun.* East Lansing: Michigan State University Press, 1962.

McDonnell, Janet A. *The Dispossession of the American Indian, 1887–1934.* Bloomington: Indiana University Press, 1991.

Michelson, Truman, ed., and William Jones, comp. *Ojibwa Texts.* Vol. 7, pt. 1, Publications of the American Ethnological Society, ed. Franz Boas, ix–xxi. New York: E. J. Brill, Ltd., 1917.

Meyer, Melissa L. "American Indian Blood Quantum Requirements: Blood Is Thicker Than Family." In *Over the Edge: Remapping the American West*, ed. Valerie J. Matsumoto and Blake Allmendinger. Berkeley: University of California Press, 1999, 231–44.

———. "Race and Identity in Indian Country." Review essay. *Ethnohistory* 51, no. 4 (Fall 2004), 799–809.

———. *Thicker Than Water: The Origins of Blood as Symbol and Ritual.* New York: Routledge, 2005.

———. *The White Earth Tragedy: Ethnicity and Dispossession at a Minnesota Anishinaabe Reservation, 1889–1920.* Lincoln: University of Nebraska Press, 1994.

Mooney, James. *The Ghost Dance Religion and Wounded Knee.* 1896; reprint, New York: Dover Publications, 2011.

Nabokov, Peter. *A Forest of Time: American Indian Ways of History*. Cambridge: Cambridge University Press, 2002.

The New American Webster Handy College Dictionary. 3rd ed. Edited by Albert and Loy Morehead. New York: Penguin Books, 1995.

Nichols, John D., ed. *"A Statement Made by the Indians": A Bilingual Petition of the Chippewas of Lake Superior, 1864*. London, Ontario: Center for Research and Teaching of Canadian Native Languages, 1988.

Nichols, John D., and Earl Nyholm. *A Concise Dictionary of Minnesota Ojibwe*. Minneapolis: University of Minnesota Press, 1995.

"No More Business as Usual in the Minnesota Chippewa Tribe." *Ojibwe News* (Bemidji, MN), October 27, 1995.

Northrup, Jim. "Fond Du Lac Follies." *The Circle: Native American News and Arts* (Minneapolis), December 2002.

———. "Fond Du Lac Follies." *The Circle: Native American News and Arts* (Minneapolis), February 2006.

O'Brien, Jean M. *Dispossession by Degrees: Indian Land and Identity in Natick, Massachusetts, 1650–1790*. Cambridge: Cambridge University Press, 1997.

O'Brien, Sharon. *American Indian Tribal Governments*. Norman: University of Oklahoma Press, 1989.

Officer, James E. "The Bureau of Indian Affairs since 1945: An Assessment." *Annals of the American Academy of Political and Social Science* 436, no. 1 (March 1978), 61–72.

Ortiz, Simon J. "Towards a National Indian Literature: Cultural Authenticity in Nationalism." *MELUS* 8, no. 2 (1981), 7–12.

Palmater, Pamela D. *Beyond Blood: Rethinking Indigenous Identity*. Saskatoon, Canada: Purich Publishing Ltd., 2011.

Parker, Robert Dale, ed. *The Sound the Stars Make Rushing through the Sky: The Writings of Jane Johnston Schoolcraft*. Philadelphia: University of Pennsylvania Press, 2007.

Peacock, Thomas, and Marlene Wisuri. *The Good Path: Ojibwe Learning and Activity Book for Kids*. Afton, MN: Afton Historical Society Press, 2002.

Peterson, Edward Michael, Jr. "That So-Called Warranty Deed: Clouded Land Titles on the White Earth Indian Reservation in Minnesota." *North Dakota Law Review* 59, no. 2 (1983), 159–81.

Pflug, Melissa A. *Ritual and Myth in Odawa Revitalization: Reclaiming a Sovereign Place*. Norman: University of Oklahoma Press, 1998.

Pierpoint, Mary. "Seminole Nation Changes Tribal Enrollment." *Indian Country Today*, July 19, 2000. Http://www.indiancountrytoday.com/archive/28198814.html.

Radin, Paul, comp. *Some Myths and Tales of the Ojibwa of Southeastern Ontario*.

Memoir 48, no. 2, Anthropological Series. Ottawa: Government Printing Bureau, 1914.

Raibmon, Paige. *Authentic Indians: Episodes of Encounter from the Late-Nineteenth-Century Northwest Coast.* Durham, NC: Duke University Press, 2005.

Rave, Jodi, "Tribal Enrollment a Contentious Issue for Native People." *Missoulian,* October 31, 2008. Http://www.missoulian.com/articles/2008/10/31/jodirave/rave16.txt.

Resnik, Judith. "Dependent Sovereigns: Indian Tribes, States, and Federal Courts." *University of Chicago Law Review* 56 (1989), 671–759.

Robertson, Tom. "Chippewa Bands Can't Agree How to Split Multi-Million Dollar Settlement." *Minnesota Public Radio,* July 22, 2008. Http://minnesota.publicradio.org/display/web/2008/07/17/mctsettlement.

Roediger, David R. *Working toward Whiteness: How America's Immigrants Became White: The Strange Journey from Ellis Island to the Suburbs.* New York: Basic Books, 2006.

Ruppert, James. "Meditation in Contemporary Native American Writing." In *Native American Perspectives on Literature and History,* ed. Alan R. Velie. Norman: University of Oklahoma, 1994, 7–24.

Schaaf, William, and Charles Roberts, in conjunction with the Minnesota Chippewa Tribe Curriculum Development Committee. *History of the Minnesota Chippewa Tribe.* N.d.

Schenck, Theresa M. *William W. Warren: The Life, Letters, and Times of an Ojibwe Leader.* Lincoln: University of Nebraska Press, 2007.

Schoolcraft, Henry R. "Shingebiss." *The Hiawatha Legends.* Reprint. AuTrain, MI: Avery Color Studios, 1984.

———. *The Indian in His Wigwam, or Characteristics of the Red Race of America from Original Notes and Manuscripts.* New York: Dewitt & Davenport, 1848.

———. *The Myth of Hiawatha and Other Oral Legends, Mythologic and Allegoric, of the North American Indians.* Philadelphia: J. B. Lippincott & Co., 1856.

"Shawanima or Divide and Conquer? Constitutional Reform at a Crossroads." *Ojibwe News* (St. Paul, MN), March 28, 1997. Http://proquest.umi.com/pqdweb?did=493781951&sid=1&Fmt=3&clientId=2256&RQT=309&VName=PQD.

Shoemaker, Nancy. "Urban Indians and Ethnic Choices: American Indian Organizations in Minneapolis, 1920–1950." *Western Historical Quarterly* (November 1988): 431–47.

Simpson, Audra. *Mohawk Interruptus: Political Life across the Borders of Settler States.* Durham, NC: Duke University Press, 2014.

Simpson, Leanne. *Dancing on Our Turtle's Back: Stories of Nishinaabeg Re-Creation, Resurgence and a New Emergence.* Winnipeg, Manitoba: Arbeiter Ring Publishing, 2010.

———. "Our Elder Brothers: The Lifeblood of Resurgence." In *Lighting the Eighth Fire: The Liberation, Resurgence, and Protection of Indigenous Nations*, ed. Leanne Simpson. Winnipeg, Manitoba: Arbeiter Ring Publishing, 2008, 73–88.

Smith, Linda. *Decolonizing Methodologies: Research and Indigenous Peoples*. New York: Zed Books Ltd., 1999.

Soderstrom, Mark. "Weeds in Linnaeus's Garden: Science and Segregation, Eugenics, and the Rhetoric of Racism at the University of Minnesota and the Big Ten, 1900–45." PhD diss., University of Minnesota, 2004.

Spruhan, Paul. "Indian as Race/Indian as Political Status: Implementation of the Half-Blood Requirement under the Indian Reorganization Act, 1934–1945." *Rutgers Race and the Law Review* 8, no. 1 (August 2006).

———. "A Legal History of Blood Quantum in Federal Indian Law to 1935." *South Dakota Law Review* 51, no. 1 (2006), 1–50.

Stark, Heidi Kiiwetinepinesiik. "Marked by Fire: Anishinaabe Articulations of Nationhood in Treaty Making with the United States and Canada." *American Indian Quarterly* 36, no. 2 (Spring 2012), 119–49.

Strum, Circe. *Blood Politics: Race, Culture, and Identity in the Cherokee Nation of Oklahoma*. Berkeley: University of California Press, 2002.

Swentzell, Rina. "Testimony of a Santa Clara Woman." *Kansas Journal of Law & Public Policy* 14, no. 1 (2004), 97–102.

Tallbear, Kimberly. "DNA, Blood Quantum, and Racializing the Tribe." *Wicazo Sa Review* (Spring 2003), 81–107.

———. *Native American DNA: Tribal Belonging and the False Promise of Genetic Science*. Minneapolis: University of Minnesota Press, 2013.

Thornton, Russell. *American Indian Holocaust and Survival: A Population History since 1492*. Norman: University of Oklahoma Press, 1987.

Treuer, Anton. *"Everything You Wanted to Know about Indians but Were Afraid to Ask."* St. Paul: Borealis Books, Minnesota Historical Society, 2012.

———. "What's in a Name: The Meaning of Ojibwe." *Oshkaabewis Native Journal* 2, no. 1 (Fall 1995), 39–42.

"Tribal/State Pact Keeps Kids with Indian Families." *Anishinaabeg Today* (White Earth, MN), March 7, 2007.

Turner Strong, Pauline, and Barrik van Winkle. "Tribe and Nation: American Indians and American Nationalism." *Social Analysis* 33 (September 1993): 9–26.

United States v. Darrell Chip Wadena. United States, 8th Circuit Court of Appeals, 152 F.3d 831.

Valencia-Weber, Gloria. "Santa Clara Pueblo v. Martinez: Twenty-five Years of Disparate Cultural Visions." *Kansas Journal of Law & Public Policy* 14, no. 1 (2004), 49–66.

Van Laan, Nancy. *Shingebiss: An Ojibwe Legend*. Boston: Houghton Mifflin Co., 1997.

Vizenor, Erma J. "White Earth 2007 State of the Nation Address." *Anishinaabeg Today*, March 7, 2007.

Vizenor, Gerald R. *Earthdivers: Tribal Narratives on Mixed Descent*. Minneapolis: University of Minnesota Press, 1981.

———. *The Everlasting Sky: Voices of the Anishinabe People*. Minneapolis: Minnesota Historical Society Press, 2000.

———. *Fugitive Poses*. Lincoln: University of Nebraska Press, 2000.

———. *The Heirs of Columbus*. Hanover, NH: University Press of New England, 1991.

———. *Manifest Manners: Postindian Warriors of Survivance*. Hanover, NH: Wesleyan University Press, 1994.

———. *The People Named the Chippewa: Narrative Histories*. Minneapolis: University of Minnesota Press, 1984.

———. *Wordarrows: Indians and Whites in the New Fur Trade*. Minneapolis: University of Minnesota Press, 1978.

Vizenor, Gerald, and A. Robert Lee. *Postindian Conversations*. Lincoln: University of Nebraska Press, 1999.

Vizenor, Gerald, and James MacKay. "Constitutional Narratives: A Conversation with Gerald Vizenor." In *Centering Anishinaabeg Studies: Understanding the World through Stories*, ed. Jill Doerfler, Heidi Kiiwetinepinesiik Stark, and Niigaanwewidam James Sinclair. East Lansing: Michigan State University Press, 2013.

Walker, Cheryl. *Indian Nation: Native American Literature and Nineteenth-Century Nationalisms*. Durham, NC: Duke University Press, 1997.

Wallace, Anthony F. C. "Revitalization Movements: Some Theoretical Considerations for Their Comparative Study." *American Anthropologist* 58, no. 2 (1956).

Warren, William. *History of the Ojibway People*. Reprint. St. Paul: Minnesota Historical Society Press, 1984.

Warrior, Robert. *Tribal Secrets: Recovering American Indian Intellectual Traditions*. Minneapolis: University of Minnesota Press, 1994.

Weaver, Jace, Craig S. Womack, and Robert Warrior. *American Indian Literary Nationalism*. Albuquerque: University of New Mexico Press, 2005.

Weil, Richard H. "Destroying a Homeland: White Earth, Minnesota." *American Indian Culture and Research Journal* 13, no. 2 (1989), 69–95.

White, Bruce. *We Are at Home: Pictures of the Ojibwe People*. St. Paul: Minnesota Historical Society Press, 2007.

"White Earth Open Meeting a Welcome Change, but Questions Left Unanswered." *Ojibwe News* (St. Paul, MN), July 18, 1997.

"White Earth's Poverty Wadena's Wealth." *The Circle: Native American News and Arts* (Minneapolis), January 31, 1996.

White Earth Reservation Curriculum Committee. *White Earth: A History.* Minnesota Chippewa Tribe, 1989.

Wilkins, David E. *American Indian Sovereignty and the U.S. Supreme Court: The Masking of Justice.* Austin: University of Texas Press, 1997.

———. "Seasons of Change: Of Reforms, Melees, and Revolutions in Indian Country." In *American Indian Constitutional Reform and the Rebuilding of Native Nations,* ed. Eric D. Lemont. Austin: University of Texas Press, 2006, 35–48.

———. "Sovereignty, Democracy, Constitution: An Introduction." In *The White Earth Nation: Ratification of a Native Democratic Constitution,* by Gerald Vizenor and Jill Doerfler. Lincoln: University of Nebraska Press, 2012.

———. "Wilkins: Self-determination or Self-decimation? Banishment and Disenrollment in Indian Country." *Indian Country Today,* August 25, 2006. Https://nnidatabase.org/news/self-determination-or-self-decimation-banishment-and-disenrollment-indian-country.

Wilkins, David E., and Heidi Kiiwetinepinesiik Stark. *American Indian Politics and the American Political System.* 3rd ed. Lanham, MD: Rowman & Littlefield Publishers, 2011.

Wilkins, David E., and K. Tsianina Lomawaima. "'With the Greatest Trust and Fidelity': The Trust Doctrine." In *Uneven Ground: American Indian Sovereignty and Federal Indian Law.* Norman: University of Oklahoma Press, 2002.

Wilkinson, Charles. *Blood Struggle: The Rise of Modern Indian Nations.* New York: W.W. Norton & Co., 2005.

Williams, Brackette. "A Class Act: Anthropology and the Race to Nation across Ethnic Terrain." *Annual Review of Anthropology* 18 (1989), 401–44.

———. "The Impact of the Precepts of Nationalism on the Concept of Culture: Making Grasshoppers out of Naked Apes." *Cultural Critique* 24, no. 2 (1993), 143–91.

Williams, Mentor L., ed. *Schoolcraft's Indian Legends from Algic Researches, The Myth of Hiawatha, Oneota, The Red Race in America, and Historical and Statistical Information Respecting . . . the Indian Tribes of the United States.* East Lansing: Michigan State University Press, 1956.

Williams, Robert A., Jr. *Like a Loaded Weapon: The Rehnquist Court, Indian Rights, and the Legal History of Racism in America.* Minneapolis: University of Minnesota Press, 2005.

Wolfe, Patrick. "Land, Labour, and Difference: Elementary Structures of Race." *American Historical Review* 106, no. 3 (June 2001), 866–905.

Womack, Craig. *Red on Red: Native American Literary Separatism.* Minneapolis: University of Minnesota Press, 1999.

Youngbear-Tibbetts, Holly. "Without Due Process: The Alienation of Individual Trust Allotments of the White Earth Anishinaabeg." *American Indian Culture and Research Journal* 15, no. 2 (1991), 93–138.

Index